Contemporary Issues Series

P9-CIU-124

Politics of Power in Latin America

A Critical Overview of the Issues Surrounding United States Foreign Policy in Latin America

Carl Flaningam

NATIONAL TEXTBOOK COMPANY • Lincolnwood, Illinois U.S.A.

Contents

Introduction   4

Chapter One: Directions for Analysis in the Wording of the
1987-88 Topic   5

Terms and Phrases for Definition

Implications for Analysis

Negative Ground

Chapter Two: Generic Issues on the 1987-88 Topic   24

Inherency-Motive Arguments

Evidence and Significance

Solvency

Advantages and Disadvantages

Chapter Three: United States Policy Toward Latin
America: Principles and Characteristics;   52

The Reagan Doctrine

Bilateral vs. Multilateral Approaches

Private Sector vs. Public Sector Development

Security Assistance vs. Economic Development

Counter-Insurgency vs. Human Rights

Chapter Four: Themes and Problems in Latin
America   78

Political Stability

Human Rights

Population, Food, and Unemployment

International Debt

Civilian vs. Military Governments

U.S. Support of the Contras

Appendix: Bibliography   108

Appendix: Bibliographic and Research Note   126

Appendix: Final Round NDT Debate, 1983   128

MAY   1988

Introduction

In July 1983, a New York Times-CBS poll revealed that only one-fourth of the people interviewed knew that the Reagan Administration supported the government in El Salvador, only thirteen percent knew that it supported the Contras in Nicaragua, and only eight percent correctly answered both questions.

The 1987-88 high debate topic addresses United States policy toward Latin America, a region of considerable interest to the President and the Congress but for which the public apparently has great difficulty in filling in the right names of the countries on the map and separating our friends from our enemies on the political scorecard.

This book attempts to provide a frame of reference for members of the debate community when analysing Latin American-oriented affairs. Chapters One and Two are the more "debate-oriented" chapters, with Chapter One examining topic wording interpretations and their effects on the division of argumentative ground and Chapter Two discussing arguments which are likely to be recurrent on the topic. Chapters Three and Four are more focused on the substantive issues of Latin American affairs. Chapter Three considers tendencies in Reagan Administration policies toward Latin America, while Chapter Four addresses major issues in Latin American political stability.

Would a repetition of the 1983 poll show a higher percentage of correct answers? The task for debaters in 1987-88 is deeper than that: in considering questions of how to promote Latin American political stability (and how not to do so) the topic requires not only a knowledge of the principal facts but an understanding of the possible goals of U.S. Latin American policy and the factors influencing the effectiveness of these policies. It is the objective of this book to be of assistance in helping accomplish this task.

Directions for Analysis in the Wording of the 1987-88 Topic

This chapter attempts to provide a framework for the application of the materials in the other chapters to the 1987–88 topic. The first section considers key terms and phrases in the topic; the second section addresses implications for analysis from the juxtaposition of several of these phrases; and the final section discusses the effects of topic wording on the delineation of argumentative ground and basic positions consequently available to the negative on the 1987–88 topic.

TERMS AND PHRASES FOR DEFINITION

There are four key sets of terms for interpretation on the 1987–88 topic. These are: (1) United States government; (2) adopt a policy; (3) increase political stability; and (4) Latin America. The effect of articles and prepositions on interpretation is discussed in the next section.

United States Government

Although at first glance this appears to be a noncontroversial phrase, "United States government" provides some limited room for alternative interpretations. The topic is not limited to "the President," "the executive," "the executive branch," or even "the federal government." The word providing latitude is "government," "United States" is defined by Black's Law Dictionary (Fifth Edition, 1979, p. 1375) as the "collective name of the states which are united by and under the Constitution." "Government," however, is less precise.

Black's defines "government" as follows: "(i)n the United States, government consists of the executive, legislative, and judicial branches in addition to administrative branches." (p. 625) It goes on to say that "(i)n a broader sense, (it) includes the federal government and all its agencies and branches, state and county governments, and city and township governments." (Id.)

This provides some slight latitude in interpretation, in two different directions. First, the topic is not limited to executive branch–legislative branch actions but includes the judiciary as well. Interpretations of the topic involving the role of United States policy in Latin America and the effect of international law would not have required this. The branch of government implicated by those cases is the executive, principally the State Department. However, the actions of United States courts are of relevance to Latin American affairs in at least two ways:

the Alien Tort Claims Act, under which civil suits can be filed
by foreign nationals in U.S. courts for actions in violation of
international customary law or United States treaties; and,
second, criminal proceedings by the Department of Justice against
the sanctuary movement in U.S. Federal courts.

Few independent regulatory agencies (with the exception of
the Federal Reserve Board) are of independent significance to
political stability in Latin America. Several agencies within
the executive branch should be of great relevance. In addition
to the obvious examples of the National Security Agency and the
Central Intelligence Agency, activities of the Immigration and
Naturalization Service, the Agency for International Development,
the Export-Import Bank, and the Office of the U.S. Trade Representative will play varying roles in discussion of the topic. Of
course, "United States government" would also include activities
of the U.S. armed forces and embassy personnel.

A second way in which the topic is broadened by the use of
the phrase "United States government" is that the topic is not
limited to activities of the federal government alone. Black's
Law Dictionary distinguishes the more general term, "government"
from a subcategory, "federal government." It defines the latter
as "(t)he government of the United States of America as distinguished from the government of the several states." (p. 625)
Inclusion of state and local governments probably only provides
breadth in that it permits topical changes requiring enforcement
and implementation actions by such governmental entities. This
could be of relevance in several situations: where state and
local law enforcement officials are involved along with federal
agents in dealing with illegal immigration or drug law enforcement; control of National Guard troops (currently among those
training in Honduras) which are under the control of the governor
of their respective states; and state and city trade representatives and offices in foreign nations.

The implications of "United States government" are explored
further in the next section, under agent of action analysis. The
topic appears to focus on governmental action, as opposed to
action by nongovernmental organizations (NGO's) or by multinational bodies. Whether either form of action, particularly the
latter, is actually precluded is unclear. While an affirmative
policy does not appear to be able to use them directly, it could
"adopt a policy" which utilized the services of nongovernmental
organizations. For example, the United States could adopt a
policy concerning human rights which specified that the·Inter-
national Committee of the Red Cross or Amnesty International play
a role in monitoring of the implementation of the policy.
Another example would be a policy which mandated that the United
States take part in the Contadora Peace Process.

Although not part of the "United States government," United
States private entities would be within the jurisdiction of the
affirmative as part of the policy adopted. Under extraterritorial
theories of jurisdiction, the activities of private citizens or
groups in Latin America would be subject to the mandate of the
affirmative. Examples would include the AFL-CIO's American

Institute for Free Labor Development (AIFLD) as well as any of the private groups aiding the Contras in Nicaragua.

Adopt A Policy

The term "adopt" according to <u>Black's Law Dictionary</u>, means "to accept, appropriate, choose, or select . . . To accept, consent to, and put into effective operation." (p. 45) A "policy" according to the same source, consists of "(t)he general principles by which a government is guided in the management of public affairs, or the legislature in its measures." (p. 104) <u>Webster's Third New International Dictionary</u> (1966, p. 1754) defines a policy as "a definite course or method of actions."

Within the context of the topic's wording, "adopt a policy" appears to mean only that the affirmative must choose or select to put into operation some course of action which is guided by a set of coherent principles or objectives.

"Adopt a policy" has relevance for agent of action, multiplicity of actions, and solvency considerations discussed later in this chapter. The resolution only mandates the adoption of a policy which has a definable set of objectives related to the attainment of political stability in Latin America. The policy could entail cooperation or coordination with governments other than the United States. Like other recent topics, the topic is "two-tiered" in form. As opposed to a "single-tiered" topic, in which resolutional mandates are spelled out in the topic wording (e.g., ban hand guns, require installation of passive restraints in automobiles), this topic creates a policy mandating actions which will be the source for attaining political stability in Latin America. The two topic options rejected ("Resolved: that the United States government should significantly decrease its military involvement in Latin America," and "Resolved: that the United States government should significantly increase its non-military assistance to Latin America.") were both examples of single-tiered resolutions. By implication, the selection of this topic suggests a preference on the part of the debate community for more expansive options. How "adopt a policy" and the two-tiered character of the resolution expands affirmative options is discussed further in the second section of this chapter, under effects topicality.

Increase Political Stability

This is the key phrase of the topic, both because it spells out the end-result to be achieved through affirmative action and, at the same time, because it indicates that the topic is nondirectional. The topic mandates no particular direction to the Latin American policy of the United States government. Either decreased or increased United States involvement could be argued to "increase political stability." The shifting nature of affirmative ground, from team to team and debate to debate, will be a unique and problematic feature of this topic.

Black's Law Dictionary defines "stabilize" as "(t)o keep steady, fixed, as distinguished from fluctuating, shifting." (p. 1259) Similarly, Corpus Juris Secundum defines "stability" as

> A relative term which does not connote a position which is fixed and unchangeable, but merely means a tendency to remain in a given position. It is the state or quality of being firm; strength to stand or endure without material change; steadiness; firmness. (Vol. B1A, p. 251. 1977)

"Political" is a somewhat harder term to define. Scruton's A Dictionary of Political Thought identifies two meanings to "political," both of which distinguish it from other concepts. First, it is contrasted with "social," with "political" meaning "pertaining to the state and its institutions," while "social" (as in "social system") encompasses collective organizations and activities generally. Second, "political" refers to a model of government, under which government operates through a system of representation and conciliation of competing interests, as opposed to theocratic, monarchic, and other models of government. (p. 359) Plano, et. al.'s The Dictionary of Political Analysis comments that "politics" refers to "(h)uman activity concerned with the authority of the society for which the decisions are made" but that "(n)o single phrase can capture the many meanings assigned to the word." The same source comments further that "(i)n most political discourse, however, politics refers to public policies and allocations rather than the internal processes of private organizations." (p. 110; emphasis in original) Further, Plano, et. al. state that a "political system" is the collectivity of relationships comprising government and the political processes of a state, although a broader definition would include any social relationship where influence is exercised or authoritative decisions are made. (p. 108)

"Political stability" may turn out to be an unhappy choice for a central phrase in a topic. The end-point of affirmative action is to augment whatever the current level of "political stability" in Latin America happens to be. The discussion of "political" above should indicate that a wide variety of subject matters are germane to the achievement of "political stability." Moreover, it is not necessarily the case that "political stability" is a positively-valued condition. If by "political stability" one means (as determined by the definitions provided above) the absence of fluctuation or resistance to material change in public policies or governmental structures, a number of regimes in history could be described as "politically stable" which were not known for their enlightened rule, respect for civil rights, or social and economic progress. The Soviet Union, for example, has been free of challenges to its political process since the death of Joseph Stalin; closer to home (and the topic), Francois "Papa Doc" Duvalier's Haiti and General Stroessner's Paraguay could reasonably be said to have been absent fluctuations in the form of governmental rule.

In fact, Scruton's <u>A Dictionary of Political Thought</u> notes that the political (as opposed to the economic) meaning of the term "stabilization" has an established meaning for United States policy in Latin America:

> Stabilization is a major preoccupation of U.S. foreign policy in Latin America, where precarious regimes are stabilized through economic and military support.
> (p. 445)

Two primary interpretations of "increase political stability" appear possible. First, a negative interpretation would view increasing the steadiness or firmness of political institutions as reducing the hazards of instability: death squads, "disappearances," the inability of governments to protect their own citizens would be reduced by the affirmative policy. This is a relatively narrow vision of the topic: the focus of topical action would be reducing the consequences of political instability.

The second, affirmative interpretation of "increase political stability" is much broader. This interpretation would focus on the view of "political" as related to state or state-related activities and organizations relevant to social or economic values within the society. The meaning of the phrase "increase political stability" from this point of view would be that of augmenting the ability of governmental institutions to provide for the social and economic needs of citizens. The end result of increased political stability would be the development of a more cohesive social order. The distinction between the two views of "increase political stability" in some ways parallels contrasting first world and second world views of human rights, discussed in Chapter Four. The affirmative view of "increase political stability" would encompass such diverse programs as land reform, provision of basic medical care, agricultural technical assistance, literacy training, and reform in the police, the military and other governmental institutions.

The two rejected topic options would have narrowed the focus of debate to either United States military involvement or non-military assistance. The topic chosen instead deals with a broad variety of institutions, programs, and practices connected to the degree of strength and endurance of Latin American governments and their ability to respond to the social, economic, and political needs of their citizens.

Latin America

"Latin America," in contrast to "political stability," has a reasonably narrow and accepted meaning. Rossi and Plano's <u>The Latin American Political Dictionary</u> (1980, p. 13) defines Latin America as follows:

The name most commonly given to the group of twenty
republics of the Western Hemisphere that were former
colonies of Spain, Portugal, and France. By extension,
but less often, the term "Latin America" is used to
refer to all territory in the Western Hemisphere south
of the United States, thus including the present and
former possessions of Great Britain, the Netherlands,
France, and the United States. The traditional "Latin"
states are: Argentina, Bolivia, Brazil, Chile,
Colombia, Costa Rica, Cuba, the Dominican Republic,
Ecuador, El Salvador, Guatemala, Haiti, Honduras,
Mexico, Nicaragua, Panama, Paraguay, Peru, Uruguay, and
Venezuela. The Commonwealth of Puerto Rico . . . is
often included with the independent Latin republics as
part of "Latin America." (p. 13)

Rossi and Plano further comment that "Latin America" is "not
geographically precise" (Id.) but that "the term can justifiably
be used with respect to the twenty republics because these states
see themselves as different from the 'Anglo-Saxon' cultures of
North America." (p. 14)

"Latin America" is probably a better choice than "Western
Hemisphere," the choice of the colleges in their 1982-83 topic.
This resulted in the occasional affirmative case dealing with
American Indian reservations. Depending on the geographical
definition of "Western Hemisphere," this sometimes included
debates about Northern Ireland, Morocco and the Western Sahara,
and Antarctica as well. However, as is discussed in later
chapters, the topic combines what are really three connected
geographic regions with related but different problems, particularly economic problems. "Latin America" encompasses states in
the Caribbean, Central America, and South America. "Central
America" might have been a narrower and more focused topic.
Certainly the bulk of recent United States governmental and
public concern has been on El Salvador, Nicaragua, and, to a
lesser extent, the other Central American republics. However,
the topic chosen includes Central America and much more. In
particular, by encompassing all of Latin America, the topic
addresses the problem of international debt in a manner which is
radically different than a topic concerned with Central America
alone.

IMPLICATIONS FOR ANALYSIS

This section of the chapter examines the influence of the topic's
wording on its breadth and limitations. There are five principal
influences, some of which deal with the absence of terms, as well
as their presence. The areas are: (1) effects topicality and
solvency-topicality; (2) agent of change; (3) site of mandates

versus site of effects; (4) absence of modifiers; and (5) multi-plicity of options.

Effects Topicality and Solvency-Topicality

The wording of the 1987-88 topic, specifically the conjunction of the phrases "adopt a policy" and "increase political stability," creates two effects on topicality and solvency analysis. First, the topic appears to explicitly sanction topicality by effect as an affirmative topicality approach; second, the topic seems to give rise to a confusion of topicality and solvency as issues.

Topicality by effect (occasionally referred to as "topical-ity once removed") occurs when implementation of the affirmative plan in itself does not result in the adoption of the affirmative resolution. Rather, the consequences of the operation of the plan (its "effects") result in the resolution's adoption. In contrast, where resolutions do not require such an additional step, adoption of the plan is synonymous with adoption of the resolution. For example, on the resolution, "Resolved: that the Federal Government should adopt a program of comprehensive medical care for all U.S. citizens," affirmative plan mandates would be examples or functional equivalents of the resolution. In the case of topicality by effect, plan mandates are inter-mediate steps, the successful operation of which will subse-quently result in the adoption of the resolution. An equivalent example for medical care would be, "Resolved: that the Federal Government should adopt a policy which will reduce the incidence of cancer among U.S. citizens."

The 1987-88 topic requires affirmatives to rely on an effects interpretation of topicality. No affirmative plan through its mere adoption ("adopt a policy") would bring the resolution into being ("increase political stability," just like "reduce the incidence of cancer"). Instead, it will always be the case that the consequence of adopting the affirmative policy, if it functions as contemplated, will be that Latin American political stability will be increased. This can be differen-tiated from either of the two topic options which were rejected. Mere adoption of the affirmative plan mandates would be suffi-cient to either "significantly decrease military involvement" or to "significantly increase non-military assistance."

The effects nature of the topic has two consequences for the manner in which it will be debated. First, there is a necessary broadening of affirmative plan options. Where an affirmative resolution is single-tiered, like the two options rejected, there is a finite number of policy proposals which are fair equivalents of the type of action mandated by the affirmative resolution. The only limitation imposed on policy proposals under a two-tiered or effects-form resolution is that the affirmative must be able to argue successfully that the plan to be adopted will have the effects claimed, i.e., it will result in the adoption of the resolution. In the case of the 1987-88 topic, this means being able to demonstrate that affirmative plans will have the effect of increasing Latin American political stability. In the case of single-tiered resolutions, the limit on plan possibilities is linguistic; in the case of effects resolutions, the limits are to be found only in the imagination, artfulness, and evidentiary support available to the affirmative.

The second consequence of effects topicality is the second result of the conjunction of "adopt a policy" and "increase political stability," that the topic confuses topicality and solvency as issues. Had either of the other two topic options been chosen, this would not have been the case. In the case of the "decrease military involvement in Latin America" topic, an analyst could separate topicality (i.e., is the affirmative plan reasonably synonymous with the affirmative resolution?) from solvency (i.e., can it be predicted that the affirmative plan will achieve the benefits claimed for it?). On the topic selected, these issues become parts of the same discussion: achievement of predicted benefits is a necessary precondition for increasing political stability, hence solvency is a prerequisite for the attainment of topicality. On other resolutions, the outcome of one issue was independent of the outcome on the other.

The result of this fusion of issues is that all debates on the 1987-88 topic will be topicality debates, unless solvency is conceded. The companion result is that topicality arguments will be less arguments about the linguistic analysis of the resolution than they will be substantive arguments about the solvency predictions of the affirmative. For example, were the affirmative to argue that modified United States immigration policies (granting political asylum to refugees from Central America on a more extensive basis) would increase political stability, the debate would only be in part about what is meant by "political stability." It would primarily be about whether the affirmative policy, if adopted, could achieve increased "political stability." An affirmative team could "win" the more traditional linguistic interpretation topicality argument ("what is political stability?") and still lose the topicality argument should it be unable to respond to the substantive, solvency-based topicality argument. Argument on the substantive portion of this argument ("would modified immigration policies increase political stability?") would be precisely the same as solvency argumentation, considering the reasonableness of affirmative predictions, countervailing factors, and alternative causes.

The 1987-88 topic wording, through the absence of some key wording, will have a further impact on this discussion. No level of "political stability" is required by the topic. The topic does not say "significantly increase," for example. Hence, any solvency demonstration sufficient to predict some increase in Latin American political stability satisfies the requirement of adopting the resolution. Whether that increase is enough to justify the adoption of the resolution in the sense of outweighing costs of adopting the resolution would be a different question, answered by balancing the benefits attributable to the achievement of political stability against the cost of such achievements.

Agent of Change

The agent of change or action in the 1987–88 topic would appear to be quite clear, the "United States government." On closer examination, however, the topic only requires that the "United States government" (or portions thereof) be an initiating or participating agent of change. In other words, the resolution only requires that the government of the United States adopt policies which involve it in actions to increase political stability in Latin America. It does not restrict the affirmative to unilateral United States efforts or restrict it from multilateral or international cooperative endeavors.

To use a fairly basic example, how would topicality analysis proceed if the affirmative proposed that the United States should endorse the efforts of the Contadora group of nations? This series of diplomatic initiatives has been carried on exclusively by four Latin American nations attempting to resolve the dispute between the United States and Nicaragua. An agent of action could reasonably be said to have been those nations, acting in concert. Under the wording the 1987–88 resolution, that does not matter. So long as the "United States government" can be said to "adopt a policy" with the result of increasing political stability, United States adoption or ratification of third party efforts would fit within the topic. It would be the affirmative's burden to show that by adopting a policy of endorsing and complying with Contadora efforts, political stability in Latin America would be increased, and that such U.S. cooperation would be essential to the success of Contadora efforts. The United States need not have initiated these efforts, nor need it have acted exclusive of the actions of other nations or organizations in achieving political stability. It need only adopt a policy to accomplish this result.

Additional examples of this type of affirmative approach would include efforts which involved such organizations as the Organization of American States, the International Monetary Fund, or the General Agreement on Trade and Tariffs. As with the Contadora example, the policy adopted could simply be United States compliance with proposals concocted by other parties. Collateral examples could include the regional nuclear nonproliferation treaty for Latin America, as well as endorsement of the United Nations Law of the Sea Treaty.

The only limitation provided by the topic is that affirmative fiat is limited in scope to actions of the United States government. The affirmative can mandate only that the United States will adopt the policy it has outlined. It cannot mandate, for example, that Nicaragua would agree to Contadora verification procedures or that Brazil would comply with a nuclear nonproliferation treaty. Compliance with United States-adopted policies by other nations would be a matter resolved by evidence about the likelihood of other nations following suit after the United States acted in a particular manner.

Site of Action versus Site of Effect

Similar to the discussion above about the agent of change, this would appear to be an easily-resolved question: the resolution appears to focus on actions taken in Latin America. Again, on closer examination, the resolution provides much greater latitude. The resolution only requires that the effect of the plan (increased political stability) take place in Latin America. It does not so limit the site of the actions mandated by the affirmative.

The political asylum case mentioned earlier provides an example. The thesis of such an affirmative case would be that modifications in U.S. immigration policy, granting asylum more freely to refugees of the interal strife in El Salvador, for example, would increase political stability in Latin America (although the primary benefit would be a humanitarian one to the refugees). The policy adopted by the affirmative would operate exclusively within the United States. The claimed benefit (satisfying topicality requirements) would be the effect of such domestic United States actions on Latin America.

Similar examples would be provided by cases dealing with Latin American debt and other economic issues. Although the result of modified IMF or World Bank debt repayment policies (taken at the behest of the affirmative policy) would be that Latin American economies would be improved, the "action" of the affirmative plan would take place entirely outside of Latin America. While some additional actions might need to be taken by Latin American nations as a quid pro quo for debt restructuring (e.g., decreased public sector spending), those could not be mandated by the affirmative, for the reasons given above. The affirmative could only attempt to establish that the actions of Latin American nations would be the inevitable consequence of the adoption of the affirmative policy.

The effect this will have for debate will be one of broadening the topic from merely consisting of debates about United States activities in Latin America to activities having consequences for Latin America. This is a principal difference between the topic selected and the two options rejected. Instead of being restricted to United States military involvement in Latin America or non-military assistance to Latin America, the affirmative may discuss policies which will have some effect on the degree of political stability in that region.

That affirmatives are not limited to Latin America as the site of plan mandates is in part the consequence of the effects nature of the topic. It is only a question of evidence, not of language, whether United States policies adopted anywhere in the world will have an effect on the political stability of Latin America. This promises debates about whether the possible effects of a proposed United States policy on Latin America are too attenuated to fulfill the loose requirements of the topic (some increase in political stability). For example, would a unilateral ban on nuclear weapons testing by the United States have an impact on Latin American political stability? This would be answered only by the probative nature of affirmative evidence on the relationship between the policy and the topical effect. Of course, this also opens up the topic to policies taken "to increase political stability in Latin America" which would have much more direct and substantial benefits in parts of the world other than Latin America, which would be true of the nuclear weapons testing example.

Absence of Modifiers

The 1987–88 topic is relatively devoid of limiting modifiers. Some of these have already been discussed. The topic is somewhat broadened by the use of the phrase "United States government" instead of "United States federal government." The topic wording has an effect on the nature of topicality disputes by not including "significantly" before "increase." In a different sense, two phrases in the topic provide greater breadth for debate where substitute choices could have produced significant narrowing of options. "Latin America" provides much wider choices for argument that "Central America" and "political stability" is broader (and more amorphous) than any of a variety of other possible end-points for affirmative solvency (e.g., reduced poverty, reduced guerrilla warfare and terrorism, reduced human rights abuses).

There are two other omissions of modifiers of consequence for topic interpretation. First, "policy" is not modified in any fashion. For example, the policy apparently need not be a "comprehensive policy," which means that policies limited to a particular substantive area (e.g., "economic policy") will satisfy the topic. At the same time "policy" was not modified by a restrictive substantive classification (such as "economic"). Therefore, any type of policy (economic, military, agricultural, diplomatic, humanitarian, etc.) would appear to be included under the topic.

The second modifier not included is a time-line modifier. The topic does not specify the point in time at which "political stability" must be achieved. This could have been achieved through such phrasings as "short-term policy," "long-term policy," or "long-term political stability."

The result of the absence of a time-line modifier is that the point at which "political stability" is to be achieved is simply a matter of judgment on the part of the affirmative: more immediate benefits could be persuasive to a decision-maker, but so could benefits which would be more long-lasting but which would take a longer "start-up" period to achieve. There are two implications of this for topic analysis. First, no resolutional ceiling is placed on the amount of time necessary for the affirmative to obtain topicality. For the purposes of claiming superior levels of net benefits over negative positions, the sooner increased political stability is attained the better for the affirmative. However, the affirmative is not limited by the topic to "quick fix" options to increase Latin American political stability. It need only indicate that the policy to be adopted will increase political stability at some point, and convince a decision-maker that waiting for that point is a more desirable policy option than the alternative defended by the negative.

The second implication is that affirmative options could have short-term or immediate destabilizing consequences, so long as their predicted long-term effect would be that of increasing political stability. This is important in that virtually any policy proposal has immediate dysfunctional effects attributable to policy transition and implementation problems. Affirmatives are not held to such near-term consequences in the evaluation of whether their proposals meet the resolution.

Time-line issues are another consequence of the effects nature of the resolution. Simply put, while the affirmative policy is implemented by the resolution, increased political stability need not be attained until a later date. To some extent this is true of any policy resolution. What is different about the 1987-88 topic is that the later-achieved effects (increased political stability) are necessary for the adoption of the resolution.

The time-line analysis could be used to describe the Reagan Administration's support of the Contras in Nicaragua. Whether one views the ultimate objective of such efforts as getting the Sandinistas to the bargaining table or overthrowing them, two things are already clear: (1) it will take several years for these effects to be obtained; and (2) the activities of the Contras will have the initial effect of decreasing political stability before political stability is restored.

Multiple Options or Interpretations

A final consideration has to do with the impact of topic wording on the multiplicity of affirmative interpretations. The conclusion drawn here is that the wording of the 1987-88 resolution produces two effects: (1) it should be possible for affirmatives to argue that they can interpret the topic to permit them to adopt policies of relevance to as few as one Latin American nation or to one issue of relevance to political stability; and (2) it should be difficult for affirmatives to present multiple policies or examples of the resolution in the same debate.

An issue which has appeared from time to time in college as well as high school debate is whether a policy resolution which prescribes a type of action for an identified audience or community should be taken as requiring the affirmative to justify the taking of such action inclusively for the entire audience or community or subsets of the class. In the case of the topic under discussion, this would mean that the affirmative would be required to establish justifications for the adoption of a single policy for all of Latin America.

This is not a reasonable interpretation of the 1987-88 high school topic for three reasons. First, as noted above, this topic does not include the term "comprehensive." Policies to be adopted under this resolution should be seen as contrasted with those intended to be comprehensive in scope or in breadth. While

affirmatives could adopt policies which would in fact be comprehensive and might cover all major issues and Latin American
nations, the topic does not place such an obligation on them.

A second factor has to do with the use of the word "in" in
the topic. <u>Black's Law Dictionary</u> states that "in" is "(a)n
elastic preposition . . . expressing relation of presence,
existence, situation, inclusion, action" and is synonymous with
the expressions "in regard to," "respecting," and "with respect
to." (p. 682) Policies to be adopted under the 1987-88 resolution need only increase stability in Latin America. This means
that increments in political stability resulting from the affirmative plan must be experienced within Latin America as a geographic entity. The resolution does not stipulate that either
the policy or the effects of the policy be universal in their
impact on all portions of Latin America, only that increases in
political stability be experienced somewhere in Latin America.
Of course, the benefits of the affirmative plan could be achieved
within Latin America or any other part of the world. Those would
be the results of the plan attaining political stability, and
would not be limited to Latin America in terms of the audience
receiving the benefit.

Finally, the analysis of solvency-topicality requirements
discussed earlier suggests that affirmatives need not deal with
Latin America as a whole. Given the effects format of the
resolution, solvency must be attained to establish topicality.
If the affirmative were able to establish that, for example,
conceding the U.S. Naval Base at Guantanamo to the Cuban government would result in increased political stability throughout
Latin America as a result of its positive effects on United
States-Cuban relations, why should the affirmative be required to
meet additional proof requirements to establish that the resolution's adoption has been justified? Any affirmative explanation
which established that the result of the adoption of the policy
it proposed would be to increase political stability in Latin
America would have fulfilled the requirements of the resolution.
To require that the affirmative plan apply to all, nearly all, or
even two Latin American nations would be a convention not
explicit in the wording the resolution. In addition, some plans
might propose actions not even explicitly mentioning Latin
America but which would have major influences on Latin American
nations. This would be true of international debt or economic
development cases which modified debt repayment or loan provision
policies.

On the other hand, the wording of the resolution appears to
make it very difficult for affirmatives to introduce multiple
policy alternatives in the same debate. This is because of the
simultaneous presence of the word "a" with the absence of the
word "comprehensive." <u>Black's Law Dictionary</u> states that "a" may
mean "one where only one is intended, or it may mean any one of a
great number. . . (it) is not necessarily a singular term; it is
often used in the sense of 'any' and is then applied to more than
one individual object." (p. 1)

Two interpretations could be given to the resolution: (1) the persons who wrote it intended that affirmatives propose the adoption of a single policy (although, as mentioned above, that single policy need not apply to all of Latin America); and (2) the persons who wrote the resolution intended that "a" policy proposed by the affirmative be one of a number of possible policies. The absence of the term "comprehensive" makes matters difficult for the affirmative which would like to propose multiple policies in the same debate: while the single proposal of the affirmative might have multiple, comprehensive effects, there is not comprehensiveness language permitting, much less requiring affirmatives to propose multiple policies. Hence, the affirmative team which would like to propose multiple, divergent policies in the same debate will have difficulty establishing that this is "a policy," as required by the resolution. At best, the affirmative could argue that these divergent elements are separate components of a single "policy."

NEGATIVE GROUND

This section examines the effect of topic wording on the argumentative ground available to affirmatives and negatives and the resultant options open to negatives. The overall conclusion drawn here is that isolation of negative ground is more problematic on this resolution than others, for a number of reasons. Negative ground is hard to identify because of the ambiguous effects nature of resolutional mandates; because of the low threshhold of change required ("increase political stability"); and because no precise area of affirmative ground is identified (actions having the effect of increasing political stability). The remainder of this section discusses the five basic positions available to negatives on this topic: (1) defending decreased political stability in Latin America; (2) defending actions producing no effect on the degree of political stability; (3) defending a policy of non-involvement in affairs relating to Latin America; (4) defending policies precluded by increased political stability in Latin America; and (5) on-point positions separated from affirmative ground by affirmative interpretations of increases in political stability. The first three policy positions, while logically available alternatives to the resolution, are unlikely to be of much practical value to negatives. The problem faced by negatives is one of avoiding defending approaches that can be characterized as topical. Given the broad nature of "political stability," this will be difficult. Some international options might avoid this problem, and are discussed at the end of the section.

Decreased Political Stability

The most direct contrast to the affirmative topic would appear to be that of defending a policy of decreasing political stability.

This appears to be a clearer option than is actually the case, simply because increased political stability is itself an ambiguous phrase in terms of the policies actually to be implemented. For example, both increasing and decreasing aid to the Contras could be argued to increase political stability. Decreasing political stability in practice ultimately has no more precise meaning that "doing the opposite of the affirmative." And even at that point, the negative position could be argued to be simply an alternative example of the resolution.

Decreasing political stability might be a useful negative position in a narrow range of cases. It should be remembered that, as discussed in the first section of this chapter, "political stability" is not always a positively-valued condition. The position adopted by the negative would be one of arguing that the achievement of increases in political stability would have undesirable consequences. This would not be easy to do, and is probably limited to a few situations.

As one example of this position, it could be argued that opposition to the Sandinistas and to Cuba is destabilizing and that there are positive effects to this. However, it would be difficult to count up benefits to this approach without including some that are traceable to net increases in political stability in Latin America. The Reagan Administration has defended its support of the Contras in part on the basis that its policy puts the Sandinistas on the defensive and reduces their ability to foment revolution elsewhere in Central and South America. This is susceptible to the response that aid to the Contras, although billed as decreasing political stability is in fact a policy to increase political stability in Nicaragua as a means to that end.

Therefore, the real test of this option is whether the negative can isolate benefits to decreased political stability which cannot be characterized as increasing political stability: given the breadth of what is included in "political stability," this will be difficult in most cases.

Policies Not Affecting Political Stability

While this appears to be a logically distinct alternative to the resolution, a policy defending no change in the level of political stability would in fact merge with the fourth set of options described below, defending policies in competition with increased political stability in Latin America. For example, an affirmative case based on the concept that increased U.S. technical assistance to agricultural cooperatives, together with land reform, would have the effect of increased political stability in most Latin American nations. Defending a policy of maintaining current levels of political stability would only be competitive with the affirmative if the negative were able to argue that the affirmative approach would produce countervailing disadvantages. Turned around, this is the same thing as saying that increased political stability would endanger or preclude other policies of the United States. It is possible for the negative to defend keeping the level of political stability at its current levels by

defending the continuation of existent programs. However, a
decision for the negative would be based on the cost of programs
or policies sacrificed or precluded by affirmative plan mandates
being greater than the benefits of affirmative action: this is
indistinct from the argumentative position described in the
fourth subsection, below.

Noninvolvement in Latin America

As a negative position, this suffers some of the same problems as
the "decreased political stability" stance. It would be difficult to argue that minimizing the presence of the United States
in Latin America would have no effect on political stability
there; it would be easier to argue that its effect would be to
decrease political stability, making it the same as the first
negative position described.

The fundamental difficulty with defending the absence of
United States involvement is that the negative would be susceptible to the argument that the absence of a policy is itself a
type of policy. The justifications for not providing military
assistance or training, or economic development aid, would be
difficult to phrase in terms that could not be characterized as
in some manner increasing political stability in Latin America.
For example, it could be argued that the effect of eliminating
United States military assistance and training would be to
decrease the control of the military on governments in Latin
America, encouraging pluralism in Latin American politics. While
this might initially be destabilizing, the argument for political
pluralism and a decreased political role for the military in
Latin America is one of increased political stability from
greater continuity of forms of government, more responsiveness to
public problems, lessened appeal of extremist groups, etc.
Hence, this approach would amount to a policy impacting political
stability. Like the first negative position described, it would
be a topical option to the degree that it had positive effects on
Latin American political stability.

Policies Precluded by the Affirmative

This is a position which can be argued in effect even when not
articulated as such by the negative. While this can be defended
as a full-blown counterplan position, the negative can also
attempt to minimize affirmative significance and then win the
debate on the strength of disadvantages. Since the disadvantages
really amount to benefits of alternative policies precluded by
efforts to increase political stability in Latin America, this
amounts to the same position as if it were argued as a counterplan.

For example, if the affirmative argued for a policy of
expanded efforts to guarantee human rights in Latin America, the
negative could phrase its response in one of two ways. First, it
could present a counterplan, defending a policy of "quiet
diplomacy" and refusing to link human rights conduct with other

foreign policy considerations in dealing with other nations, in Latin America and elsewhere. The position could be described as nontopical in that it would be a policy to secure U.S. strategic interests, not a policy to increase Latin American political stability. Competitiveness could be established through the mutual exclusiveness and philosophical contradictions between the affirmative and the negative approaches to human rights abuses. The negative could argue a net counterplan advantage of better securing U.S. strategic interests through not linking them to human rights performance by other nations. The negative could argue that the affirmative degree of solvency in dealing with human rights abuses would be no greater than that of "quiet diplomacy."

Should the negative not wish to phrase this as a counterplan, it could nevertheless argue all of the same issues. It could argue that "quiet diplomacy" minimized the significance of affirmative advantages. However, its major argument would be the foreign policy linkage position, which would be presented as a disadvantage. The decisional calculus at the end of the debate would be the same in both cases: do the benefits of decreased human rights abuses (measured in comparison with the degree of affectiveness of Reagan Administration "quiet diplomacy" efforts) exceed the costs of such a policy to the attainment of U.S. foreign policy objectives?

This negative policy position also brings to light a set of arguments that can probably be presented in most debates on the 1987-88 topics. Although the topic focuses on Latin America, there can be collateral effects on all parts of the world. Negatives in defending a position that affirmative efforts to increase Latin American political stability will preclude other important values will attempt to find harms to the United States in other parts of the world. This is because such harms will be difficult for the affirmative to match in terms of significance and because they will have the tactical value of pulling the focus of the debate from Latin America, the area of the affirmative's advantages, to the disadvantages. In the human rights linkage example given above, the negative could argue that although the affirmative's policy benefits would be limited to Latin America, linkage would have worldwide effects. The negative could argue that the affirmative policy would be extended to other areas of the world as a matter of policy consistency or that there would be a snowball effect from Latin American affairs to other parts of the world. Based on that premise, the negative could then argue foreign policy harms to the United States in other parts of the world.

Also affirmatives can argue collateral worldwide effects to policies increasing Latin American political stability, although it may be more difficult for the negative than the affirmative to do so. Such advantages would not be extratopical. The topic requires that the affirmative adopt policies increasing political stability in Latin America but does not limit the affirmative to advantages occurring in Latin America alone. So, for example, increased Latin American political stability through decreased

United States military assistance to Honduras and to the Contras could be argued to improve United States relations with Western Europe. The theory would be that Western Europeans worry about the ability of the United States to conduct a competent European foreign policy while preoccupied with military adventurism in some other part of the globe, e.g., Southeast Asia or Central America.

On-point Positions

As has been discussed, "political stability" will probably take on distinctly different meanings from debate to debate. As a result, negatives can develop positions for individual debates that they will not be able to retain as generic positions on the topic. The most prominent example of this is how different affirmatives might choose to define "a policy to increase political stability" with respect to Nicaragua. The policy proposed by the affirmative could involve withdrawal of support to the Contras. It could just as easily involve increasing support to them, given the absence of directionality in the topic.

Depending on the option chosen by the affirmative, the negative's options would change as well. However, given the slipperiness of "political stability" as a concept, the negative would have to defend alternatives which could not be characterized by the affirmative as simply another example of the affirmative resolution. In the Nicaraguan example, if the affirmative proposed withdrawal of support to the Contras and the negative defended a position of maximizing support to them, the affirmative could argue that the negative position was in effect a topical counterplan, since its putative result would be restoring political stability to Latin America. The negative could choose to deal with this in one of three ways. First, it could argue that it was reasonably nontopical in that its policy would decrease political stability, at least in the short-term. However, the same thing can be said of nearly all affirmative options on this topic. A second response would be to say that the resolution separates policies to increase political stability in Latin America from other types of policies: the critical feature is the purpose or objective of the policy. In this case, the objective would not be one of increasing political stability in Latin America but of decreasing Cuban-Soviet influence in Central America. This is arguably artificial: on this basis, every counterplan would be nontopical, so long as the negative was sufficiently adroit to think up a policy objective it could contend was distinct from increasing political stability.

A final more likely response to be argued, given the breadth of the topic and the policy-making paradigm orientation of the debate community would be that the affirmative has defined the operational meaning of "a policy to increase political stability" for the purposes of the debate in progress. Negative options need only be nontopical by the standards operating within that debate. Therefore, if the affirmative and negative positions are clearly distinct alternatives on the basis of the definitions advanced by the affirmative, a decision-maker must evaluate the negative as a nontopical option, even if it might be advanced as an affirmative case in another debate. The difficulty with this approach is that the definitional standards under which an affirmative would fulfill topicality will often make the negative position topical as well. This is particularly true with regard to "political stability." Hence, it is up to the negative to find ways of describing its position as "reasonably nontopical" in some manner.

In addition to the negative options described above, there are some additional positions based on alternatives to "United States government." The agent of action in the topic is the United States government. It could be argued that an alternative to the resolution would be nongovernmental or private efforts. The negative would run the risk of having this approach being argued to be a topical counterplan if the United States government was involved in any way. For example, if the negative position in a human rights debate were to have the United Nations fund human rights monitoring, the affirmative might argue that this was topical action, given United States support of the United Nations. The question would be how attenuated the connection between the counterplan and the United States government would be. This would be true of negative positions generally which involved international organizations of which the United States was a member.

A position which has been debated on a number of topics, world government, may reappear here as well. In contrast with the option described above, the negative can argue that it has superceded "United States government" action by creating a world federation of states. The competitiveness argument used by negatives presenting world government counterplans on other topics can be presented here as well. The topic sanctions unilateral nation-state activities by a superpower, enhancing national sovereignty as a force and retarding movement toward world government.

REFERENCES

Jack C. Plano, Robert E. Riggs, and Helena S. Robin, The Dictionary of Political Analysis. Santa Barbara, ABC-Clio, 1982.

Ernest E. Rossi and Jack C. Plano, The Latin American Political Dictionary. Santa Barbara, ABC-Clio, 1980.

Roger, Scruton, A Dictionary of Political Thought. New York, Harper and Row, 1982.

Generic Issues on the 1987-88 Topic

This chapter explores what are predicted to be recurrent issues on the 1987-88 topic. These predictions are based on the following assumptions: (1) most cases on the increased political stability topic will fall into the categories of decreasing United States military assistance to Central America, increasing economic assistance to Latin America, or attempting to reduce the Latin American international debt repayment burden; and (2) the benefits claimable from affirmative cases will be ones of savings in lives, increased political freedom, increased standards of living, improved United States-Soviet relations, and improved economic growth. In addition, there will be subcategories and variations of all of these case types. Assuming that these are the general case types, a number of recurrent issues can be predicted. These issues fall into four areas: (1) inherency; (2) evidence and significance; (3) solvency; and (4) advantages and disadvantages.

INHERENCY-MOTIVE ARGUMENTS

Affirmatives will for the most part be contrasting proposed Latin American foreign policies with current policies. In most cases, this will involve analysis of the "Reagan Doctrine" discussed in Chapter Three. As a result, paradigmatic differences as to the meaning of inherency may not be quite as important on the 1987-88 topic as on other topics. Whether one conceives of inherency as uniqueness of benefits accruing to alternative systems, as competing policy systems, or as impediments to change, the immediate focus of affirmatives and negatives will be on the Reagan Administration's conduct in Latin American affairs. This will be particularly true of cases dealing with military assistance and human rights, but will also be true of most other affirmative cases.

As is discussed in Chapter Three, there is a coherent Reagan Administration view of foreign relations which has been applied to Latin America. There is a similar set of views as regards international economic relations, although these are somewhat less detailed. Depending on one's paradigmatic perspective, this means that inherency can be characterized as the degree of commitment to these policies, or in terms of the motives behind the adoption and maintenance of them. It seems highly unlikely that there will be any radical shift in Reagan Administration Latin American policy between the current date and mid-1988. As is discussed in Chapter Four, this is probably even the case as regards U.S. aid to the Contras in Nicaragua, the least popular and most controversial of the Reagan Administration's foreign

policies. The Reagan Administration appears steadfastly committed to a policy of providing extensive military assistance to
Central America to combat insurgents it sees as connected to
supporting the Contras and funding covert operations directed
against Nicaragua. Consistent with its ideological positions in
other policy arenas, the Reagan Administration also appears
committed to largely unilateral or bilateral policy initiatives,
a "free enterprise" view of economic development, and to seeing
human rights as a concern secondary to the development of internal security in Latin American nations. At a deeper level, these
policy positions reflect motives connected to the maintenance of
national security and to U.S. protection of the region from
Soviet influence (or, thought of a different way, United States
hegemony over Latin America).

Two additional comments can be made about inherency that are
specific to the 1987-88 topic. First, if one thinks of affirmative policy positions as departures from current Reagan Administration policies, it will probably be easier to conceptualize
affirmative case positions which run in the opposite ideological
direction of those policies. Therefore, it will probably be the
case that affirmatives will propose cutbacks in military assistance, augment human rights efforts, reorient U.S. efforts toward
land reform, or do other things contrasting with Reagan Administration policies and priorities.

Since the topic is nondirectional, affirmatives are not
required to oppose current policies. The affirmative could just
as easily augment current Reagan Administration Latin American
policies. Especially from a hypothesis-testing perspective,
modification of current administration policies is the wrong way
of thinking about inherency. Inherency, from this paradigmatic
orientation, means contrasting policies to increase political
stability in Latin America with other, nonresolutional policies.
As was indicated in Chapter One, this means such negative positions as non-U.S. organizations increasing Latin American political stability, or U.S. efforts to do something other than
increase political stability in Latin America. Also, the wording
of the topic makes both of these positions problematic, as both
could be argued to be productive of topical counterplans.
"Political stability" is an opaque term which can describe a
variety of policies, and the topic does not preclude international and multilateral efforts done in concert with the United
States. For example, a negative which defended a free trade
counterplan would have to show not only that this was competitive
with the affirmative but also that free trade would not be a
means of increasing political stability in Latin America.

Should affirmatives choose to augment current policies to
Latin America, they also would run into a conception of inherency
prevalent in the debate community: policy propositions always
involve the proposing of change. There is no a priori reason why
a policy proposition must do this. Certainly, affirmatives could
defend continuation of existent Reagan Administration policies as
productive of increased political stability in Latin America.
However, inherency as traditionally conceived of would run

counter to this. The topic does not require that a new policy be adopted, only that a policy be adopted. One can make the semantic argument that a policy which already exists cannot be proposed to be adopted. However, there certainly is no preclusion in the topic to enhancing assistance to the Contras as a means of increasing political stability. Affirmatives which adopt such a position must expect that, from a narrow policy-making perspective, they will be regarded as proposing something that is already being practiced to a large degree. This will lead to debates about whether the "present system" can be "expanded" to include the affirmative augmentation of current policies. It is probably conceptually easier simply to adopt affirmative positions counter to current policies.

A second comment derives from the same kind of policy-making perspective on inherency. The point of departure for inherency analysis is the current state of affairs, i.e., Reagan Administration Latin American policy. It is a chronological accident that the high school debate community will be discussing Latin America close to the end of the Reagan Administration's existence. This should not be seen as justifying a pseudo-inherency argument that "the present system" will change with the inauguration of a new President in 1989. The extension of this view would be that the proposals of the affirmative will be adopted by the new administration once it takes office, so there is no reason to adopt the affirmative. A variation on this theme would be that the affirmative is indicting policies of the Reagan Administration, which is about to come to an end: a policy-maker should wait to see what the next administration will do with regard to Latin America before deciding to adopt the affirmative proposal.

These are nonpositions. The negative is in the position of defending against whether affirmative policies to increase Latin American political stability are preferable to alternative, nontopical positions. Whether a future administration will (or will not) modify the current administration's policy toward Latin America in several months does not matter. The negative has to evaluate the affirmative with something concrete, either because it already exists or because it is a counterplan proposal which the negative is willing to defend. There is no guarantee that a future administration (e.g., a Bush Administration) would modify current U.S. policy toward Latin America in any case. U.S. policy toward Southeast Asia took on a life of its own and continued through several presidencies, so U.S. support of the Contras and military assistance to Central America could do the same thing. The only relevance of the positions of a Gary Hart or a Jack Kemp on Latin America is in their suggestion of a competing policy view which would have to be proposed and defended by the negative. Arguing that future administrations may do something and we should therefore wait does not oppose the topic in the sense that it does not say adopting a policy to increase political stability in Latin America is a bad idea and should be rejected. Rather, it says that the affirmative resolution is a good idea, but some different set of policy-makers will adopt it at a later point in time. The negative is, in essence, defending a studies counterplan without the study.

EVIDENCE AND SIGNIFICANCE

An inevitable feature of the 1987-88 topic will be a number of debates about the truth and accuracy of the evidence used. This is not a comment about the integrity of the debaters using the evidence; it is a comment about the "real world" debate which is raging about the integrity of a number of the sources being quoted. The only integrity implication for debaters is how they use such evidence once they have the knowledge that it is of doubtful accuracy. Whether the debates become acrimonious or not will be a matter determined by the participants. Since much of the evidence that can be introduced has been the subject of dispute by the "real world" participants, the debate world experience should not be expected to be radically different.

Every topic has biased and dubious evidence: the 1987-88 topic may be different in the degree of vitriol and animosity expressed by some of the courses cited toward each other. This is primarily the case in debates about U.S. military involvement in Central America, safeguarding human rights, and United States support of the Contras. Human rights organizations monitoring the situation in El Salvador, including Americas Watch and Amnesty International, have contended that they have been the target of verbal abuse by the Department of State since mid-1985. They also have accused the Department of State of distorting facts and selective reporting in its "Country Reports," which are the basis for certification of human rights improvements neces- sary for Congressional funding. The State Department has re- torted that human rights groups also exaggerate claims of abuses and accept uncritically information supplied by members of guerrilla organizations. El Salvador has also been the focus of a dispute about whether the Air Force of that country has con- ducted a bombing campaign against civilian targets.

The evidence issue has a Washington front as well. The Reagan Administration State Department has accused the Washington Office on Latin America (WOLA) of being a public relations office for the Sandinistas. Several groups in New York and Washington opposed to Reagan Administration Latin American policies have reported break-ins of their offices, with documents being searched for or stolen. The FBI has disagreed with the groups, finding no pattern to the burglaries. The debate in Congress about aid to the Contras has been affected by name-calling on both sides. Former White House Director of Communications Patrick Buchanan negatively affected the outcome of one Congres- sional vote through an Op-Ed article in the New York Times dis- paraging opponents of aid, which House Speaker Tip O'Neill referred to as "McCarthy-like" in tone. Proponents of aid have linked the Contras in similar fashion.

The Reagan Administration has not helped its credibility on Latin American policy through engaging in conduct and making statements from time to time which have embarrassed White House and State Department officials. The revelations about Colonel North and the diversion of funds from arms sales to Iran to CIA activities in Central America are simply the latest episode in a series of events serving to draw a distinction between official and actual policy. It should be remembered that the Reagan Administration denied any connection between itself and the Contras until a November 1982 magazine expose revealed that the U.S. Ambassador to Honduras, John Negroponte, was overseeing the arming and training of Nicaraguan exiles. It was later revealed that a CIA agent calling himself "Tony Feldman" interviewed candidates for Contra leadership roles. Incidents in Nicaragua ascribed to Contra operations (the mining of harbors, the bombing of Managua) have since been revealed to have been carried out by the CIA. The Reagan Administration has attempted to maintain the fiction that the Contras are an indigenous group which we are merely aiding, and would exist without U.S. support. The various revelations have made this position harder to sell. In 1981-82 the Administration was embarrassed on several occasions when it announced that it had proof of Cuban and Nicaraguan support of the guerillas in El Salvador and was then unable to make good on its allegations. On one occasion, in March 1982, the State Department produced a Nicaraguan, Orlando Jose Tardencillas at a press conference to support such charges. Instead, Tardencillas recanted earlier statements attesting to Cuban and Nicaraguan involvement as having been made under duress by department officials.

For its part, it should also be remembered that the Sandinistas take a distinctively different view of the role of the press and of media information than is familiar to most Americans. The Sandinistas have clamped down on press freedoms because of its view that in a revolutionary society, the press is to be an agent of education, promoting the revolution. Since the revolution and the government act in the best interests of the people, press criticism impedes national progress and must be suppressed. Although referred to by mass media theorists as the "Soviet" theory of the press, this view is quite common among single-party, post-revolutionary governments in the Third World. It is also a convenient excuse for prepublication censorship of bad news, slanted reporting where convenient, and suspension of the publication of newspapers (such as La Prensa) which say unpleasant things about the government.

Part of the problem with evidence on human rights abuses and the conduct of insurgency and counterinsurgency efforts in Central America is the difficulty in reporting. Western reporters are dependent on the government, whether it is Nicaragua or El Salvador, in being allowed to see certain parts of the country. Governments will always act in their own best interest, permitting reporting showing their country in the light most favorable to them. News which does not come from the government may come from secondary sources, or is based on interviews of witnesses or survivors of atrocities which must be carried on through an interpreter. And while Amnesty International and the American press generally have no political or ideological agenda to which information is molded, a number of political groups engage in this activity. The State Department under Assistant Secretary of State for Inter-American Affairs Elliott Abrams and his predecessors Thomas Enders and Langhorne Motley have been accused of being result-oriented in their analyses of the situation in Central America, reading events as establishing the existence of a network of Soviet and Cuban support for guerillas in El Salvador and elsewhere, describing an improving but still dangerous situation in which the presence of an insurgency movement justifies U.S. aid and the use of extreme measures by local governments, while the human rights record is simultaneously improving. The American Library Association's <u>Newsletter on Intellectual Freedom</u> annually publishes a "top ten" list of stories that were unreported or reported in a distorted fashion compiled by the journalism faculty of a California university: the war in Central America has been at or near the top of the charts since the beginning of the Reagan Administration. The same poll also found U.S. media coverage of the elections in Nicaragua inaccurate.

Outside of an object lesson in the reasons for not taking evidence at face value and considering the motives of sources, debaters should find the evidence credibility issue on the 1987-88 topic relevant to disputes about significance. The real impact of evidence challenges should be on the level of significance which can be ascribed to affirmative and negative disadvantage arguments. Here there may be a reprise of arguments first heard on the arms sales topic: what is the level of human rights abuses; have they decreased; if so, to what extent have human rights abuses decreased? No one seriously disputes that there have been human rights abuses by virtually all the governments in Latin American countries, just as no one seriously disputes that the assorted Latin American Marxist insurgencies have also engaged in atrocities. The question for significance is both the extent and frequency of such activities and their causes. Without some notion of casual explanations, the numbers of human rights abuses themselves are of little value in determining the effectiveness of responsive policies. This should be remembered during debates which focus on whether the number of death squad casualties in El Salvador has dropped to two hundred persons per month or if the figure is actually one hundred.

Debaters also should draw a distinction between current evidence which attempts to attach firm numbers to specific events and evidence attempting to describe general tendencies and trends over longer period of time. While there is some justification for using whatever sketchy information is available in the first situation, there is no excuse at all for doing so in the second case. Latin American history and Latin American political affairs are the subjects of serious study and scholarly research at a number of major American universities. Special interest groups of any political complexion need not be relied upon for support of theoretical and historical positions. And while there is no shortage of biased publications to be cited on this topic, there are also a number of publications which strive to be balanced: Rosset and Vandermeer's <u>The Nicaragua Reader</u> (1983) is one such book.

While debaters with any level of experience should be familiar with biased evidence, they should detect a special patriotic fervor about some of the materials they will read this year, especially by conservative writers supportive of anti-Cuban, anti-Soviet U.S. activities in Latin America. They may also detect a note of righteousness and moral superiority in the writings of both opponents and proponents of Reagan Administration human rights and military assistance policies in Latin America. The task for debaters in performing research is recognizing biased and distorted evidence when they see it, and not basing arguments upon it. This may be asking a great deal of high school students, especially if they have to divorce personal opinions from research. On the other hand, debaters should see a special credibility to admissions against interest by different parties. When the Salvadoran guerillas admit that they use forced conscription in rural areas to fill their ranks, or the United States concedes that it bombed a hospital during the invasion of Grenada, this is classic "reluctant testimony" and should have heightened persuasive value. As mentioned above, debaters should distinguish between evidence disputes which are quibbles about differences in numbers and those which undercut the authority or validity of a theoretical position.

Finally, debaters should distinguish between other debaters who misapply or overclaim evidence and those who, in good faith, rely on evidence which misapplies or misstates the facts. While debaters are always responsible for the quality and veracity of the evidence they rely upon, there are distinctions between the debater who makes tortured use of evidence, the debater who uses evidence he or she knows to be of dubious quality, and the debater who uses evidence he or she believes to be credible which is subsequently challenged.

SOLVENCY

Three generic types of solvency arguments will be present on the 1987-88 topic, owing to its international character, its implication of security assistance and covert operations agencies and issues, and to the relationship between plan mandates and attainment of advantages for this topic. The three types of solvency arguments will be: (1) circumvention; (2) absence of "follow-through" by nations other than the United States; and (3) resistance to or ineffectiveness of monitoring and verification procedures by nations other than the United States.

Circumvention

As was mentioned in Chapter One, the topic by its language limits affirmative fiat to actions of the United States. In other words, the affirmative can avoid questions of whether legislation

will in fact be adopted or implemented, funds will be appropriated, etc., only as regards the United States. The effect of the
resolution's wording is to suspend for the sake of argument
considerations of whether the President or Congress will take
special measures to increase political stability in Latin America
in order that the merits of those special measures can be articulated by the participants in the debate. The resolution's
wording does not suspend consideration of whether other nations
will modify their policies, legislation, or behavior in response
to the affirmative proposals in the manner predicted by the
affirmative: fiat power extends to the United States government,
not to the Argentine military or the Shining Path guerillas in
Peru. This limitation on fiat power is critical to solvency
analysis because the affirmative can only mandate that policies
will be adopted which have the intention or objective of increasing political stability in Latin America. However, as was also
mentioned in Chapter One, for this topic, solvency is a precondition for topicality. The affirmative must establish that the
policies adopted are reasonably likely to increase political
stability in order that the topicality of affirmative proposals
can be established.

The other reason that the limitation on fiat power to
actions of the United States is critical to solvency analysis is
that it differentiates the first generic solvency argument,
circumvention from the other two types of arguments. Both the
"follow-through" and the monitoring-verification arguments stem
from the international character of the resolution, with the
United States adopting policies which will have differing degrees
of effectiveness based on foreign (and, as a result, uncontrollable by fiat) responses to those policies. Circumvention, a
familiar argument to the debate community, is instead an argument
based on whether selected agents or audiences of the resolutions
obey the edicts of the affirmative or find ways of ignoring them.

In its 1987-88 incarnation, the circumvention argument will
take on the following forms: (1) where the affirmative ends
covert operations by the CIA in Central America, the agency will
find a way to sidestep plan mandates and continue such operations; (2) where the affirmative seeks to end military assistance
which promotes counterinsurgency methods productive of human
rights abuses (e.g., the provision of aircraft and aircraft parts
necessary for the bombing of zones inhabited by guerillas and
noncombatants) will nevertheless find a way of providing such
assistance; and (3) where the affirmative prescribes U.S. policies to modify social and economic conditions (e.g., land reform
measures, modified trade or immigration laws), Congress or the
President will be influenced by interest groups or lobbies to
either not carry out these measures or to utilize other powers of
authority to blunt the effectiveness of these measures.

Variations of all of these forms of arguments have been
heard on other topics. The position taken here is that these are
theoretically unsound interpretations of solvency as an issue,
running counter to the "should-would" distinction made by fiat as
a concept. All of the examples used above have one common theme:

the affirmative plan will not be adopted, or, more precisely, although the literal language of the plan will not be adopted, it either will not be given practical effect or alternative measures explicitly precluded by the affirmative plan and diammetrically opposed to it will also be adopted. This is a misunderstanding of solvency as a concept. The notion of solvency arguments is one of testing whether the affirmative ideas for solving problems, if put into effect as the affirmative has conceived of them, are capable of producing the results the affirmative has predicted for them. The circumvention arguments described above are nonsequiturs. They answer the question, "If the affirmative did x, would it have y effect?" by saying, "x will not take place." Given its focus on public policies and examples of legislative and governmental executive decision-makers, it is sometimes easy for debaters to lose sight of the fact that policy proposition debate is about the evaluation of alternative forms of solutions to problems. So although it is factually accurate to say that the CIA, the Defense Department, and virtually every other governmental agency acts to circumvent policies they oppose, this is not suggestive of solvency arguments. Instead, the reasons for the opposition of such agencies to affirmative policies is creative of the disadvantages of such policies, once implemented.

Another way of examining circumvention arguments is to note the distinction between agents of change and audiences of change. For example, consider an affirmative case on the 1987–88 topic which proposes that the United States cease covert military operations in Central America. The agent of change or action would be anyone or anything that was reasonably synonymous with the topic phrase, "United States government." Hence, the affirmative could by fiat stipulate that the President, the Contras, and their designated agencies, the Department of State, the Department of Defense, the CIA, the Defense Intelligence Agency, the National Security Agency, etc., would cease involvement in covert operations in Latin America. The audience of change would be groups or individuals to be affected by the taking of action. In the language of the 1987–88 topic, this would be one or more nations in Latin America, where political stability is to be increased. Solvency arguments are properly directed at the behavior of the audience of change, not the agents of change. This is because in testing the capability or effectiveness of a problem-solving method, a policymaker is concerned with the results of the application of this method will have in practice.

From a games-simulation perspective, solvency analysis involves efforts to conceptualize what would happen if a policy were put into effect. Hence, it has to be presumed that agents of change will put the policy into effect: otherwise, no accurate test of the capabilities of the policy proposal can be conducted. It is, however, relevant to consider how the persons to be affected by the implementation of the proposal (the group for whom the problem will be "solved") are likely to behave in response, as it is their reactions which will be the basis for the level of effectiveness of the proposal. Circumvention arguments directed at whether the agent of change will prevent the putting into effect of an action (such as the examples given above) do not test the capabilities of proposals were they to be adopted in the form specified by the affirmative and are therefore "should-would" arguments (i.e., you should not do this because you would not do this). On the other hand, arguments which focus on noncompliance and circumvention motives of the audience of change test the worth of the proposal. They assume that the plan will be adopted as intended by the affirmative, i.e., the agents of change will act as mandated and consider the likely responses of the audience of change. The other two generic solvency arguments on the 1987-88 topic fall into this category.

Follow-through

The "follow-through" solvency argument will be applicable to a variety of cases, including debt restructuring and human rights observance. In both examples, the affirmative will propose that the United States take certain measures which will have the effect of inducing Latin American states to respond in ways attaining solvency (and topicality). In the examples given, the United States might adopt policies of making interest rate reductions on international loans dependent on modified Latin American government policies, such as currency devaluation or cut off military and economic assistance to Latin American countries guilty of specific types of human rights abuses. The key factor here is the distinction between affirmative fiat (what the "United States government" can do in adopting a policy) and "follow-through" responses (how Latin American governments will respond to plan provisions). In the examples provided, the affirmative cannot topically fiat that Latin American nations will clean up their human rights practices or that they will devalue their currencies. It is a question for affirmative proof whether Latin American nations will respond to affirmative fiat measures (military assistance fund cutoffs or debt payment modifications) in a manner productive of affirmative advantages, i.e., reduced human rights abuses and currency devaluations.

"Follow-through" solvency arguments can be evaluated on the basis of evidence predicting likely foreign and international responses to affirmative mandates. This is an issue which has appeared on occasion on other topics, chiefly with cases involving transnational pollution. For example, if the United States bans fluorocarbons or the burning of high sulfur coal for electrical power generation, will other nations follow suit? The question is critical to solvency because, without "follow-through," there will be no accrual of benefits. This is even more the case with the 1987-88 topic than with the transnational pollution cases, as the responses of Latin American nations will be largely determinative of whether affirmative mandates will have any impact on the problems they attempt to solve. Evidence on this issue is generally sketchy. This is not quite as true on the 1987-88 topic, as there is some discussion of how Latin

American states respond to U.S. policy initiatives. The news is generally not good for affirmatives. The most analogous set of examples, the responses to the military assistance cutoffs by the Carter Administration for human rights violations by Latin American nations was generally one of indignation and acceptance of cutoffs, not modification of human rights practices.

The two plan examples given above, interest rate reductions in debt and assistance are also examples of the two types of approaches affirmatives can take in attempting to attain "follow-through." Interest rate reductions are an example of the reward-carrot approach, while assistance cutoffs are an example of the punishment-stick approach. Which approach will be more effective is dependent on the substantive features of the situation addressed by the affirmative. There is a generic issue here as well, though: Latin American perception of how long-term the American commitment is to a policy, or how credible the United States position has an impact of how effective "stick" policies will be. This is discussed further with regard to United States human rights policy in Chapter Three.

"Follow-through" will also bring into play different judges' theories of presumption. There clearly is a burden on affirmatives to establish solvency: the issue is how much evidence of likely Latin American responses is necessary to rebut. Given situations where there is relatively little evidence, judges may be faced with situations in which affirmatives have minimal evidence and negatives have nothing but bare assertions. Since there is no presumption in favor of solvency, judges must decide if minimal evidence is enough evidence. On the other hand, negatives who simply assert that Latin American nations will not follow through on the affirmative policy fall into the "he (or she) who asserts must prove" category. The heart of the issue will be the explanations provided by both teams for likely responsive behavior: i.e., what motives on the part of Latin American governments would cause them to modify their national economic policies in exchange for lowered interest rates on international debts or to alter human rights practices in response to threatened military assistance cutoffs? The evidence which can be presented chiefly consists of opinions based on past examples and past behavior.

Monitoring and Verification

The final generic solvency issue is that of monitoring and verification difficulties. While this argument is most directly applicable to a negotiated agreement between governments and insurgents in several Latin American countries, most notably Nicaragua and El Salvador, it also is relevant to cases setting human rights conduct standards and to those attempting to modify Latin American domestic economic practices. Like the "follow-through" argument, the basis for this solvency argument is that the resolution does not permit affirmatives to stipulate plan compliance by the targets of plan mandates, the nations of Latin America.

As one example, consider an affirmative plan which adopts a policy of researching a negotiated settlement of the United States-Nicaraguan dispute in Central America. Under the resolution, the affirmative could fiat U.S. participation in such a process: it could not fiat Nicaraguan participation. Hence, the affirmative would in effect be limited to peace provisions which the Sandinista government is either on record as saying that it would support or adhere, or provisions for which it could make a case that the Sandinistas would have sound motives for compliance. Solvency would be dependent on the degree to which the contracting parties complied with these provisions. The type of circumvention argument described above would be used in this example to argue that the United States would use covert means to get around the treaty, continuing to conduct guerrilla operations to destabilize the Sandinista government. Besides the fiat responses discussed earlier, the affirmative could also answer that U.S. benefits from a negotiated settlement (as well as world opinion costs if the United States is discovered to have violated the agreement) would impel it to comply with plan provisions.

The situation is more difficult with regard to the Nicaraguan end of the plan. Since fiat power is not available under the language of the resolution, the affirmative is dependent on Nicaraguan compliance with plan mandates based on rational perception of interests by the Sandinistas. While part of the policy to be adopted could include provisions for on-site monitoring by third parties, there is no guarantee that the Nicaraguans would accept the affirmative policy under those conditions. The affirmative would have to suggest reasons why it would be perceived to be in the best interests of the Nicaraguan government to accede to such on-site monitoring. It would also have to establish that, if the Nicaraguans agreed to such provisions, that such on-site monitoring would be adequate to obtain affirmative advantages.

An issue which pervades literature on arms control treaty enforcement is how high the level of compliance needs to be to obtain the expected benefits of the treaty. The physicist Freeman Dyson in his book Weapons and Hope has contended that persons who argue that arms control agreements must obtain extremely high levels of mechanical compliance are in effect opposing the treaty. Those levels are either technically unattainable or, if attainable, would artificially inflate the number of violations, as very low-level actions capable of alternative explanations would constitute apparent treaty violations. Dyson is primarily referring to test ban treaties but his point is applicable to a U.S.-Nicaraguan agreement as well: an agreement under which use of armed force by the Nicaraguan government constituted a treaty violation would trigger reactions by the United States to very low levels of the use of force (e.g., patrolling borders, gruelling civil disturbances) which arguably would not be sufficient justifications to consider the treaty to have been abrogated. Affirmatives in this situation would be wise to be precise about what conduct is expected of the Nicaraguans (or in other cases, of Latin American governments in meeting human rights objectives), who is to enforce plan-proposed measures. However affirmatives must be careful not to set conduct requirements unreasonably high. For example, a large degree of compliance by the Nicaraguan government with a treaty may be sufficient to obtain affirmative advantages (increased stability in the area, lessened tensions): some technical or low level violations could be tolerated. The critical factors are that the affirmative be able to demonstrate that its monitoring-verification procedures would be acceptable to the parties and that such procedures are capable of working sufficiently for affirmative advantages to be obtained.

A final note about solvency has to do with counterplan solvency. If counterplans use international or multilateral organizations for solvency, the fiat discussion above would simply be reversed. The reasoning behind this is that negatives in proposing counterplans are defending the non-resolution. Hence, negatives are in the position of saying that a competitive alternative to the affirmative resolution would achieve a superior level of net benefits and should be chosen instead. In order to determine the accuracy of this statement. The same kind of solvency-testing process has to be engaged in for the counterplan. Therefore, the same suspension of "would this actually take place" arguments has to be indulged in for the counterplan. In the case of counterplans in which increased political stability would result from the operations of international or multilateral organizations (a relatively narrowly drawn counterplan), this would mean assuming that the organization would enact the affirmative mandates as prescribed by the negative. However, to be nontopical, the counterplan could not fiat U.S. adoption of the same mandates. As the mirror image of the U.S.-Nicaraguan agreement example given above, the negative would have to argue that there would be an adequate basis for predicting that the United States would comply with the counterplan agreement.

It is sometimes argued that negatives do not counterplan fiat power or threat collective action cannot be assumed to take place. An example occasionally given is that of a Constitutional Convention or an interstate compact. It cannot be assumed, the argument states, that all the states would behave in the manner specified by the counterplan. This argument stems from an artificial distinction between affirmative resolutions which specify a single agent of action (typically, the federal government) as opposed to the counterplan, which involves the collective action of multiple agents which do not have precisely the same interests (typically, the states). The 1987–88 resolution is different only in that the resolution and the non-resolution contrast the "United States government" with international or multilateral bodies. While it is true that Panama and Venezuela do not have exactly the same interest, this misses the point of fiat: it is to exempt a policy debate from arguing issues unrelated to the merits of a proposal. Arguing about whether the assorted Latin American governments would cooperate in reaching an agreement is unrelated to the merits of their cooperation as an alternative to the affirmative resolution. It could just as easily be argued that, although it superficially appears to be a single agent of action, the "United States government" is really a collection of competing constituencies, either the separate states being represented there, or the different branches of government. If there are to be meaningful non-resolutional alternatives on this topic, multilateral, non-U.S. actions must be included.

ADVANTAGES AND DISADVANTAGES

The following areas will probably be the focus of affirmative advantage and negative disadvantage arguments, all stemming from the assumption that affirmative plans will work and increased political stability will actually be obtained: (1) effects on U.S.-Soviet relations; (2) effects on sovereignty; (3) effects on economic growth; (4) effects on U.S. trade deficits and trade policies; (5) effects on nuclear proliferation; (6) effects on repayment of international debt; and (7) effects on the provision of human rights. The last two areas are discussed fully in Chapters Three and Four and are not discussed here. It is sufficient to say at this point that, in addition to affirmative cases adopting policies to produce changes by Latin American countries to deal with these problems, virtually every other affirmative plan will have some impact on these problems triggering additive advantages and disadvantages arguments. The first five advantages-disadvantages argument areas are discussed below.

U.S.-Soviet Relations

A frequently stated rationale of the Reagan Administration for its policies toward Latin America is opposition to Soviet-Cuban Adventurism. Domino theory-like descriptions are given of Soviet objectives, with the Communist presence in Nicaragua being linked to the insurgency in El Salvador and elsewhere, eventually leading to the Red Army being at the Texas border. The Soviets, through their proxies, the Cubans, are said to be behind most of the unrest in the Western Hemisphere.

The question for debaters will be whether United States policies to increase political stability in Latin America will have any impact on U.S.-Soviet relations. The principal ways such relations can be implicated are the following: (1) decreased U.S. military involvement would improve U.S.-Soviet relations, since the Soviets see Marxist groups there as fellow socialists; (2) decreased U.S. military involvement in Latin America would reduce a source of friction impeding U.S.-U.S.S.R. arms agreements, since the Reagan Administration has been shrill in its rhetoric about Soviet culpability for problems in the region; (3) decreased U.S. military involvement would encourage Soviet adventurism in Latin America and other regions in the world, since it would be an indication of weaknesses in U.S. resolve in its own backyard; and (4) decreased U.S. military involvement in Latin America indicates to the Soviets that there is a cost to their expansionist policies and also serves as a bargaining chip for future diplomatic talks with the Soviets, particularly as regards the Soviet occupation of Afghanistan.

All of these possible descriptions share a common view of Soviet involvement in Latin America as being significant in proportions and a policy of major importance to the Soviets. While an argument can be made in favor of this position based on the magnitude of Soviet arms shipments to Nicaragua and Soviet subsidization of Cuba, equally persuasive arguments can be made in the opposite direction. The Soviets have been selective in the kinds of arms they have (and have not) provided to Marxist groups. For example, while the Soviets have provided small arms and helicopters to the Sandinistas, they have turned down their requests for MIG aircraft. This is consistent with a view that the Soviets are willing to give the Sandinistas weapons useful in defeating the Contras, but are unwilling to provide weapons which would be perceived by the United States as being useful in a regional conflict. Similarly, the FMLN in El Salvador has been unable to obtain surface-to-air missiles useful in responding to the current emphasis of government forces on bombing guerrilla-controlled areas. Since Soviet SAM's have a good reputation in the international arms markets and have been made available to Cuba, Libya, and others, that they have not been made available to the FMLN (or to third parties who would ship SAMs to them) suggests Soviet reluctance to be involved in the escalation of the civil war there.

There are several arguments that support the position that what the United States does in Latin America will not have a major impact on U.S.-U.S.S.R relations, short of a U.S. invasion of Cuba (notably, Cuba has said that it would not become directly involved militarily in the event of U.S. military intervention in Nicaragua). First, empirically, U.S. criticism of Soviet support of Cuba and Nicaragua has had no effect on arms control and other negotiations. Second, the argument is made that the Soviets perceive Latin America as a "no lose" situation. They are willing to provide minimal assistance to Nicaragua because they receive a good return on their investment in terms of both good public relations with the Non-Aligned Movement and the degree of irritation produced in Washington. However, their strategic interests in Central America are too minimal to justify the sacrifice of other objectives. There are also indications that the Soviets view Nicaragua as another Mozambique: a Marxist nation whose assistance needs far outstrip its value to the Soviets. The Soviets may not be able to subsidize a second Cuba in Latin America. The Cubans themselves have advised the Nicaraguans to keep open trade channels with Western nations because of the diluted amount of trade and assistance the Soviet Bloc can provide. Finally, the Soviets, like the United States, are much more willing to support causes close to home (e.g., Afghantistan) than those close to a superpower rival.

Sovereignty

One of the preemptory norms of international law is the right of the nations to self-determination and self-government. The resolution can be read to effectively call for the affirmative to infringe on the sovereignty of other nations. The United States government is to adopt policies which will have the effect of causing modified behavior on the parts of Latin states, for the purpose of producing increased political stability. This is true of such diverse interpretations of the resolution as increased assistance to the Contras and economic assistance policies which seek to modify Latin American land ownership policies. Most affirmative mandates will to some degree impose U.S. priorities on internal Latin American policies. It is a well established principle in international law treaties that sovereign states have the right to be free from foreign intrusion as to purely domestic concerns, except for a very narrow range of cases. This concept is embodied in the U.N. Charter.

There are a number of responses to this argument within the context of Latin American political affairs. First, it is not a violation of sovereignty when nations voluntarily enter into agreements in which they agree to place limitations on their rights or property in exchange for negotiated benefits. Nicaragua, for example, stated that is was willing to sign the Contadora Peace Treaty, under which it would have had to have asked Eastern European and Cuban military advisers to leave its territory, reduce the size of its army, and accept some system of foreign monitoring to verify that is was complying with the agreement. Either the Sandinista regime thought that this agreement was a worthwhile exchange for the removal of the Contras and de facto U.S. recognition of its legitimacy as a government, planned to violate the Treaty, or was bluffing, guessing that the United States would back away from the Treaty if the Nicaraguans accepted it. If the affirmative could argue that nations would be making voluntary choices in acceding to a proposed policy instead of dealing with coercion, no sovereignty issue would be present.

Second, a cynical response would be that few Latin American countries, the Central American republics especially, have much independent control of their future. Central America, from this view, is a collection of client states, either those of the United States, or, in the case of Nicaragua and Cuba, those of the Soviet Union. Affirmatives arguing for a lessened U.S. military presence in Central America or economic development attuned to the social and economic needs of the population could argue an aggregate increase in the freedom of these countries from determinations of their future by foreign powers.

Affirmatives dealing with Latin American external debt can point to the austerity measures instituted as quid pro quo for World Bank or International Monetary Fund loans and other assistance. A threshold question, then is what residual level of national soverignty existed prior to the adoption of the affirmative proposal. If economic decisions are in effect being

dictated to Latin American nations by international organizations, their level of national self-determination cannot be
decreased. This may also be a case area in which time-line
analysis is relevant. Affirmative measures might impose
limitations on the independent decision-making capacity of Latin
nations in the short term in order to make them economically
self-sufficient and independent nations in the long run.

A different approach to this issue is to ask whether
decreases in sovereignty would be a bad thing. The debate
guaranteeing human rights implicitly is about prioritizing those
rights over the right of sovereign states to make determinations
about how it will police its citizens. The International Convention on Genocide is an example of this type of prioritization,
limiting the right of a nation to govern by excluding from this
power acts of group-based atrocities against its own citizens.
It should be noted that the United States Senate only recently
ratified the Genocide Convention, although it was signed during
the Truman Administration. The Senate ratified the Convention
only after several "understandings" were added to the ratification resolution which reflect a United States view of a limited
international law role in domestic matters. The Senate's resistance to the Convention stemmed precisely from its fears about
infringement on U.S. sovereignty, for example, in dealing with
state civil rights practices.

The sovereignty argument can take several other twists and
turns. One is for negatives to argue world government as a
disadvantage. Instead of arguing that the affirmative impedes
national sovereignty, the argument would be that the resolution
enhances it, because it operates through unilateral action by the
United States. For example, instead of dealing with human rights
through international forums, the affirmative imposes U.S.
conceptions of human rights on Latin American nations. The plan
has the effect of augmenting the individual nation-state force of
the United States. As with the world government counterplan, the
thesis of this argument is that such augmentation impedes progress
towards international government which is "vertical" in nature,
with power and regulatory authority. The affirmative effectively
substitutes a bilaterally-enforced regime for an international
one.

An alternative approach for the affirmative would be to
argue that its actions decrease nation-state sovereignty by
bringing United States conduct closer to international legal
norms, This would be the case where the affirmative argues for
the reduction of U.S. military involvement in Central America.
Non-government organizations, especially human rights observers,
have contended that the United States and its allies in Central
America have violated a number of international conventions for
the conduct of states in civil wars. These include attacks on
civilian noncombatants in war zones and the forcible relocation
of those persons, which has occurred in El Salvador and in
Guatemala. The United States has also been found to have been
in violation of international law in its mining of Nicaraguan
harbors: the United States refused to accept the jurisdiction of

the International Court of Justice (ICJ). The affirmative position would be that voluntary adherence to international law norms is a predicate step for the development of supernational institutions. Hence, the plan would have the additive advantage of enhancing respect for international conventions, with the Untied States setting a good example for conduct by nation-states instead of a bad one.

A final affirmative approach to sovereignty attacks was suggested in Chapter One: although the topic calls for the "United States government" to "adopt a policy", it does not preclude that policy from involving U.S. accession to conventions or treaties drawn by international or multilateral organizations. The resolution's wording also does not preclude U.S. action in concert with other nations, although the amenability of those nations to the affirmative proposal would be a question for affirmative proof. For example, affirmative human rights approaches could occur through the Inter-American Conference on Human Rights, while economic development measures could be administered through the Economic Committee for Latin America and the Caribbean (ECLAC) of the United Nations Economic and Social Council (UNECOSOC). To the extent that affirmative proof demonstrated that plan mandates represented an international consensus, it would at least be able to claim a "progress toward world government" additive advantage: that its mandates would be carried out as a result of shared decision-making would at least blunt the argument that the plan was imposing U.S. norms on Latin in nations.

Economic Growth

Effects of affirmative mandates on patterns of economic growth have been argued on a succession of debate topics. Growth can be argued on the 1987-88 topic under at least three scenarios: a disadvantage scenario, a general effects advantage scenario, and an appropriate development scenario.

Under the disadvantage scenario, negatives will argue that all affirmatives will have at least secondary effects on economic growth. A case arguing for decreased U.S. military involvement or improved human rights conduct in Latin America could be argued to have consequences for the rate of economic growth, as military activity and political repression could be argued to be impediments to potential economic development. The effect of civil wars and insurgencies is misallocation of government resources to internal security from the development of infrastructure and aid to business and industry; the wars themselves result in the destruction of bridges, power utilities, and factories, as well as the displacement (voluntary and forcible) of populations, destruction of crops, and significant emigration. Concomitant repressive measures by governments have similar dysfunctional economic effects. Finally, countries involved in hostilities are less attractive to foreign investment.

Reduced military assistance cases are examples where growth

effects are relatively remote. Cases attempting to reduce Latin American debt payments and to otherwise increase the viability of Latin economies would have a direct impacts on rates of growth. Such cases overlap with the next disadvantage section, effects of U.S. trade policies, as such growth would be related to the exports of such countries.

The focus of growth disadvantages, whatever the chain of causation, will be on the ecological side effects of economic growth on Latin America. Much of Latin America is tropical rain forest and ecologically fragile. Some parts of Latin America have already experienced deforestation, either as a result of development or meeting subsistence needs. Deforestation is associated with erosion, decreased soil fertility, siltation of water supplies, and the extinction of plant and animal species. The situation is worst in Haiti, where over ninety percent of the nation's forests have been cut down for charcoal. Brazil, Honduras, and Costa Rica have also experienced significant deforestations. Environmental regulation in Latin America varies from weak to nonexistent, causing increased industrial production to have greater ecological impacts than similar levels of increased production in the United States or Western Europe. There are also variations in water supplies, ranging from generally good in South America to inadequate in Mexico and the Caribbean, which would be impacted by increased economic growth.

As was mentioned in Chapter One, the 1987–88 topic is conducive to effects topicality-oriented approaches. This is the source of the second scenario, under which affirmatives would argue that economic growth is good and that affirmative policies having the effect of stimulating economic growth in Latin America would increase political stability there. In addition to having to counter environmental disadvantages on the effects of growth, the affirmative would also have to demonstrate that increased growth would have a positive effect on political stability. There is evidence to the contrary, that industrial growth stimulated by external investment tends to have disproportionate effects in Latin American economies, having its greatest effects in countries which have an existing industrial base (Mexico, Brazil, and Argentina) and having little effect on Latin American poverty. Latin American wealth distribution patterns are considerably more skewed than those of the United States: increases in aggregate wealth tend to intensify those distribution patterns rather than ameliorate them. Latin America is an extreme case of "trickle down" economics. Unless targeted at industries using semi-skilled or unskilled workers or at agriculture, development programs have relatively little effect on poverty. Hence, if increased growth results in increased social stratification, it may decrease, not increase political stability. Latin American economic growth in the 1970's was accompanied by increased environmental degradations, but also by increased urbanization and pressure for trade unionization, both factors which contributed to political discord between working class populations and elites. The Reagan Administration's Caribbean Basin Initiative, which is emphasized investment incentive, which emphasized investment incentives and trade policy adjustments, could be characterized as an example of a pro-growth, pro-stability policy.

The final economic growth scenario is an appropriate growth-slow growth model. Under this model, the emphasis would be on export of technology appropriate to the internal economic needs of Latin American economies. The concept would be one of slow but steady growth oriented towards subsistence agriculture and light industry. Like the second scenario, affirmatives would have to establish the link between such growth and increased political stability. The argument for this approach is that slow growth would place less pressure on the environment while being more responsive to the problems of poverty (especially in rural areas) and income maldistribution. A slow growth model would produce as many, if not more jobs within the reach of the unemployed and underemployed in Latin America than would a heavy industry or export-oriented growth model.

This growth scenario might have its greatest relevance for Central America and the more agrarian South American republics. It does not provide a solution for nations which are dependent on the foreign exchange necessary to repay commercial debts; it also does not respond to the need of Latin American countries for the hard currency that foreign trade brings for the development of public works. This is a model that would require integration with foreign assistance programs for the development of infrastructure of debt repayment programs which restructured loan repayments.

Trade Deficits and Trade Policies

Two sets of facts create this issue. First, the United States trade deficit is currently running at an annual rate of about $170 billion. Each $1 billion change in the trade balance affects at least twenty-five thousand jobs in the United States (according to Alfred E. Eckes of the United States International Trade Commission, cited in Trade: U.S. Policy Since 1945, 1984, p.3). A "real world" debate which will be taking place in Congress concurrent to the 1987-88 topic will be about United States trade policy and whether protectionist legislation, such as that proposed by Rep. Gephardt of Missouri should be enacted.

A second fact is that Latin American economics have grown increasingly dependent on the United States as an export market. Sales to the United States and other foreign markets are necessary to pay off large international debts and to obtain hard currency to finance future economic development. During the 1970's Latin American economies grew at average annual rates of about six percent. As the United States and Western Europe went into recession in the early 1980's, Latin American nations' economic growth shrank to between one and two percent in 1981, followed by a one percent contraction in gross domestic product in 1982. These economies have experienced growth rates of about one percent per year since then. Factors aggravating this situation have included the decline in world oil prices, a major factor in the problems of Mexico, and a number of natural disasters affecting Colombia, Mexico and other states.

As the United States attempts to deal with its trade imbalance Latin America will be affected, either unintentionally or intentionally. Unintentional effects will come about as a result of a continued policy of letting the dollar weaken against other currencies, which has the effect of making foreign goods, including Latin American ones, more expensive relative to U.S. domestic products. Protectionist measures aimed at Japan and Western Europe will afflict Latin America as well. For example, restriction on imported steel would affect not only Japan and West Germany, but Brazil and several other Latin American states. Retaliation by Western Europe and Japan for U.S. protectionist measures might include the erection of trade barriers injurious to Latin American trade.

Protectionist trade policies on the part of the United States may also have Latin American exports in mind. The Latin American nations, particularly those in the Caribbean and Central America, are in a position to exploit low production costs because of their geographic proximity to U.S. ports in the Gulf of Mexico. Between 1982 and 1984, the United States absorbed ninety-five percent of the increase in merchandise exported by Latin American nations. U.S. exports prior to 1982 had accounted for only about half of Latin American exports. Between 1981 and 1983 the United States went from trade surplus of $7.5 billion to a deficit of $14 billion with Latin America. Although a drop in the $170 billion trade deficit bucket, a $20 billion-plus shift accounted for a loss of over four hundred thousand U.S. jobs. Congress has already stiffened import quotas on textiles and agricultural commodities such as sugar, major components of Latin American exports. Further such protectionist policies could have the effect of cutting off Latin American sources of economic growth altogether.

The Reagan Administration and the Congress have been working at cross-purposes with respect to Latin American trade policy. The administration has encouraged Latin American economies to become more export-dependent as a means of helping such nations meet their debt obligations. This is also consistent with the Administration's private enterprise orientation, discussed, in Chapter Three. Dependency on U.S. export markets also gives the United States more leverage with Latin Aerican nations. The Reagan Administration has pressured Congress to open up U.S. markets to copper from Chile and tin from Bolivia as part of this process.

Congress and affected industries view Latin America in a different fashion, seeing them as a competior for United States jobs, and competing according to different rules. Latin American exports reflect substantially lower wage costs and costs of governmental safety and environmental regualtion; they are also subsidized by their governments. Congressional lobbies appear strongest as regards imports of minerals, textile, and steel, although all of those industries have already been devastated by foreign competition. There is an irony to this in that a number of these industries are dominated by multinational enterprises (MNE's) which have been cutting back their United States operations, while increasing their sales to United markets for their South American subsidiaries. One such example is Kennecott Copper, which has shut down its Utah operations but still maintains mining and smelting facilities in Chile. a related factor as regards minerals is that there is a world-wide glut, expecially in copper, and Latin American nations have been cutting their price to maintain the existence of these industries.

Trade will affect debate on the topic in several ways. First, unless focused on internal development, economic assistance Latin America will have the primary effect of increasing production for export to the United States. Even development limited to creating industrial production for domestic consumption affects the trade issue, as it competes with U.S. export sales to Latin America. Second, protectionish trade policies will have a counteracting effect on negative ecomomic growth disadvantages. Such policies will also conteract the effects of current United States and international organization efforts to stimulate Latin American growth and development.

A final effect of the trade issue on the topic would be similar to the second growth scenario discussed above. Affirmatives may argue that efforts to increase Latin American exports are an example of the resolution, as the ecomomic growth produced by such exports will increase political stability in Latin America. Affirmative mandates could take the form of U.S. unilaterial trade concessionsor efforts to create across-the-board reductions in import restrictions through the General Agreement on Trade and Tariffs (GATT). Such an approach could also include expanded U.S. development assistance and, like the second ecomomic growth scenario, be somewhat similar to the Reagan Administration's Caribbean Basin initiative. Like the growth scenario, the concept would suffer difficulties in establishing that export-oriented economic growth would have a positive effect on Latin American political stability, as well as inheriting growth disadvantage problems. If done unilaterally, such a program would amount to preferential treatment of Latin american economies in violation of the "most favored nation" principle of the GATT. Under the GATT Agreement, signatories are required to accord the treatment they provide to their most favored trading partner to all signatories, unless exceptions are permitted under the Agreement. In practice, there are numerous expections to this principle, but it seems unlikely that Western Europe and Japan would accede to United States exceptions for Latin American imports in the midst of United States Measures increasing trade barriers to their exports. United States action could set off another round of trade wars. In addition, this approach would result in the loss of American jobs, a factor behind organized labor's opposition to the Caribbean Basin initiative.

Nuclear Proliferation

Nuclear proliferation is another argument which has been debated on a variety of topics. The 1987-88 topic implicates proliferation in several ways: first, current Reagan Administration policies have an effect on the likelihood that Latin American nations (i.e., Brazil and Argentina) will become members of the nuclear club; second, increased political stability in Latin America arguably might have an effect on the likelihood of nuclear proliferation in other parts of the world; and, finally, policies adopted by the affirmative could generate nuclear proliferation (especially in Latin America) as a disadvantage. Before discussing these possibilities, this section discusses the Treaty of Tlatelolco (or, as debaters will probably refer to it, the Treaty of T) and the Brazilian and Argentine nuclear programs.

The prospects for nuclear proliferation in Latin America are set against the background of the 1968 Treaty of Tlatelolco, which created the Latin American Nuclear Weapon Free Zone Agreement. All Latin American nations have signed and ratified the agreement except Argentina, which has signed but not ratified the Treaty, and Cuba, which has done neither. In addition, while Brazil and Chile have signed and ratified the agreement, they have taken the position that their ratification remains provisional until all nations complete the process. Brazil and Argentina, the chief candidates for proliferation, also have not signed the Nuclear Proliferation Treaty (NPT). Brazil and Chile have also taken the position that the regional agreement does not prohibit the development of Peaceful Nuclear Explosives (PNE's), an interpretation not shared by the other parties to the agreement.

The Treaty of Tlatelolco also permits non-Latin nations to sign and ratify the agreement. The United States has done so, although it took thirteen years to do so. It has not ratified an Additional Protocol. Argentina has announced that it will not ratify the agreement until all other nations have done so, which is probably pretextual.

The Treaty also created the Agency for the Prohibition of Nuclear Weapons in Latin america (OPANAL). The Agency provides for more stringent regulation of nuclear technology than does the NPT. Under the Treaty, parties are to follow the guidelines for safety of the United Nations' International Atomic Energy Agency (IAEA) in their handling of nuclear materials for peaceful atomic uses. The parties are also to submit semi-annual reports to the IAEA and OPANAL; they are to submit special reports on request by OPANAL; last, they are to submit to special inspections by the IAEA if OPANAL requests them. Protocol I of the Treaty prohibits storage or deployment of nuclear weapons in Latin America; Protocol II provides that signatories will not contribute to acts involving Treaty violations.

Both Brazil and Argentina have had nuclear power reactors for a number of years. The United States, through Westinghouse, Inc., was involved in the construction of nuclear reactors in both nations. The Argentines also built a reactor in 1968 with assistance from West Germany. This reactor, which has been operational since 1973, is capable of producing weapons-grade plutonium. West Germany also entered into a fifteen-year agreement with Brazil in 1975 to sell Brazil sensitive nuclear technology and to build a pressurized water reactor. Both nations have imported heavy water from the Soviet Union; in 1985, Senator Cranston reported that he had had information that the People's Republic of China was aiding five nations by exporting nuclear technology, among them Brazil and Argentina. The latter are unusual steps for Second World nations. The Soviets have traditionally refused requests for nuclear technology by Third World nations with the hard currency to obtain them, such as Libya.

What has the role of the Reagan Administration been with regard to nuclear proliferation in Latin America? The Reagan Administration has adopted a much different perspective on nuclear proliferation than was true of its predecessors, particularly the Ford and Carter Administrations. The Ford Administration attempted to get West Germany to rescind its agreement with Brazil in 1975. It subsequently founded the Nuclear Supplier Group, also known as the London Club, which includes the United States, France, The United Kingdom, Canada, Japan, West Germany and the Soviet Union. This group has acted to coordinate supplier policies, restricting the sale of nuclear technology to Third World nations. The Carter Administration also opposed nuclear proliferation, getting Congress to pass the Nuclear Non-Proliferation Act (NNPA) in 1978. This Act placed restrictions on the export of nuclear materials and increased United States support of the IAEA.

At one point during the 1980 campaign, candidate Reagan responded to a question that he thought it was none of the business of the United States whether other nations were attempting to acquire nuclear weapons. The Reagan Administration's policy on nonproliferation has been more sophisticated, supporting the letter of the NNPA but seriously eroding its spirit. A possible explanation for this changed policy is that the United States lost its position of near monopoly over the nuclear export market in the mid 1970's. The sale of technology to Brazil by West Germany was part of this competition, although West Germany also received favorable concession prices on Brazilian uranium as part of the deal, which was also a motivating factor. The Reagan Administration has authorized sales of both materials and equipment with nuclear-related uses to Brazil, Argentina, Chile, despite the absence of full IAEA safeguards on their use by those nations. This has been interpreted by the Administration not to violate the NNPA on a narrow technical ground and signals that it will not impede the nuclear industry's efforts to regain supremacy in the international market.

The Reagan Administration's policy on nonproliferation has two primary features. First, it has taken an approach of permitting liberal U.S. exports of nuclear technology to allies which it considers to be low proliferation risks, while restricting such exports to those nations which it considers to be high proliferation risks. The rationale supporting this approach is that it increases U.S. leverage over recipients, and helps the United States prevent those nations from exporting nuclear technology to higher proliferation risk nations.

The problem with this theory put into practice is that it has caused the United states to invite demands for equitable treatment by nations we have not put into the low risk category but which we do not wish to offend. It has also given the impression to nations which have not signed the NPT that the United States is no longer as committed to the Treaty, since it has helped increase the flow of nuclear technology. On the other hand, the Reagan Administration praised Egypt when it signed the NPT. Finally, the United States has not in practice used its leverage: recipients of U.S. nuclear technology, following our lead, have continued to export technology to other nations.

The other policy imperative of the Reagan Administration has been that the United Stated should be a reliable supplier of nuclear exports, something which it sees as having been inter- fered with by the NNPA. Critics of the Administration have contended that it has been deeply affected in its proliferation policies by the nuclear industry, which has suffered reverses in the domestic market and is in tough competition with France and West Germany for Third World markets. Critics have also charged that, while the Reagan Administration will not admit to it in public it has concluded that more nuclear proliferation is inevitable. This being the case, the Reagan Administration sees no reason for impeding the U.S. nuclear industry in garnering a share of the market. Since the NPT has no realistic prospect of preventing proliferation, the Administration will give it lip service but will not let advocacy of the Agreement get in the way of other foreign policies. This was the thesis of Lewis Dunn of the Hudson Institute in Controlling the Bomb (1982), who later became a special counselor to the Administration. Dunn's addi- tional argument is also consistent with the "two-track" approach of the Administration. By being the supplier of nuclear mater- ials, the United States will be in a better position to control the subsequent uses of such materials. An implicit assumption of this position is that direct United States relations with nuclear recipients is to be preferred over international regulations. The Reagan Administration does not appear to have much confidence in the IAEA.

Whether Brazil or Argentina actually obtain nuclear weapons is in part tied to two factors discussed further in Chapter Four: international debt and the strength of the military in democratic regimes. Both nations are experiencing severe economic diffi- culties and are carrying large external debts. Both have also recently replaced long-ruling military regimes with elected civilian leaders. Brazil at one time had projected that it would have sixty nuclear reactors on line by the year 2000: it has scaled back those numbers and shifted to the development of non-nuclear technologies as the cost of constructing nuclear facilities has escalated. The 1975 agreement between Brazil and West Germany apparently has yet to have resulted in the construction of commercial-scale enrichment and reprocessing facilities.

Brazil and Argentina pursued nuclear weapons under military leadership as part of the effort of both nations to be identified as world major powers. The economic difficulties afflicting both nations and the inability of their military leaders to deal with them resulted in their replacement by civilians. An explanation for the Falkland Islands–Malvinas War is that the Galtieri government was looking for an external enemy (and a victory) which would unite the people and take their attention off of the economy. The nuclear power programs were associated with the military's rule. Civilian opposition has grown around the lofty goals, inept performance, cost overruns, and corruption associated with the programs. The building of nuclear devices at an estimated additional cost of $6 billion have been seen by civilian opponents as one more military extravagance. Finally, one reason for going nuclear, the rivalry between the nations, appears to have abated. Brazil and Argentina reached agreement on the use of water in the Rio Plata, a major issue dividing the two nations. The treaty process itself seems to have improved relations between them.

Both nations, however, have nuclear programs which have been progressing toward the development of nuclear weapons capabilities for over a decade. There is an internal force behind such programs, fueled by the industries which have a commercial interest in their completion. Both nations already have delivery systems in the form of Mirage jet aircraft. The Sarney and Alfonsin governments in Brazil and Argentina are not so firmly established that they do not have to worry about appeasing the military: letting the military have its way on nuclear weapons development (or simply not opposing it vigorously) would be a not likely concession. It should also be taken into account that a nuclear technology has foreign and economic policy value to both nations. Brazil, despite an offshore drilling program, is dependent on foreign oil imports. It has supplied nuclear technology to Iraq in exchange for favorable rates on imported oil.

A nuclear proliferation effect which is largely unrelated to the discussion above is the impact of increased political stability in Latin America on world proliferation. This argument, which would probably be best cast as an affirmative additive advantage, would posit that United States preoccupations with an unstable Latin America increases the probability that West Germany and Japan will acquire nuclear weapons. The rationale behind this is that both nations are reliant on U.S. strategic defense guarantees but fear that it will become overwhelmed by a military commitment to Central America. If the United States started taking steps which seemed to make a long-term, extensive military commitment to Central America inevitable, both West Germany and Japan would perceive it as being in their best interests to develop an independent nuclear deterrent. The argument for the affirmative would be that if the United States were to clear the deck of actual and potential options for military involvement in Central America, it would reduce the impetus for developing nuclear status on the part of West Germany and Japan. Both nations possess the technical capability to acquire nuclear weapons. Acquisition by West Germany would lead to a heightening of tensions in Central Europe, as the Soviets see a nuclear Germany as a real threat. A Japanese nuclear force would set off similar tensions between it and the People's Republic of China.

There are also a number of affirmative plan options which could be productive of proliferation disadvantages. It has been argued that Brazil and Argentina's nuclear weapons programs received a major boost when the Carter Administration was openly critical of their human rights records. Both voluntarily abrogated their military assistance programs with the United States. Indignation at what was seen in elite and military circles as meddling in the domestic affairs of both countries provided support for the development of nuclear weapons capabilities, which would cause them to be treated as equals, not as client states of a superpower.

Heavy-handed affirmative mandates could be argued to produce similar results. This is true not only of affirmatives dealing with human rights abuses, but also those seeking to modify internal economic development programs or to alter the domestic budges of Latin American debtor nations (of which Argentina and Brazil are charter members). One such proposal would be that of linking United States assistance in reducing the commercial debt of Brazil and Argentina to a pledge not to build nuclear weapons or their signature and ratification of the NPT. The negative could argue that such mandate would increase, not decrease, the likelihood of nuclear proliferation.

A final comment on proliferation in Latin America has to do with Cuba. Cuba has almost no prospect of ever developing its own nuclear weapons. It's opposition to the NPT and abstinence from the Treaty of Tlatelolco stems from its self-identification as a leader of the Non-Aligned Movement. It views the NPT as a scheme by the nuclear "haves" to keep a strategic edge over the non-nuclear "have nots".

Since the official position of Brazil, Chile, and Argentina is that less-than-universal acceptance of the Treaty of Tlatelolco makes it non-binding on the first two and precludes ratification on the part of the third, Cuban abstinence at least provides a pretext for the continuation of current development programs. It is an open question whether Cuba's ratification of the Treaty of Tlatelolco would actually lead these other nations to modify their positions. Cuba currently enjoys good relations with both Argentina and Brazil, although this is a recent development.

Cuba has given some indications that it might sign the Treaty of Tlatelolco under certain conditions. The Treaty was the idea of Mexico, a nation with whom Castro has always enjoyed good relations, along with Panama. Although critical of the NPT, the Cubans have not criticized the Treaty of Tlatelolco, simply not signing it. The conditions under which Cuba might sign the Treaty involve concessions on the part of the United States, such as the closing of the Guantanamo Naval Base and the shutting down of Radio Marti, the U.S. propaganda station (popular in Cuba for its broadcasts of baseball games). These items are more irritants than serious policy matters to Cuba. Their strategic value to the United States is dubious but the Reagan Administration appears committed to the retention of both items. The Naval Base will only last until a ninety-nine year lease runs out in 1997. A reasonable question in whether Castro has hinted that he would sign the Treaty under these conditions because he is certain that the Reagan Administration will not accede to them and may be somewhat embarrassed in explaining its position to Mexico.

Given the wording of the resolution, affirmatives could mandate the United States adopt these policy changes with regard to Cuba but, as mentioned in the solvency section, would be powerless, to require "follow-through" by Cuba. The closing of Guantanamo and other policy changes (e.g. lifting of U.S. trade sanctions against Cuba) have also been linked to benefits other than non-proliferation, such as the pullout of Cuban troops from Africa and decreased support of Latin American insurgent movements.

The disadvantages section of the chapter has not mentioned such "old reliable" disadvantages as cuts in social spending and effects on global climate. Both arguments are problematic under the 1987-88 topic. Whether there would be an impact of affirmative plans on social spending above and beyond those of the Reagan Administration under Gramm-Rudman would be a function of affirmative selection of policy options requiring significant economic assistance or subsidies to Latin America. Generally, affirmatives should be able to argue a turnaround on social spending, as most teams will probably reduce the aggregate amount of spending on Latin America. Teams arguing for decreased military assistance have this position available to them; teams which reorient rather than simply increase economic development should have this position open as well.

Teams which wish to argue climate should realize that they will probably have to devote most or all of their time to it. This is because they would have to work their way through several stages of causation to get from affirmative mandates to some effect on global warming or cooling. It is also because it will be difficult to separate plan effects on warming or cooling from other (and more direct) chains of causation having the same effect. The negative is in the position of arguing that Latin American growth is the necessary and sufficient condition for the passing of the threshold level to climate impacts, which will be difficult to establish.

United States Policy Toward Latin America: Principles and Characteristics

The 1987-88 topic asks high school debaters to examine the Latin American foreign policy of the Reagan Administration in its final year of existence. This chapter identifies principal features of the "Reagan Doctrine", which appear to have its greatest import for Latin America. Initially, the chapter attempts to describe what the "Reagan Doctrine" is; the ensuing section describe tendencies and preferences of the Reagan Administration in its conduct of foreign policy in Latin America. These policy preferences are: (1) bilateral as opposed to multilateral action; (2) private sector over public sector development; (3) security assistance before economic development; and (4) counter-insurgency and anti-terrorism as higher priorities over human rights. This is not meant to be pejorative: the Reagan Administration has articulated policy explanations for these preferences; preference does not mean exclusion of lower priorities, only that they play a secondary role with a policy framework.

THE REAGAN DOCTRINE

Latin American foreign policy is an area in which there have been major differences between the Reagan Administration and its predecessor, the Carter Administration. These differences are partially due to the greater latitude the Carter Administration enjoyed in Latin America than in other parts of the world, as well as less in the way of countervailing strategic interest to impede its policies. As is discussed in the human rights section of this chapter, the Carter Administration, While different on paper with regard to human rights than the Reagan Administration was quite similar in practice in parts of the world other than Latin America. These policy differences can also be traced to the distinctions of the the ideological positions of the two administrations on a wide variety of issues. while the most prominent features of this ideological difference as regards Latin America were in human rights and in policy toward Nicaragua, the Reagan Administration has had a coherent perspective which has influenced all phases of United States relations with Latin America. Variations of this world view have been played out in other parts of the world, but not to the extent that has occurred in Latin America. Like the Carter Administration, the Reagan Administration · has felt less constrained in its own backyard than in other parts of the world. It has also been influenced by some long-standing animosities toward Cuba held by different groups within its constituency: members of the military and intelligence communities, the Cuban community in Florida, and a number of conservative political organizations.

The Reagan Doctrine is largely negative in nature. It appears to promise unyielding opposition to groups, movements, and nations identified as pro-Soviet anywhere in the world. The reality is that this is easier to do in Central America than in Afghanistan. It should also be noted that the Reagan Doctrine, while assertedly anti-Communist and pro-Democratic, can more accurately be described as anti-Soviet and pro-Capitalist. The Reagan Administration has been able to rationalize support of Communist and Marxist groups in opposition to the Soviets and Soviet client states. This has meant support of the coalition in Kampuchea opposing the Soviet-backed Vietnamese, even though the largest group in the coalition is the remnants of the Pol Pot-Ieng Sary regime, the Communist group responsible for a reign of terror in the mid- and late 1970's. In Africa, the Reagan Administration supports the UINTA insurgency group of Jonas Savimbi in Angola. UINTA is a Marxist group whose other benefactor has been the People's Republic of China. The Reagan Administration opposes a government with strong ties to the Soviet Union and whose security is maintained by thirty thousand Cuban troops. And while the Reagan Administration encourages democratic elections, it has been tolerant of military regimes and one-party political systems where the economic climate has been hospitable to capitalism.

❡In Latin America, the Reagan Doctrine has meant opposition to Cuba and to the Sandinistas in Nicaragua as exporters of Cuban and Soviet adventurism. As the President argued in a speech on March 16, 1986, "(u)sing Nicaragua as a base, the Soviets and Cubans can become the dominant power in the crucial corridor between North and South America. Established there, they will be in a position to threaten the Panama Canal, interdict our vital Caribbean sea lanes and ultimately move against Mexico." A variety of insurgent groups in different Latin American nations (El Salvador, Guatemala, Peru, Colombia, primarily) are seen under the Reagan Doctrine as extensions of the Soviet-Cuban-Sandinista cause.

Of course, there are haunting memories of the domino theory pronounced for Southeast Asia by President Johnson, among others in the Reagan Administration's view of Latin America. However, there is an even stronger hint of the "roll-back" view of anti-Soviet foreign policy and military strategists of the 1950's, during the early years of the Cold War. What was to be "rolled back" then was Soviet influence in Eastern Europe, although in practice this did not occur in Hungary and other Eastern European nations which from time to time openly attempted to extricate themselves from the Soviet Union's influence. The domino theory and support for South Vietnam can be described more as an expression of containment, preventing the spread of Communism in Southeast Asia, on the model of NATO containment of communism in Western Europe. While the Reagan Administration certainly intends to contain communism in Latin America, it also seems to intend to "roll-back" Communism in Nicaragua, if possible. From this perspective, the removal of Cuban influence from Grenada (as opposed to actions limited to the rescue of U.S. nationals) was consistent with U.S. global policy. U.S. support of the Contras in Nicaragua is the 1980's edition of the CIA-backed overthrow of the Arbenz government in Guatemala in 1954.

A central policy dichotomy for Latin America which may be the focus of debate is the choice between containment and roll-back of communism. The Reagan Doctrine in fact waffles between the two. While the Reagan Administration in its public pro-nouncements appears offended by the continued existence of the government in Managua, it has also engaged in diplomatic talks with the Sandinistas from time to time. The public position of the Reagan Administration on the Contadora Peace Process, a containment-oriented agreement, has not been that it is opposed to an agreement in principle but that the agreement is not enforceable against the Sandinistas under the monitoring provi-sions contemplated. One could describe roll-back as an ultimate purpose of the assorted economic sanctions and covert operations of the Reagan Administration against the Sandinistas. However, it could also be said that the Contras are instruments of a containment policy, keeping the Sandinistas on the defensive (as the President himself once said, U.S. policy is aimed at getting the Sandinistas to say "uncle."). The United States has long mounted similar economic sanctions, as well as a propaganda campaign through Radio Marti and covert operations (though on a less public basis than those against Nicaragua) against Castro's Cuba.

A difficulty in describing Reagan Administration foreign policy objectives is that varying explanations have been provided for them over a period of time, even when the policy initiative itself remained unchanged. U.S. support of the Contras is one example of this. Initially, the American people were told that the Contras were being aided because they were fighting to protect El Salvador from the Sandinistas, who were sending supplies, weapons, and advisers to the Farabundo Marti Liberation Front (the FMLN) in El Salvador. Since El Salvador and Nicaragua do not share a common border, few if any of the Contras had ever been to El Salvador, much less expressed an interest in defending it, and (perhaps most important) the administration was unable to present convincing evidence of the existence of "rebel supply lines" between the two nations in 1981 and 1982, this rationale was abandoned. The Reagan Administration then moved toward a position which it still exposes, that its aid to the Contras places the Sandinistas on the defensive and will help bring them to the bargaining table. Who else will be at this bargaining table is unclear. It apparently will not be the Contadora nations; the United States has occasionally said that the Contras should be represented in negotiations, which the Sandinistas are unlikely to find acceptable under any circumstances. The Reagan Administration has been less vocal about the "force them to the bargaining table" explanation since the revelations of fund diversions from arms sales to Iran and the role of the CIA in the supplying of the Contras, partly because of the unpopularity of the topic but partly because the operations engaged in by the CIA (including the mining of harbors, bombings in 1982-83 and the current attack on Nicaraguan infrastructure) is explainable if our objective is to overthrow the Sandinistas but are hard to explain otherwise. The United States has disavowed that its objective is that of overthrowing the Sandinistas, a roll-back view. If true, this seems cruel to the Contras, implying that the United States is willings to support them to the extent that they are a distraction to the Sandinistas but apparently no more than that. This may be a cynical lesson of Vietnam. The American people will not be upset by support of a proxy group fighting (and dying) in an unwinable fight, so long as Americans themselves (in numbers greater than Eugene Hasenfus and assorted others) are not directly involved.

As a doctrine opposing the presence of Soviet Communist-supported groups, the Reagan Doctrine makes a number of assumptions, each of which enjoys some support but each of which is open to argument. First, the doctrine assumes that different communist groups are connected and supportive of each other. This is an extension of the "monolithic Communist threat" and "international communist conspiracy" views of the 1950's. There is support for this assumption in the Soviet Union's subsidization of Cuba; there is also evidence that Cuba at least in the late 1970's and early 1980's aided the FMLN in El Salvador and the M-19 organization in Colombia. The rebuttal is whether this evidence validates the conclusion that Communist groups are like-minded, must be opposed, and must be opposed in the same manner. While the Cubans can be depended on to support the Soviet Union in public arenas such as the United Nations (and in boycotting the 1984 Summer Olympic Games), it is also true that the Cubans are members of the Non-Aligned Movement (NAM) and that the Cubans have considerable standing and respect among NAM nations. The Cubans have also led the Soviets in taking positions on Third World issues. And while the Cubans have supported the Sandinistas, the latter appear to resent the implication that they are the ideological children of the Cubans, given their own long revolutionary tradition.

A related assumption is that Cuban-Soviet support is the key element in the prospects for success of a communist insurgency in Latin America. Evidence in support of this assumption is mixed at best. While the Cubans supported the Sandinista revolt against Samoza, their success can easily be attributed to the Samoza government alienating most sectors of Nicaraguan society. It is easier to support the proposition that leftist governments receive Soviet support after they come to power, and not before.

A final assumption is that a non-Communist government is always preferable to a Communist government. This is a non-controversial assumption for nearly all Americans, given the paradigm cases of communist governments they have in mind, chiefly that of the Soviet Union. The assumption becomes more controversial when it is stated in the terms used by Ambassador (then Professor) Jeane Kirkpatrick in 1979: a distinction can be drawn between totalitarian-Communist regimes and authoritarian-

Capitalist ones on philosophical grounds, with the former always demanding our opposition and the latter always meriting our support. As a result, a repressive (but non-Communist) regime should nevertheless receive support in the form of military assistance, lest it become communist. This distinction then leads to the differing positions of the Carter and Reagan Administrations on human rights, discussed in the final section of this chapter. The unstated correllary of the assumption, and the totalitarian-authoritarian distinction, is that U.S. foreign policy and strategic interests are always better served by the presence of a non-Communist as opposed to a Communist government. This presumes the validity of both earlier assumptions, that all Communist governments are more or less alike, make common cause with each other and are hostile to non-Communist governments because they owe their primary allegiance to the Soviet Union. A criticism of the Reagan Doctrine in this regard is that it is a self-fulfilling prophecy. Economic sanctions and support of the Contras can be argued to have guaranteed that the Sandinistas would seek Soviet bloc support. A question at this point is whether this debate has become moot, given the degree to which the Sandinistas have gravitated toward Cuba and the Soviet Union, although Nicaragua is considerably more pluralist than Cuba. This still leaves unanswered the original question: Is it always the case that U.S. interests are better served by the existence of a non-Communist as opposed to a Communist government? In the case of Nicaragua, is it necessarily the case that the Samoza regime was always a superior option over coalition governments which included the Sandinistas in terms of meeting U.S. strategic and policy objectives? As another example, although the New Jewel Movement in Grenada produced its own downfall, it should be noted that is replaced the government of Sir Eric Gairy, who was known more for his interest in the study of UFO's than anything else. One difficulty in describing the Reagan Doctrine as containment is that it seems to resist dealing with Latin American Marxist governments as an unpleasant reality, something it is forced to do in Eastern Europe and Northern Asia. In this regard, the Reagan Administration is no different than the Nixon Administration, which found the Allende government in Chile intolerable; the Johnson Administration, which opposed a Marxist role in the government of the Dominican Republic; and the Kennedy and Eisenhower Administrations, which sought the overthrow of Castro.

The Reagan Doctrine in fact could be characterized as the lineal descendant of the Cold War policies of John Foster Dulles, Secretary of State under President Eisenhower (and his brother, Allen, head of the CIA until the Bay of Pigs debacle.) In addition to a shared view of Communism as monolithic, the Reagan Administration shares with its predecessor opposition to countries seeking to remain neutral or non-aligned where their support could be of value to us: this is true of the Reagan Administration's treatment of Guatemala, Honduras and Costa Rica, which would like to remain neutral as against Nicaragua, as well as the less-than-hearty enthusiasm the United States has displayed toward the Contadora nations. Another point of similarity, discussed further in a later section of this chapter, is the carryover between ideological views to economic and development assistance policies.

The issue to be addressed by affirmative teams is whether the Reagan Doctrine is the most effective policy response to the problems of Western Europe, or alternative policy approaches can be suggested. Containment was an effective policy in Western Europe in the 1950's. The question is whether Cold War policies are equally appropriate for Latin America in the 1980's and 1990's. A related question is whether the convert operations policy of presidencies since the Eisenhower Administration remain effective today.

The final question to be asked about the Reagan Doctrine is what vision it has of the future for the nations affected by it. Besides non-Communist, the Reagan Administration's view of what it would like Latin American nations to be has remained unclear. A later section of this chapter discusses the Reagan Administration's preference for private sector economic development and minimal state economic activity. The administration's economic and development policies have taken on secondary status to its military and security policies. Support for such programs as land reform have been subordinated to counter-insurgency progams, especially in Central America. And while it prefers democratic regimes, the Reagan Administration was less than vigorous in pushing Argentina and Brazil's juntas toward civilian rule, and seemed genuinely surprised when democratic regimes came to power. As the final section of the chapter indicates, human rights were at best a secondary concern to the Reagan Administration when it took office. It was embarrassed by the amount of criticism it received for its positions: whether there was a real or only cosmetic change in its view of human rights after 1981 is a subject for dispute. In either case, the the Reagan Doctrine views provision of human rights as a subject connected with interal security, rather than an independent foreign policy objective.

A consistent policy position which colors much of the remaining analysis in this chapter is that security against Soviet and Cuban subversion is the first order of business, as economic development and human rights objectives will not be attainable without such security. The opposite point of view is that the military security orientation of United States policy competes with and precludes economic development and human rights. From this perspective, continued increases in funding and in material support of the military in Latin America will in fact be counterproductive. As Clifford Krauss of The Wall Street Journal wrote in Foreign Affairs in 1987,

> United States policy is supposedly designed to
> promote security in the region, but in practice it
> makes the isthmus less stable. A policy of containment
> ensures the security of the isthmus by blocking the
> spread of communism, without increasing the risk of war

in Central America. Containment is not an ideal
solution, but it is a feasible one. The task for 1987
is to work for a diplomatic complement to containment.
("Revolution in Central America?" Foreign Affairs,
vol.65 (1987), p. 581)

BILATERAL VERSUS MULTILATERAL APPROACHES

A primary feature of Reagan Administration foreign policy
has been a reluctance to use multilateral arrangements, including
international organizations, in the pursuit of its most important
foreign policy objectives. This has not been universally the
case. The United States has acted through international and
multilateral organizations where it has been in its interests to
do so. Nevertheless, only ten percent of its fiscal 1985 budget
request for international security assistance was to be in the
form of aid channeled through multilateral agencies. The last
two budget requests have reflected actual decreases in U.S.
voluntary contributions to United Nations agencies. The focus of
U.S. efforts in Latin America has been on unilateral initiatives,
whether through the proposed Caribbean Basin Initiative, the
study of the problems of Central America by the Kissinger Commission, or its won diplomatic initiatives. This section addresses
the reasons for the Administration's preference for a "go it
alone" approach, then looks at the effects of this approach on
Reagan foreign policy for Latin America.
    Conservatives, the President among them, have seldom been
avid supporters of the United Nations. The Administration's
reluctance to use international offices as a vehicle for dealing
with Third World and Latin American problems goes deeper than
that, although there has been a spate of "UN bashing" by conservatives during the Reagan Administration. There are three
explanations for the Administration's preference for unilateral
as opposed to multilateral foreign policy programs. First, the
Administration has been highly critical of the manner in which
the United Nations and other international organizations have
been run. These criticisms include charges that United Nations
agencies are inefficiently administered: the United Nations
Economic, Social, and Cultural Organization (UNESCO) has a been
major target. The United States has ceased participation in
UNESCO and other organizations it considers to be ineptly run,
arguing that the withholding of United States funds is necessary
as leverage to force internal reforms by such agencies.
    A second reason that the Reagan Administration has been
critical of the UN and other international organizations is that
it has disagreed with the political orientation of the policies
developed by them. Membership in the UN General Assembly is
heavily weighted toward Third World and Non-Aligned Movement
nations. Policies of UN organizations often reflect the perspectives on development of the New International Economic Order
(NIEO), a Third World group usually shrill in its criticism of

the United States as a neo-colonial power. United States charges of "inefficiency" sometimes mean that organizations are seen as spending too much time or money on NIEO-oriented policies.

A related and highly controversial item is UN funding. The Reagan Administration has supported what can be termed a "one dollar, one vote" position in international organizations. The UN has made member assessments for funds on an ability to pay basis, tied to gross domestic product. United States contributions accounted for twenty-six percent of the funds budgeted for by the United Nations in 1985, although the United States has less than five percent of the world's population. The United States share represents a decline from the one-third share it paid in the 1970's and the over-forty percent amount it paid in the early days of the UN after World War II. The shrinking U.S. proportion of the budget represents decreases in contributions by the United States, but primarily reflects increased contributions by other nations. Despite this, the Reagan Administration has taken the position that other nations, notably the Soviet Union, have not paid their fair share, and the other nations have disproportionate influence for their level of contributions. An often-repeated statistic is that sixty-seven UN members account for less than on percent of the budget.

The funding position of the Reagan Administration was embodied in the Kassenbaum amendment of 1985, which puts a ceiling on United States contributions of twenty percent of the budget to organizations which do not give the United States a vote proportional to its financial contributions, especially to NAM and NIEO-oriented organizations. It also has used the threat of decreased U.S. contributions in negotiations with UN Secretary General Perez de Cuelhar over the shape and objective of UN organizations. In response, the United Nations has hired a Washington lobbying firm to campaign for support in Congress and a public relations firm to design an advertising campaign for U.S. news media, hoping to boost American support for the UN in the post-Reagan era.

The second explanation for the U.S. preference for unilateral action is the flip side of its disagreement with NAM-NIEO positions in the UN. Most of its foreign policies toward Latin America are in conflict with the majority of members of the UN. As is discussed further in the section on private versus public sector initiatives, the United States has ideological and policy-based disagreements with other members of the IMF on the nature of development assistance, which has resulted both in U.S. efforts to use its weight as a key contributor to reorient such assistance but also in the U.S. relying on bilateral, U.D.-controlled development initiatives instead. Although a case can be made for the Reagan Administration's view of development assistance, it is a minority view within international organizations. Hence, the Administration increasingly allocates development funds on a bilateral basis.

U.S. foreign policy toward Latin America of a military nature has even less support in the UN and other international forums. The United States has been regularly criticized for its military assistance to Central America and the use of those funds in ways violative of international conventions. The hardest criticism has been reserved for U.S. support of the Contras and covert operations in Nicaragua. In April 1984, the United States was forced to veto a UN Security Council resolution condemning its mining of harbors in Nicaragua. Nicaragua subsequently took its case to the International Court of Justice, where the United States lost a jurisdictional argument and then refused to argue the case on its merits. It subsequently refused to recognize the jurisdiction of the Court in its findings against the United States.

A final explanation for U.S. preferences for unilateral over multilateral approaches has to do the a U.S. view of international organizations which predates the Reagan Administration. At least since World War II, the Unites States has considered such organizations as instruments of U.S. policy, useful to the extent that they fulfill U.S. requirements. Where they have no such value, the United States has ignored international organizations. The Johnson Administration, for instance, invoked the SEATO agreement to justify to Congress its sending of troops to South Vietnam: Kennedy Administration manipulation of the OAS in dealing with Cuba is another example. The Reagan Administration has used international organizations in a similar fashion. United States military involvement in Grenada, after all, was at the request of the Organization of Eastern Caribbean States, an organization few Americans were aware existed. Although the OECS requested assistance because of legitimate fears about the effects of the coup in Grenada in which one Marxist group overthrew and executed another, the OECS Treaty under which the United States intervened only permitted the organization to ask for outside assistance against external aggression. The best explanation the United States could offer of how the Treaty required its response was that its actions were in "anticipatory self-defense" against possible aggression by Cuba and the regime which had just come to power in Grenada (the United States used roughly the same argument in the International Court of Justice in defending its Nicaraguan operations, arguing that El Salvador was a party to the dispute). The OAS approved U.S. action in Grenada three weeks after it had occurred. The United States was heavily criticized by United Nations members, including such allies as the United Kingdom.

Similarly, the United States has attempted to revive the Central American Defense Council (CONDECA). This organization was founded by Nicaragua and Honduras in 1913, but had been moribund for years. The Reagan Administration has attempted to use it as a vehicle for coordinating joint training exercises of the troops of different Central American nations in Honduras.

The "go it alone" approach has had two effects on U.S. foreign policy toward Latin America. First, its participation in international development organizations has reflected its political policies toward the region. As is discussed in the section on human rights policy, the Reagan Administration does not believe that human rights practices by its allies should restrict the availability of loan funds to them. On the other hand, it has placed pressure on the IMF and the World Bank to cut off loans to Nicaragua. During the brief tenure of Maurice Bishop in Grenada, it encouraged the same policies toward that nation. The Reagan Administration has placed an embargo import quota to its allies. The Administration also imposes tariffs on nations which export products to the United States which contain nickel obtained from Cuba.

The second effect is on diplomatic initiatives. The United States has preferred ad hoc diplomatic initiatives between itself and other Latin American countries, rather than working through the OAS or other multilateral organizations. Despite its opposition to both, the Reagan Administration has engaged in negotiations with the FMLN and the Sandinistas on a nation-to-nation basis. It also has held talks with Cuba about returning the prisoners and mental patients the Castro government included in the 1980 Mariel harbor boatlift, although at one time it denied the existence of such talks.

The major example of the U.S. preference for "going it alone" diplomatically has been the Contadora Peace Process. Contadora was initiated by Mexico, Panama, Colombia, and Venezuela in January 1983. These nations sought a negotiated end to hostilities in Central America between the United States and Nicaragua. The Contadora Group may have been motivated by fear of continued escalation in fighting in Central America and the polarization of the political situation there; they may also have concluded that U.S. preoccupations with a military conflict would detract from its attention to the economic problems of the region, including those of the Contadora group.

During 1983-84, the Contadora nations conducted talks between the five Central American nations and the United States. It produced documents stating the objectives of the parties as being reduced hostilities, eliminating foreign military intervention in Central America, and emphasizing democratic government in the region. In September 1983, the Sandinista government announced that it would accept the second of these draft proposals on the condition that the United States agree to this statement without any changes. The United States refused to do so, on the basis that this version contained inadequate procedures for verifying whether Nicaragua was in compliance with Treaty provisions in such areas as the departure of foreign military advisors, reductions in the size of its armed forces, and cessation of aid to the FMLN in El Salvador. When later draft agreements were proposed, the Sandinistas refused to accept them.

As mentioned elsewhere, it is hard to discount the likelihood that the Sandinistas were engaged in strategic behavior, assuming that the United States would not accept change was a draft proposal, not a finalized document. On the other hand, the Reagan Administration is unlikely to get much better terms than those provided by the draft treaty. If there is a risk of Nicaraguan noncompliance, the Nicaraguans can reply that the Treaty held an equal risk of noncompliance by the United States and the Contras.

Since the Contadora Peace Process has been the chief alternative to U.S. military initiatives, it has been supported by the Democrats in Congress. While the President has been publicly supportive of Contadora, the Administration has criticized as naive those who believed that the Sandinistas were sincere in saying that they would abide by negotiated agreements. After talks were broken off between Nicaragua and the other Central American nations at the end of 1985, the U.S. reverted to its use of unilateral initiatives, sending retired diplomat Philip Habib to Central America for a round of talks with different government leaders.

The issue for debaters on the 1987-88 topic in this regard is whether multilateral diplomatic initiatives such as Contadora hold more promise for increasing political stability in Latin America than the Administration's "go it alone" approach. As with international development programs, a major factor in U.S. analysis of such proposals is the degree of control it retains over the process. The Reagan Administration has preferred unilaterally approaches because it can govern the terms of such agreements, given its overwhelming power over bilateral negotiating partners. The choices open to such nations are to accept U.S. terms or not negotiate. There is a risk in this, that other nations will determine that no agreement is better than one dictated by the United States. In a sense, that has occurred with Nicaragua. At this point, it would appear that the President may have been correct in his assessment that the only way in which the Nicaraguans will negotiate with the United States will be when they have been forced to say "uncle."

PRIVATE SECTOR VS. PUBLIC SECTOR DEVELOPMENT

Consistent with its conservative domestic political outlook, the Reagan Administration has emphasized aid to Latin America which would encourage capitalism and the development of free market economies. It has opposed aid programs of international institutions and agencies which it has viewed as encouraging socialist models of economies for the Third World, those featuring central economic planning and state ownership of the means of production. Many of the same factors explaining the Reagan Administration's preference for bilateral as opposed to multilateral aid are relevant here as well.

When the Reagan Administration took office, it gave serious consideration to reneging on Carter Administration aid pledges to international organizations, including the International Development Agency (IDA) of the IMF. The IDA focuses on aid to the poorest nations. The Reagan Administration has opposed IDA projects as overly focused on large state-owned public works programs. Although the administration ultimately decided to honor the Carter Administration's ultimately decided to honor the Carter Administration's earlier pledges, it has resisted repetitions of these projects. In 1984, the United States resisted the consensus of opinion of other IMF members and opposed a $12 billion replenishment to IDA funds. A reduced replenishment of $9 billion was eventually agreed upon. Taking inflation into account, this meant a decrease in IDA funds for development in real terms of forty percent. For similar reasons, the Reagan Administration also opposed the recapitalization of the Inter-American Development Bank (IADB). Like the IDA, the IADB has focused on the construction of large public works projects, primarily the building of hydroelectric power stations and irrigation projects. Such projects have long-term completion dates and projected benefits. The United States has been critical of the expense of these projects and the allocation of IADB funds to them.

The centerpiece of early Reagan Administration private sector-oriented projects was the Caribbean Basin Initiative, unveiled by the President in a speech to the Organization of American States in February, 1982. The CBI was a combination of trade and investment incentives for the region. In the form in which it reached Congress, its price tag was $350 million, a modest sum when compared with other international development programs and United States direct military assistance to the region. This was because the CBI was intended to be a free market, capitalist program, spurring economic activity. The real "funding" was to come from market transactions, with U.S. consumers purchasing Latin American products.

The CBI proposal was passed by Congress as part of a larger appropriations bill which was vetoed by the President, in part because of his objections to other items in the package and in part because of Congressional modifications of the proposal. One modification was that Congress wanted CBI funds to go into a trust fund, rather than being administered directly by the State Department. Other modifications had reduced trade incentives, responding to Congressional fears that the CBI would result in the loss of American jobs.

There are three fundamental reasons for the Reagan Administration's preference for private sector programs. The first is bluntly ideological. The Reagan Administration is opposed to what it sees as state socialism in many emerging nations in the world. It views state-owned-enterprises as being in conflict with its capitalist notions of democracy. The state which controls the economy usually leaves little room for political opposition. Economic allocations are the result of bureaucratically-developed multi-year plans, not marketplace forces. This model more accurately describes the emerging nations of Africa than it does the republics of Latin America. However, state planning has come to Latin America, especially South America, imported sometimes by military governments. The Reagan Administration sees state centralization as inimical to the best interests of the peoples of these countries and is firm in its opposition to programs it sees as furthering it. In doing so, it has to oppose most of the other members of international organizations, which partially explains its preference for unilateral action.

A second reason is connected with the first. The track record of centrally-planned economies in the Third World is dismal. Again, the best case that can be made for this proposition is in Africa, where grandiose public development and industrial projects and government inducements toward more "modern" urbanization and industrialization have been at odds with economic capacities and have ignored the human needs of populations. Brazil's search for "Grandeza" with accompanying deforestation of the Amazon River, nuclear power development, and construction of a new capitol in the middle of the rain forest is probably the closest Latin American Analog.

The Reagan Administration can make a convincing case that centrally planned economies are often inefficient, slow to respond to changed economic conditions, resistant to admit mistakes in design, and corrupt. It considers encouragement of marketplace forces a superior alternative, creating incentives for efficiency, responding to economic demand, being productive of private wealth as opposed to entranced state bureaucracy.

A third reason for the Reagan Administration's policy preference is budgetary. There have been battles within the Administration between the Department of State and the Office of Management and Budget over funding for international development, and the OMB has almost always won. Already resistant to international development projects which are to be publicly-owned, the President and his staff have been even easier to persuade when they view the funding for such projects as both large and in competion with more preferred bilateral and military assistance. When the IADB proposed a recapitalization from $20 billion to $35 billion, it was expected that the United States would provide one-third of the increased funds. Given the pressures of Gramm-Rudman and the other priorities of the Reagan Administration, it is not surprising that it prefers proposals along the lines of the CBI, which do not involve significant funding and create no ideological heartburn for the Administration.

There are several criticisms of the Administration's preference for private sector-oriented programs. First, it is almost necessarily export-oriented, which puts Latin American economies at the mercy of world economic conditions. Variations on the Reagan Administration's approach were tried in the 1950's and 1960's, with mixed results, the result of trade restrictions and world recessions. Latin American capitalist development is export-oriented because of the absence of substantial middle income groups with consumer purchasing power in most countries limits domestic markets. Latin American growth in the 1970's was assisted by the world inflation in oil prices, as well as high prices for agricultural commodities such as grain, sugar, and coffee. All of these economic trends have been reversed in recent years: increased emphasis on private sector capitalism will not be productive when the primary markets for such enterprises are already saturated.

A related criticism is that the export-orientation of private sector development creates a quasi-colonial relationship between the Latin American states and the United States. The

United States is the logical market for Latin American exports: as Cuba and Nicaragua can attest to trying to develop and export strategy exclusive of the United States is difficult indeed. Colonies are dependent on the good will of the colonizing nation. One way of looking at the economic boycotts and cutoffs of loan funds to Cuba and Nicaragua (and, briefly, Grenada) by the United States is that of economic retribution for political deviations.

A final criticism of the Reagan Administration's approach is that it ignores the very real public works needs of most Latin American countries. Lack of adequate road systems, safe sanitation and drinking water, irrigation for agriculture, and electric power stand in the way of both economic and public health in much of Latin America. Development of the kinds of economic enterprises the Reagan Administration has in mind will be difficult without first completing these projects. While MNE's do certain amount of infrastructure development in the Third world to facilitate their operations, they do no more than is necessary and are more attracted to nations where such facilities are already in place.

An example of economic dependency and private sector initiatives is provided by Guatemala. Under the Reagan Administration, Guatemala has been encouraged by changed import quotas to raise cattle for beef export. Ranching is land-intensive and competitive with land reform. Small farms, formerly tenant operations, have been turned into pastureland. In addition to being land-intensive: it aggravates Guatemala's employment problem, displacing farm workers. Cattle-raising, which the United States has also encouraged in Honduras, is heavily reliant on U.S. markets for export, even small domestic beef consumption.

Guatemala has also been the site of investment by the Latin American Agribusiness Development Corporation, a consortium of major U.S. banks and agribusiness corporations. LAAD finances and develops agricultural projects, but primarily those producing food for export, not domestic consumption. Latin America's attractions are its cheap land and labor. While LAAD projects create jobs in Guatemala, they are dependent on U.S. markets for consumption of such crops as cauliflower, peas, and other vegetables which can be raised on a factory-like basis in small land areas. In the event of oversupply, they would not substitute for crops consumed domestically (corn, beans).

There are alternatives to the Reagan Administration's preferred economic model for Latin America, but it opposes them through withholding aid and providing trade incentives for its own model. One approach is that being advanced by the Sandinistas in Nicaragua, that of government-owned cooperatives and central economic planning. The Reagan Administration has opposed peasant-owned cooperatives in other Central American nations. This is somewhat ironic, in that rual cooperatives in Guatemala and Honduras had built up around United States Agency for International Development technical assistance programs. The Reagan Administration sees cooperatives as part of state socialism. The targets of the Contras in Nicaragua frequently are such cooperatives, as will as public works projects the United States helped build under the Samoza regime.

The argument for state cooperatives and central planning in Latin America is that it is the most efficient use of limited resources, such as electrical power and petroleum. The Reagan Administration's embargo has coincided with increased use of cooperatives in Nicaragua: this may have occurred anyway, but the embargo has made it imperative. The positive way of viewing this is that labor is not used in duplicative or inefficient ways and the cooperative use of labor is necessary for the construction of public works projects in rural areas. The negative way of viewing this is that the state is making decisions about resource allocations and workers are de facto employees of the state.

The cooperative-state planning approach has been more prevalent in the rural than in the Nicaraguan urban economy, where foreign and private firms have remained. The limitations of the cooperative approach is that it seems best-suited for subsistence agricultural production and some light manufacturing. It is not suited for obtaining the foreign exchanged necessary to finance large development projects or to obtain materials not produced domestically or available. Nicaragua had relied on exports of sugar to earn foreign exchange necessary to import manufactured goods, petroleum, and other products: the U.S. embargo has had its biggest impact in this area. However, even without such economic retaliation, Latin American economies focusing on an agrarian model and domestic economic needs would be faced with the same prospects, producing at least some goods for export and attempting to obtain foreign and international development aid.

A modification of this second model is regional economic cooperation. One example of this was the Central American Common Market, which is discussed further in Chapter Four. While not avoiding all of the problems of the model just described, it would avoid the problems the problems of world market dependency which afflict the Reagan Administrations's private sector development model. Because regional cooperations would emphasize production for regional cooperation would emphasize production for regional instead of world consumption, it is less attractive to foreign investment, given a probable lower rate of return. Politically, it is less attractive to the United States precisely because it decreases U.S. leverage over these economies. The real stumbling block to regional economic cooperation, both in Central and South America, has been the degree of rivalry among the different nations.

What are the implications of the Reagan Administrations's private sector economic emphasis for the 1987-88 topic? At a basic level, it explains the Administration's commitment to certain types of programs and opposition to others, particularly international development projects. Critics of the Reagan Administration have considered its private sector emphasis as misconceived, ignoring the nature of Latin America's economies and their problems. Particularly for the Central American republics, this has ominous implications. The problems there can

be viewed as economic rather than political, those of unemployment and hunger. Military assistance can at best sustain governments against insurgencies, but it cannot make up for the inef-
fectives of such governments in meeting their population's
economic needs.

SECURITY ASSISTANCE VS. ECONOMIC DEVELOPMENT

A clear emphasis of the Reagan Administration has been on military assistance, including foreign military sales and the presence of U.S. military advisors in El Salvador, as opposed to
economic development aid. Much of what has been categorized as
economic aid has been targeted for nations also receiving significant U.S. military assistance. PL 480 Food for Peace shipment
also always seem to be in large amounts to countries where U.S.
allies are engaged in civil conflicts, which was true of El
Salvador and Guatemala today. This is an area of the 1987-88
topic in which most of the emphasis will be on Central America as
opposed to South America. Despite the presence of guerrilla
movements in Peru and Colombia, the lion's share of U.S. military
assistance has been to Central America, particularly El
Salvador.

The Reagan Administration's budget for fiscal 1987 included
a request for $11.3 billion in international security assistance
funds. $6.1 billion of this was to be in foreign military sales
credits (i.e., Department of Defense transfers to U.S. defense
contractors for weapons and equipment shipped to U.S. allies),
$1.0 billion was to be for direct military assistance, and $4.1
billion was for economic support funds. The latter was to be
focused on nations with security concerns, i.e., insurgency
movements. The budget request represented an increase of $1.0
billion over the previous year. Meanwhile, the Agency for
International Development was budgeted for $2.1 billion, with the
admonition to use the private sector as a vehicle for economic
growth.

The current request for FY 1988 included a request for a
supplemental appropriation of $1.3 billion, plus an increase in
the budget authorization level over the previous year of $1.0
billion. The FY 1988 request indicated that economic assistance
would be targeted at "four Central American democracies." The
real jump in U.S. security assistance funds occurred in 1985,
after the landslide reelection of the President: security assistance funds were increased by five percent.

Increases in the level of funding for military aid for
Central America alone have been much more dramatic. U.S. aid to
El Salvador increased from $50 million in 1980 to $514 million in
1986; the United States sent more aid to Central America between
1981 and 1983 than in the Johnson, Nixon, Ford, and Carter
presidencies combined. This aid does not include Department of
Defense funds spent on U.S. military training exercises in
Honduras, conducted in conjunctions with the troops of Central

American nations. It also does not include funds for the U.S. Southern Command in the Canal Zone, where nine thousand U.S. Army troops have been stationed, eight thousand at the U.S. Jungle operations Training Center in colon (although under the Panama Canal Treaty, the U.S. did have to turn over Ft. Gulick to the government of Panama in 1984 and transfer its training school for Latin American officers to Ft. Benning, Georgia. The training school, "the School for the Americas', was popularly referred to as "the school for dictators.") U.S. assistance figures also do not include the $100 million for the not-so-covert operations of the Contras in Nicaragua.

U.S. military assistance still primarily consists of foreign military sales, both of light infantry weapons and of helicopters and spare parts for aircraft purchased at earlier dates. Military aid also includes so-called "non-lethal" assistance, such as jeeps, uniforms, medicine, and other equipment. U.S. assistance has played a major role in the expansion of the Salvadoran Army from seven thousand troops in 1979 to thirty-seven thousand in 1985, with security forces also being increased for twenty-five hundred to thirteen thousand during the same period.

The United States Army is limited to a noncombatant role in Central America. While most attention has focused on U.S. advisors in El Salvadors, other advisors are present in Honduras and Costa Rica. The "advisory" limitation sometimes takes on odd features. U.S. advisors in El Salvador are limited by law to the regions in which they can accompany Salvadoran troops and have been reprimanded for being armed while in the field. When Honduran troops were transported to an area where the Nicaraguan Army had been reported to have crossed the border in December 1986, they were taken there by U.S. helicopters on loan from U.S. training exercises, which were unarmed.

The Reagan Administration has emphasized security assistance over more traditional economic development aid on the theory that the primary problem confronting El Salvador and other Central American nations is that of guerrilla insurgencies. An additional recreational is that security against guerrilla attacks is necessary before economic development efforts can be made viable. Since the FMLN, the Salvadoran guerrilla organization, has made a point of destroying electrical power stations and bridges and cutting off major transportation routes, there is some support for this position.

There is an alternative perspective on U.S. military assistance and its effect on the economic situations in Central America. In both Guatemala and El Salvador, a principal objective of the military has been to separate the guerrilla movements from the civilian populations which might provide support to them. In Guatemala, this has meant the forced relocation of rural Indian populations into "Model Villages", reminiscent of the "Strategic Hamlets" program of the Vietnam War. U.S. helicopters were useful in counter-insurgency warfare against the guerrillas during Guatemalan Army sweeps of Indian areas in Western Guatemala during 1982 and again in 1984. U.S. assistance has also helped the Guatemalan government pay for "Civil Patrols" which control the "Model Villages." Riding in U.S. jeeps and armed with U.S. weapons, the Civil Patrols are a reminder of the Reagan Administration's abrupt shift on aid to Guatemala, which had been cut off by the Carter Administration for human rights abuses in 1977. From one perspective, the Civil Patrols, which are not part of the regular army and are made up of members of Indian tribe members, protect the Model Villages from guerrilla attacks; from another perspective, the Model Villages are concentration camps, with Civil Patrol members guilty of human rights abuses and extortion from village inhabitants.

In El Salvador, separation of civilian populations from the FMLN has meant Salvadoran Army operations on the Honduran border, in what was until a few years ago a sparsely populated area. El Salvador, the smallest of the Central American republics outside of Belize, has the highest population density (this has been the source of tensions between El Salvador and Honduras for a number of years, with Honduras fearing Salvadoran expansion). Salvadorans have been displaced from subsistence farming, as in Guatemala, by a transition to cash crops for export: in El Salvador, the crops are cotton and sugar.

In the early 1980's, the FMLN announced it was creating a "Free El Salvador" in the border regions with Honduras. There had been some population migration to the area as other farming areas had become unavailable. Salvadoran Army operations have been aimed at removing civilian populations from these areas, and have included "scorched earth" operations, destroying crops and houses in an effort to deny the FMLN a base of support. The Salvadoran Army regards civilians in these areas as guerrilla sympathizers. The Salvadoran Air Force has been accused by human rights observers of conducting an air war against these regions, bombing villages. The military has denied these reports, saying only that there have been occasional accidents on their part. Again, U.S. support, particularly of helicopters used in such operations, has been instrumental in the outcome of this campaign.

The United States does not appear to have clearly articulated objectives for its economic assistance to Central America. It currently sees such assistance as an adjunct to its military assistance program. The hope is that guerrilla activities can be reduced to a level at which private sector-based initiatives will not be disrupted. As was discussed in an earlier section, this has occurred in Guatemala. However, the prevailing impression is that of a U.S. policy which is military and counter-insurgency in orientation, with economic development an afterthought.

The major question raised by the Reagan Administration's emphasis on military assistance is whether this carries with it the seeds of direct intervention by U.S. troops. Secretary of State Haig at one time refused to rule out such an option: the rest of the Reagan Administration has been more circumspect. The Joint Chiefs of Staff, while maintaining a low profile on the subject, have opposed U.S. military involvement in Central America. Their position has been based on a reading of American public opinion as being apathetic towards the region or opposed to the involvement of U.S. troops. One effect of the Vietnam War experience is that the Joint Chiefs are reluctant to commit the U.S. military to a cause which lacks widespread public support.

The practical aspects of U.S. military intervention into Central America are daunting as well. In some respects, Central America is a more favorable case for such involvement than was Southeast Asia. The region is closer to the United States, the nations involved (primarily El Salvador, Honduras, Costa Rica, and Nicaragua) are much smaller in population, and there is no large socialist parent nation available which would provide significant support in the event of an actual U.S. invasion. On the other hand, U.S. troops would be forced to engage in search-and-destroy missions against the FMLN in mountainous and forested areas in El Salvador. In contrast to the rhetoric of the Reagan Administration, the Contras have no base of popular support in Nicaragua. While the United States Army would win a large-scale engagement with the Nicaraguan Army, an invasion of that country would be bloody, unpopular in the United States and around the world, and only the prelude to protracted guerrilla warfare by the Sandinistas.

A closer analogy for U.S. involvement in Central America is the Soviet role in Afghanistan, not the U.S. experience in Vietnam. Like the Soviets, the United States would have to be content to keep its troops in Central America for an extended period of time and to expect that "victory" would mean keeping Marxist insurgents from coming to power. Since the Joint Chiefs are convinced that the American public would find this unpalatable, it has opposed policies which it considers to increase the probability of direct U.S. military participation in Latin American military conflicts. From this perspective, the military training exercises on the Honduran-Nicaraguan border (and the construction of landing fields for military transports) can be put in the category of "sabre-rattling", making the Sandinistas aware of a potential U.S. presence.

The most likely scenarios under which U.S. troops would become directly involved in Central America assume precipitating action by Nicaraguan forces. For example, the Sandinistas might overrun Honduras while attacking Contra forces. There is a small, Marxist insurgency movement in Honduras to which the Sandinistas have given at least moral support. It is out of fear of such scenarios that the Honduran government has pushed the United States to relocate the Contras in Nicaragua and to guarantee that Contra refugees would be given asylum in the United States should the Contra effort ever be abandoned. The Reagan Administration has demurred on the latter request; it promised to move the Contras into Nicaragua by spring, 1987. For their part, the Sandinistas have avoided giving the United States a reason to become more directly involved, minimizing its entries into Honduran territory in its operations against the Contras. It has denied reports of clashes with the Honduran Army.

Even without direct participation by the United States military, there are negative effects of the Reagan Administration's emphasis on security assistance. U.S. support of the

Contras has polarized Central America between Nicaragua and the other nations in the region. Several of these governments, including Guatemala, Costa Rica, and Panama, would prefer to remain neutral in this dispute. The United States has not permitted nations in the regions to remain neutral, using its military assistance to counter-insurgency efforts as leverage. Panama, which co-opted domestic leftist support with the signing of the Canal Treaty and which has maintained good relations with Cuba, has been able to resist U.S. pressure, but others have not been so fortunate. One example of this occurred in September 1984, when nations in the region which had endorsed the Contadora Peace Treaty had to reverse themselves after Washington refused to accept the version of the agreement which Nicaragua announced it was willing to sign.

U.S. military assistance has also had a polarizing influence within countries receiving aid. The London-based Institute for Strategic Studies has concluded that U.S. aid has had the effect of polarizing social conflicts in Latin American countries, hurting moderate and centrist groups. This is because the effect of U.S. assistance has been to strengthen the position of groups already in power, preserving their authority. Dissenting groups viewed with suspicion by the military and ruling elites become targets of repression in an environment in which U.S. military assistance has insured the continued supremacy of the government and its supporters.

One example of this is El Salvador. Although the popular conception among Americans is that Jose Napoleon Duarte won a victory for centrist moderation over the extremist policies of Roberto D'Aubuisson in 1984, the results were in fact more complex. Although Duarte was elected President, his Christian Democrat Party did not win a majority of seats in the Assembly, which is instead controlled by D'Aubuisson's ARENA Party. ARENA speaks for large landowners and political conservatives in El Salvador, whose interests have been furthered by U.S. military aid. Although President Duarte had met with opposition leaders on several occasions, ARENA has prevented him from achieving success. The basic demand of the FDR, the political arm of the insurgency, is for power sharing in a new coalition government. Ironically, the FDR representative would be Guillermo Ungo, Duarte's Vice Presidential running mate in 1972, when Duarte apparently won election but then lost in the military's count of the votes. ARENA has resisted power-sharing: since it knows it has U.S. support in this (Secretary of State Schultz once said that it would not permit the FMLN to "shoot their way to power"), it has no reason not to impede negotiations.

Lastly, U.S. preference for security assistance over economic aid has been criticized as creating conditions for its perpetuation. As was mentioned earlier, the thesis behind the Reagan Administration's prioritization is that security must precede development, in order to provide a safe environment in which the latter can take place. Increased numbers of troops and increased levels of operations usually lead instead to demands for further increases in troop levels and levels of operations.

The power of host country military leaders comes from sustaining and increasing counter-insurgency operations, not from winding them down. So long as a political insurgency group exists, there will be a justification for continued military operations, delaying the point at which emphasis can be shifted to economic development. While some private sector-oriented assistance has taken place in Guatemala and El Salvador, economic assistance to both countries has been an adjunct to security assistance. Military assistance has continued to increase to both countries, even though the level of fighting between government and guerrilla forces has declined since 1984.

COUNTER-INSURGENCY VS. HUMAN RIGHTS

Consistent with other positions described in this chapter, the Reagan Administration has prioritized the combatting of terrorism over support for human rights efforts. This position was a campaign issue in the 1980 Presidential elections, with candidate Reagan blaming the Carter Administration's stand on human rights for the loss of Nicaragua to a Communist government; its ineptness in dealing with terrorists was the basis for Republican criticism of the Carter Administration's handling of the Iran Hostage crisis. Early in the life of the Reagan Administration, it became apparent that then-Secretary of State Alexander Haig used "human rights deprivations" to describe abuses by terrorist groups and by Soviet Bloc and Marxist countries, but the phrase had no application outside of that.

Despite wholesale changes in foreign policy personnel, the perspective of the Reagan Administration remains the same as it was in 1980-81, that a more serious threat to U.S. interests comes from the activities of terrorist groups than from the human rights practices of its allies. The Reagan Administration describes itself as committed to the prevention of human rights abuses. However, it sees as counterproductive a human rights policy which hampers U.S. support of anti-Communist governments. As a reflection of Reagan Doctrine views of the world, it sees insurgents and opponents of anti-Communist governments as being closely related or the same group, and views with suspicion claims of human rights abuses by such persons. From the Reagan Administration perspective, terrorism, including state-sponsored terrorism, can be traced in most if not all cases to Soviet support: hence, support of anti-Communist governments accused of human rights violations and opposition to terrorism amount to the same policy.

In this section of this chapter, distinctions between the Carter and the Reagan Administration's approaches to human rights policy are discussed, followed by a description of the principal features of the Reagan Administrations' record concerning human rights. A section of Chapter Four also deals with human rights, but from the perspective of conflicting policy options for affirmatives in dealing with Latin American political stability.

President Carter, in a commencement address at Notre Dame in 1977 set the tone for his administration's human rights policy when he said that "inordinate fear of Communism. . . once led us to embrace any dictator who joined us in that fear." (quoted in Lacquer and Rubin, eds., The Human Rights Reader, 1979, p. 306) The Carter Administration was identified, especially by its opponents, as having adamantly supported human rights, even at the cost of offending allies and sacrificing other foreign policy objectives. The Reagan Administration's view of the place of human rights within a larger foreign policy was expressed by Jeane Kirkpatrick in her November 1979 essay in Commentary, "Dictatorships and Double Standards," distinguishing between totalitarian and authoritarian governments and pointing toward a "pragmatic" policy of support of authoritarian governments capable of being reformed, as opposed to the Carter Administration's "utopian" support of human rights, which produced the Sandinistas, a government incapable of ever embracing democracy and respect for individual liberty.

The differences between the two administrations in human rights practices are in fact more apparent than real, more rhetoric than reality. The Carter Administration was in fact selective in its use of aid termination as a club to force improved human rights practices. Its use of this policy tool was restricted to Latin America, but for reasons having to do with other foreign policy priorities, not because of its view of Latin governments' human rights abuses. When aid terminations were considered by the Carter Administration with regard to governments in other parts of the world, they were rejected because of competing foreign policy considerations, such as proximity of the nation involved to the U.S.S.R. or its allies, presence of U.S. military bases in the nation, membership of the nation in pro-Western security organizations, or exports by the nation to the United States of strategic materials. The Carter Administration announced terminations of security assistance to eight Latin American nations because no such competing policy considerations were available to justify continuation of aid to them.

The consensus of the human rights community was that the Carter Administration was long on intentions but short on having a coherent program or strategy for guaranteeing human rights. Although it created an Inter-Agency Committee to coordinate human rights policy (subsequently eliminated by the Reagan Administration) it provided little support for human rights as a policy. Human rights community members also charge that there were two Carter Administrations insofar as human rights were concerned, the one in office in 1977–78 which was publicly committed to human rights as a foreign policy priority, and the one in office in 1979 and 1980, which was preoccupied with superpower relations and, later, the hostage crisis.

The watchwords for the Reagan Administration have been "counter-terrorism" and "quiet diplomacy." The Reagan Administration's fundamental position has been that Soviet and Marxist expansion are a greater threat to human freedoms than are the behaviors of individual authoritarian regimes. The Reagan

Administration's definition of terrorists is not limited to the
Palestinian Liberation Organization, Islamic Jihad, the Red
Brigades, etc., but also includes the governments of Libya and
Nicaragua, and sees the Cubans and the Soviets behind terrorist
acts in Latin America. The Reagan Administration's attitude
toward how human rights considerations should figure into its
relations with anti-Communist governments was expressed by the
State Department in its "Country Reports on Human Rights Practices for 1982": (February 8, 1983)

> The Reagan Administration's test is effectiveness.
> With friendly governments we prefer to use diplomacy,
> not public pronouncements. We seek not to isolate them
> for their injustices, but to use our influence to
> effect desirable changes.

This leads to another watchword, "quiet diplomacy" or
"constructive engagement." The theory behind this policy is
that, for example, South Africa, will be more open to human
rights influences if the United States maintains a constructive
dialogue with that government and receives security assistance
from it in dealing with Communist or Communist-backed terrorists.
For critics of the Reagan Administration, the opposition to the
South African government is Nelson Mandela and Desmond Tutu; for
the Reagan Administration, it is the Cuban troops in Angola, who
support the SWAPO organization in Namibia and the ANC in
Zimbabwe. The criticism of this approach is that repressive
governments interpret Reagan Administration "constructive engagement" as tacit support; having received the award of assistance,
such countries have no incentive to improve their practices.
    Whether the Carter and the Reagan Administrations can be
described as functionally distinct in human rights practices was
the subject of a study by political scientists Carleton and Stohl
of Purdue University in Human Rights Quarterly in May, 1985.
They concluded that there were no significant differences between
the two administrations in degree of correlation between human
rights observance and aid distribution. However, the one exception to this generalization was for the Carter Administration aid
distribution to Latin America. Carleton and Stohl also concluded
that there were no significant differences between the two
administrations in terms of policy results. A survey of fifty-
nine nations showed improvements in five nations but worsening
situations in four countries under the Carter Administration,
with the corresponding figures being seven and eight for the
Reagan Administration. Carleton and Stohl are critical of the
Reagan Administration not for what it has done but what it has
not done in human rights, centering on El Salvador and South
Africa as cases where the United States could have been active in
promoting human rights but did not do so. They also conclude
that while the Carter Administration raised more hopes of human
rights attainment than it fulfilled, the Reagan Administration's
"quiet diplomacy" raises no hopes at all. The Carter Administration at least created an image of support for human rights

efforts by indigenous groups and non-governmental organizations, while the Reagan Administration has not done so (and, as mentioned earlier in this chapter, has actually been disparaging of such groups as Americas Watch and Amnesty International's efforts in Latin America).

In 1981, the incoming Reagan Administration engaged in a number of human rights-related acts for which it was criticized by the press, both in the United States and around the world. In 1981, the Administration ordered U.S. delegates to the World Bank to support loans to nations boycotted by the Carter Administration for human rights violations, including Chile, Argentina, Paraguay and Uruguay. It also voted with Argentina and Brazil, then both under the rule of military juntas, in an unsuccessful attempt to abolish the United Nations Working Group on Enforced or Involuntary Disappearances. It also lifted the Carter Administration's Executive Order banning military and economic aid to Argentina, Chile, Guatemala, and Uruguay. These actions were accompanied by pronouncements by United Nations Ambassador Kirkpatrick and Secretary of State Haig, among others, about the pragmatic wisdom of such policies. This period culminated with the Senate Foreign Relation Committee's rejection of the nomination of Ernest Lefever as Assistant Secretary of State for Human Affairs in June, 1981 (the job went instead to Elliott Abrams, who later became Assistant Secretary of State for Inter-American Affairs and who has been the Administration's spokesman for aid to the Contras).

Following this early criticism of its policies, the Reagan Administration began in late 1981 to articulate a public position that it had been misunderstood as denigrating the importance of human rights. The general reaction of commentators has been that any changes in the Administration's position since that time have been cosmetic rather than substantive. Some of the Reagan Administration personalities publicly associated with attacks on Carter Administration human rights policies departed during the first term of the Reagan Presidency, including Ambassador Kirkpatrick, Secretary Haig, and National Security Agency Director Richard Allen, although only Mr. Lefever's departure was associated with his stance on human rights policy. However, press criticism of Administration human rights policies became more muted once these publicly-identifiable figures left. The Reagan Administration's human rights image has also been helped by the end of the rule of several military regimes with bad human rights records in Latin America, as well as by the election of Jose Napoleon Duarte as President of El Salvador. Critics of the Administration have replied that these events took place more despite the human rights policies of the United States than because of them. Nevertheless, they removed areas of tension about human rights abuses by Latin American allies of the United States.

From the perspective of the Reagan Administration, however, it has not been disingenuous when it has said that it has been misunderstood as to its commitment toward human rights. It is simply a matter of understanding what the Reagan Administration means by that commitment. The Administration has consistently taken the position that security assistance is the best course of action in combatting insurgency activities in Latin America. Since it sees insurgency movements as the greatest threat to human rights, its support of the military in Central America constitutes a prioritization of the protection of human rights. This is coupled with patience on the part of the Reagan Administration with military governments dealing with what are difficult domestic situations. In addition, it has agreed with the characterizations those governments have made of dissenting groups as Commmunist or Communist-influenced, and so discounts reports of human rights abuses by them. One result of this has been the form taken by the "Country Reports" of the Department of State. Human rights groups have charged that these reports have been objective and well-documented, except for Latin America, where the regimes accused of abuse are American allies and not Soviet Bloc or Non-Aligned Movement nations. The reports for Latin America have been criticized for giving improper emphasis to reports of terror by guerrilla movements taken from military sources, while selectively omitting reports of military atrocities and the activities of paramilitary death squads. They are also accused of simply distorting facts. The Reagan Administration has relied on these reports in uniformly certifying that Latin American governments have made improvements in human rights practices sufficient to justify continued military assistance.

The major question to be considered by the debate community in 1987–88 in this area is whether the Reagan Administration has been correct in its emphasis on combatting guerrilla movements over support of human rights as an independent foreign policy objective. The Administration has pointed to the decreased activities of death squads (which it says are leftist as well as right-wing) in El Salvador and the accession to power of democratic regimes in Argentina and Brazil as evidence that its policies have produced results. It has also pointed to increasing political repression by the Sandinistas as proof that it was correct in its assessment of the human rights practices of totalitarian governments.

There are two basic rebuttals to this. First, an assessment of the Reagan Administration's record is premature: both human rights and counter-insurgency are policy areas where "the early returns" may not be indicative of how the final results will turn out. A defense has been raised of Carter Administration policies on human rights that four years was not nearly long enough to establish a credible pattern of U.S. opposition to governments with poor human rights performances. Since the history of U.S. foreign policy toward Central America in the twentieth century has been one of sending the Marines to occupy misbehaving countries and supporting a succession of dictators in a variety of nations, a reasonable Latin view of the Carter Administration's stated human rights policy was that it was an aberration.

Under the Reagan Administration, two of the most repressive governments in the world departed (via U.S. military transports), those of Duvalier in Haiti and Marcos in the Philippines.

Whether the role of the Administration in their departure reflected concern for human rights or a pragmatic reading of the futures of these regimes is a matter for dispute. Both governments survived the Carter Administration. The civil war in El Salvador has receded from the newspapers, in part because it has been replaced by revelations about Administration activities in support of the Contras. Some analysts have concluded that the war in El Salvador has entered a new phase, that of a "war of attrition", as opposed to the larger-scale engagements of the early 1980's: while the FMLN is no longer talking about waging its "final offensive", this does not mean that the government has won the war.

An even more basic rebuttal is whether the emphasis on counterterrorism is more productive than an emphasis on human rights in terms of guaranteeing human freedoms. Between 1969 and 1981, terrorist groups around the world are generally blamed for the deaths of about four thousand persons. This figure, while reprehensible, pales by comparison with the record of repressive regimes, such as the "authoritarian" ones the Kirkpatrick model suggests merit United States support. Over forty thousand persons have died in El Salvador since 1979, most of them through "extrajudicial executions." The military leaders on trial in Argentina have been charged with the "disappearances" of nine thousand persons, while human rights observers have put the figure at closer to thirty thousand persons. In addition to disagreeing about numbers, a counter to this argument is to re-introduce the basic Reagan-Kirkpatrick position: Argentina's authoritarian military government gave way to a democratic one, while the prospects for this taking place in Cuba seem remote or nonexistent.

There is no definitive answer to the question whether the Reagan Administration has been correct in its policy emphasis, since the answers are reflective of the values and political paradigms of the commentators. The position of the Reagan Administration in prioritizing counter-insurgency efforts over human rights as an independent foreign policy objective is both consistent with its other foreign policy positions and has a pervasive influence upon them.

Themes and Problems
in Latin America

This chapter addresses tensions in Latin American politics influencing the level of stability and unrest. These are factors which will be the subject of analysis on the 1987–88 topic, either as the focus of affirmative cases, or as impediments to solvency and the source of disadvantage arguments by the negative. These areas for analysis are: (1) human rights; (2) population and development; (3) international debt; and (4) the form of government, military or civilian. The final section of the chapter looks at the role of the United States in supporting the Contras in Nicaragua.

HUMAN RIGHTS

In the broadest sense of the term, all problems in Latin America are human rights problems. The more traditional Western conception of human rights has been to focus almost exclusively on civil liberties and political rights. The view of human rights adopted by persons in the Third World and Marxists has been to include development and affirmative social programs by governments as part of securing human rights. From a combination of these perspectives, all of the problems addressed in this chapter are human rights problems. The section on military versus civilian rule concerns individual civil liberties, while government responses to population pressures and to national economic problems implicates rights of citizens as members of the state as a collective social organization. United States support of the Contras implicates both conceptions of human rights, as well as the rights of the state as a sovereign entity to territorial integrity and self-determination.

United States and Western views of human rights have been termed "first generation" conceptions by writers in human rights theory. "First generation" rights are based on individual liberty and protection of the person from deprivations of liberty by the state and focus on civil and political freedoms and rights. From this viewpoint, the role of the state is limited to one of guaranteeing the rights of its members: states are negatively implicated in depriving the rights of their citizens. The Western view also implies that human rights are universal, to be enjoyed by all individuals, whatever the cultural and social context in which they live. This is a corollary of the position that human rights are held by individuals, and guaranteed by states: all individuals have these rights, and states are not to deprive them of these freedoms. This is somewhat in conflict with concepts of international customary law, which although Western in origin have only recognized as peremptory norms the rights of nation-states (such as the right to self-determination, which belongs to states, not individuals. Peremptory norms or universal rights applying to all nations are limited to a very short list, restricting such things as acts of genocide and slavery. Western, including U.S. views of political rights are not universally shared. African nations, for example, do not share Western notions of a right to emigrate. This "right" may have more to do with the need of Western European nations to export their "surplus" populations to other continents than some "natural right." Cultural biases influence notions of what are the human rights of the greatest importance. U.S. views reflect its historical forms of political, social, and economic organization, such as capitalism and protestant moral values.

What are referred to as "second-generation" human rights include economic and social rights and are based on equality of persons, and guarantee access of societies to essential goods, services, and opportunities. While the United States has been supportive of notions of equality of opportunity, this has not been viewed as being a matter of human rights, except where governments have systematically deprived some persons of access to social and economic values. The United States has always viewed economic and social values as being obtained by individuals, rather than as being guaranteed by governments, past minimum "floors" preventing starvation, for example. The conflict between the Reagan Administration and other nations with regard to development is that other nations view development as a right of citizens and an obligation on the part of states, while the Reagan Administration has viewed development as the result of individual, market-responsive efforts.

Marxist and Third World views of human rights add a "third generation" of rights, solidarity rights. These rights are said to be based on the notion of fraternity among peoples, obligating international cooperation by states to overcome inequalities barring the attainment of "second generation" rights (and, to a lesser extent, "first generation" rights as well). The Reagan Administration, while in some contexts amenable to "second generation" rights flatly rejects the idea of "obligations" toward other states. The "third generation" rights view can also be regarded as a cover for New International Economic Order (NIEO) writers in arguing that Western nations, including the United States, are obligated to provide economic assistance to Third World nations.

The United States therefore takes a very different view of human rights than do Second World and Third World governments. The United States prioritizes democratic political rights, such as the right to vote in free elections. Governments which are inept at providing for the economic needs of their citizens may be nonetheless viewed positively by the United States if they have accorded fundamental political freedoms to their citizens. The United States is also willing to tolerate otherwise repressive regimes if they at least make a pretense of being democratic. Correspondingly, Third World regimes focus on the rights of individuals more as members of the collective social whole than as individual right-holders. The state, not the individual, holds rights, because the state is obligated to provide for the social and economic needs of its citizens. From this point of view, the Sandinista campaign to collectivize its economy, adopting central economic planning, can be described as an appropriate state measure taken to secure the human rights of its citizens.

Latin American nations' views of human rights adopt portions of both Western and Marxist-Third World views. The issues to be confronted by debaters on the 1987-88 topic are whether Latin American governments have engaged in human rights abuses, and by what standards, as well as considering what U.S. policies with regard to human rights are the most conducive to their attainment, however those rights are conceived of. The Latin American policies of the United States can be characterized as having been productive of both first and second-generation human rights. Positions adopted by affirmative teams can be productive or counterproductive of human rights with regard to either human rights construct.

The Carter Administration attempted to be productive of both first-generation and second-generation human rights, although it was more vocal about first-generation political values. The Carter Administration experience should be advisory of future U.S. efforts. The Chilean political scientist Francisco Orrego Vicuna in "The Human Rights Debate in Latin America" in Robert Vincent, editor, Foreign Policy and Human Rights (1986), has expressed Latin American criticisms of Carter Administration policies on three grounds. First, Latin American governments saw United States human rights sanctions as being solely negative in nature: governments were punished for not meeting United States-expressed standards for conduct, but they were not rewarded for taking corrective actions. In addition, sanctions were simultaneously imposed for other reasons, e.g., on Brazil for allegedly developing nuclear weapons and Ecuador for alleged violations of fishing agreements, diluting the human rights character of the sanctions message. Second, Latin Americans viewed the United States as operating under a double standard, punishing them but exempting its allies elsewhere for essentially the same conduct. The difference between the cases was one of the presence of U.S. political, strategic, or economic interests elsewhere in the world, but the absence of such interests in Latin America. Finally, the Carter Administration failed to differentiate between protection of individual and economic and political rights. While it espoused both, it had no clear description of the standards to be met in the latter category, while it had precise standards for the former. Hence, the Carter Administration's efforts took on the character of harassment of military regimes, while exempting inept civilian democracies. This final criticism also indicates how a military regime, such as Chile's, could adopt a "second-generation" view of human rights just as easily as a Marxist regime.

The Reagan Administration, on the other hand, can be criticized as engaging in policies conflicting with "second-generation" views of human rights. As was discussed in Chapter Three, the Reagan Administration prefers private sector to public sector development. Given the export orientation of Latin American countries, something which the United States has encouraged, a private sector orientation can have the effect of meeting supranational commercial interests, while being inimical to the social and economic rights of the poor in less developed nations. United States emphasis on security assistance over economic development aid, as well as the policies discussed in this chapter on population and economic development, can also be argued to conflict with the securing of social and economic development rights of Third World and Latin American nations. The Reagan Administration is consistent with earlier presidencies, including the Carter Administration, in prioritizing first-generation, political views of human rights, and in being charitable toward nominally democratic regimes. The principal differences between the two Administrations are ones of the relationship between human rights priorities and other foreign policy objectives, and of method or strategies for securing human rights in Third World nations, which for both Administrations has in practice meant Latin America.

Finally, debaters will have to grapple with the distinction between "universal" and "relative" human rights. It is a reflection of ethnocentrism to see the values of one's own culture as universal: one can attack the application of United States standards of moral conduct to Third World situations as cultural elitism. Conversely, one can view with distrust "relativistic" explanations for nation-state human rights. This is usually a cover for egregious conduct toward politically and ethnically disfavored groups. One recurrent theme in both Central American and South American politics is the relatively greater deprivations of human rights of American Indian tribes, whatever the level of first-generation or second-generation human rights accorded to the Latino (or "European") population as a whole. Universalism versus Relativism is applicable to both first and second-generation notions of human rights. For example, the section of this chapter on population and development implicates first-generation rights notions of rights to privacy and the right to life. However, it also implicates second-generation notions of governmental obligations to provide for the social and economic needs of its citizens. The levels of needs to be provided for and the degree to which the civil liberties and first-generation rights can be infringed upon in the process is a matter for dispute. The task for debaters is one of locating "relatively universal" human rights and resolving conflicting interests.

POPULATION, FOOD, AND UNEMPLOYMENT

From one perspective, the problems of Latin America, especially Central America, are political and military, centering on counter-insurgency warfare and terrorism. From a different perspective, the problems of Latin America are human and economic, centering on an explosive increase in population, with resultant effects on unemployment and hunger. From this second perspective, political dissent and military responses to them are effects or results of those human and economic problems. This section describes the population and population-related problems, then discusses possible responses by the United States and other agencies to this problem.

Population and Population-Related Problems

The most dramatic increases in population between now and the year 2000 will be in Asia, mainly because of the much larger population base from which increases will take place. The increases in population in Latin America, while smaller in absolute terms, will be equally significant for this region. Between 1981 and the year 2000, the Office of Technology Assessment has estimated that Latin America's population will increase by roughly two hundred thirty million persons, a figure sixty-five percent of the current population total. Most of the population increase is projected to take place in just two countries, Mexico and Brazil. Mexico will increase from its 1981 total of seventy-two million to one hundred thirty-two million persons by the year 2000; Brazil will grow from one hundred thirty million persons to two hundred twelve million during the same period of time.

   Population increases cause feedback effects on the ability of nations to deal with the social and economic needs of its citizens. Latin American nations during the 1980's have struggled to deal with the problems of creating sufficient economic growth to provide jobs for their citizens and paying for industrial development to create such jobs. At the same time they have struggled to provide adequate social services for their citizens. Population increases both increase the number of jobs which must be created and the amount of services to be provided. In addition, because population increases are disproportionately located in lower income groups in Third World countries, simply because of the large percentage of the population in those groups, there is a greater drag on government social services in relation to additions to gross domestic product as a result of population growth.

   Latin American nations have high rates of illiteracy, also concentrated in lower income groups. This impedes Latin American economies in the types of jobs which can be developed for their labor forces, as well as placing a strain on limited educational services. For example, Haiti has a seventy-seven percent adult illiteracy rate: combined with poor public services and labor unrest, Haiti has only been able to attract a light assembly industry and foreign investors have been reluctant to commit funds to development there. An increase in the portion of the population poorly educated or illiterate by the sixty-five percent figure or higher would create a nearly insoluble problem in the creation of job opportunities.

There are significant unemployment and underemployment problems in Latin America. In the early 1980's, the International Labor Organization of the UN reported a thirty percent underemployment rate for Latin America as a whole. The rate has been much higher in specific countries. In Guatemala, forty percent of the work force is either unemployed or underemployed: sixty percent of the nation's jobs are in agriculture, even though that sector only accounts for twenty-five percent of the economy's production. El Salvador's unemployment rate is fifty percent, with many of those employed working at very low wages. Haiti, the poorest nation in the Western Hemisphere, has an unemployment rate in excess of fifty percent, as well as a per capita income of $125 per year.

As is discussed in the section on international debt, employment problems in Latin America have been aggravated in recent years by the international recession which has affected exports from the region, and by the diversion of revenues from exports to repay foreign loans. However, negligible (or even negative) economic growth and the problems of debt repayment should be seen as aggravating, not creating a problem. The fundamental problem facing Latin America is one of the economic demands of current population levels outstripping the abilities of traditional forms of economic organization in meeting them. In addition, some of the economic changes, such as increased emphasis on cash crops for export, as opposed to subsistence farming and production for domestic consumption, have exacerbated employment and food supply problems. Continued growth in labor force populations which cannot be absorbed through job creation will simply increase the burden of governmental and international welfare and relief services, to the extent that those services are available.

Hand in hand with employment problems, problems in food availability and hunger are also associated with increases in population. Latin America, as opposed to Asia and Africa, is fortunate to have generally good supplies of water and fertile soil for future agricultural production. Latin American nations have often squandered this potential. They have not been billing to invest the funds in road-building, bridge-building, constructing storage facilities, or extension and research facilities, or extension and research facilities for farming to take advantage of the resources for production available to them. Some governments, such as the Duvalier government when it was in power in Haiti, have engaged in short-sighted policies destructive of farmland.

Domestic food production is currently capable of meeting an average level of eighty-four percent of the nutritional needs of the Latin American population. Assuming a world-wide figure for less developed nations of three percent growth per year in food production, Latin American nations should be able to increase this slightly to eighty-seven percent by the year 2000, even with the projected population increase. Whether Latin America is actually able to accomplish this, and what meeting an average level of nutritional needs means in practical terms is dependent on four factors.

First, it is a truism that, with the exception of famines of calamitious proportions, the cause of hunger is not lack of available food supply but poverty. Latin America is no exception to this rule. Although hunger is a more significant problem in the poorer countries in the region (and among the Indians in those countries), relatively food-rich nations such as Brazil and Argentina have high rates of malnutrition among their rural poor. Latin America's income stratification, with small elite and middle-class groups and a large group ranging from marginally adequate personal income to destitution, guarantees that average levels of nutrition are poor indicators of what the actual experience will be, especially for those at the bottom end of the scale. And, as population increases will be disproportionately centered in these bottom groups, maldistribution of food will increase as well.

A second factor influencing the incidence of hunger in Latin America is the focus of agricultural and economic policy on food for export as against domestic consumption. As was discussed in Chapter Three and in the debt section in this chapter, Latin American nations need to earn revenues through exports: a primary source of such revenues is through agricultural commodities. Although in countries such as Brazil and Argentina, the primary exports (grain and beef) are also useful for at least some domestic consumption, this is generally not the case. The Central American and Caribbean nations primarily export "cash crops": coffee, sugar, cotton, bananas. Three-fourths of Cuba's export earnings, for example, come from sugar. Although these crops are useful in generating needed foreign exchange, they are of relatively little value in meeting domestic food needs. Countries such as Guatemala and El Salvador, which convert land which has been used for domestic food production to use in the production of "cash crops" for export create net decreases in the food supply available to the population.

There is also the risk that "cash crops" will become net drains on an economy: where a state has come to depend on earning revenues through exports of a commodity, it will respond to fluctuations ("valleys") in international market prices by subsidizing continued production. This is especially true where the industry employs a substantial proportion of the work force in the country or the state owns the commodity or serves as its exporting agent. There has been friction between the United States and Brazil over the latter's subsidization of grain for export which the American farm community considers unfair competition. The effect of these subsidies on the Brazilian population is that funds are diverted from some other potential use to sustain production of crops of marginal direct value to the domestic food supply.

A third factor in the ability of Latin American governments to meet food needs is the ecological impacts of both farming and industrialization programs. Much of Latin America is made up of rain forests: removal of forest canopy has occurred for both commercial purposes (tree-harvesting in the Amazon River Basin) and for agricultural purposes (clearing marginal land for subsistence agriculture in Central America). This can lead to rapid soil erosion and loss of land from productive use, as the topsoil underneath rain forests is thin and easily removed through flooding.

A final factor is the effect of civil conflicts. Warfare has a number of negative influences on agricultural production. Guerrilla warfare targets often include infrastructure on which agriculture is dependent: bridges, dams, or electric power stations. As was mentioned in Chapter Three, agricultural cooperatives themselves are the targets of guerrilla groups, including the Contras. The military in Guatemala and in El Salvador has forcibly removed persons engaged in subsistence farming from combat zones. Finally, the fighting itself leads to the destruction of crops and the forcing of persons off their lands.

Responses by the United States and Other Agencies

There are several ways in which the United States and international organizations have attempted to deal with population and population-related problems. Chapter Three discussed international development programs for the region, a primary response to employment and food productions pressures. As was mentioned, the Reagan Administration has attempted to shift the focus of solutions from public sector to private sector programs, and has emphasized production for export as a program of preference in solving Latin American economic problems. There are three other types of solutions: (1) population control; (2) food aid; and (3) technical assistance in expanding food production. The Reagan Administration's policies are open to debate in all three areas.

Despite religious and conservative political opposition to contraception and abortion, Latin America has been a major recipient of funds from international organizations to aid in family planning, receiving almost as much in funds as Asian nations. There is a certain amount of Latin American cynicism and racism involved here. While publicly opposed to birth control on religious grounds, some Latin American leaders are privately more amenable to population control where the targets are low-income, illiterate peasants, frequently Indians.

The major vehicles for population control have been the United Nations Fund for Population Activities (UNFPA) and a variety of non-governmental organizations: the International

Planned Parenthood Foundation, the Family Planning International Association, the Association for Voluntary Sterilization, and others.   The United States, until recently, funded efforts of both the UNFPA as well as the NGO's: it also provided funds directly to less developed countries.   In 1979, prior to the advent of the Reagan Administration, the United States contributed $30 million to the UNFPA, about twenty-six percent of its budget, plus gave $90 million to NGO's, and another $48 million was appropriated directly to Third World nations for population control.

Reagan Administration international positions on contraception and abortion, causing a cutoff of funds to NGO's and less developed countries for this purpose.   United States contributions to the UNFPA have been withheld under the Kemp-Inouye Amendment to the 1985 Foreign Assistance Appropriations Act. That legislation calls for the Agency for International Development to make determinations of whether recipients of funds engaged in coercive abortions or involuntary sterilizations.   AID determined that the UNFPA had provided funds to a People's Republic of China program which engaged in such practices.   While not large relative to other governmental programs, the amount the United States was to contribute to UNFPA was about one-fourth of that agency's revenues.   Moreover, the United States waited to act until after it had committed itself to this contribution and the UNFPA had prepared its budget for the year.

Here, as in other areas where the United States has opposed the manner in which UN agencies have operated their programs or the objectives of them, there is a tension between two alternative positions.   The position adhered to by the Reagan Administration is that it can best promote reforms in UN agency practices by withholding funds, "getting the attention" of the agencies in question.   This is in effect a reprise of the "one dollar, one vote" position.   Unable to affect outcomes through its vote, the United States is attempting to influence them through its economic muscle.   The alternative point of view is that U.S. behavior will be counterproductive, being seen by other nations as a blatant attempt by the United States to impose its policy views on international organizations: being forced to do without U.S. support, such agencies may ignore U.S. perspectives altogether.   This debate can be considered without reference to one's views of sterilization and abortion, especially where coerced, and the case of the PRC, where foreign observers have accused China of Draconian measures to induce sterilization and third-trimester abortions.   It is difficult to imagine solutions to Latin American employment and hunger without cutting into the rate of growth in population, and U.S. efforts have impeded international population control measures.

A second area of solutions is food aid.   Again, Reagan Administration policies can be criticized as being counterproductive.   A factor to be reckoned with is that the United States has accumulated large agricultural surpluses as the amount of U.S. grain exports has decreased in recent years.   U.S. agricultural producers see Latin America as a market for its exports; the

Council of Economic Advisers in its <u>Annual Report for 1987</u> has described the purpose of international financial programs as to "facilitate U.S. participation in world trade." Hence, the United States has accompanied its military sales and other military assistance to Latin America with PL 480 "Food for Peace" shipments. For example, Guatemala's PL 480 funds have increased from $5.3 million in 1983 to $23.7 million in 1987.

PL 480 shipments consist of Title I funds, sales of food commodities on a long-term, low-interest basis, and Title II aid, humanitarian assistance, outright gifts. The breakdown between the two Titles is about seventy: thirty. Title III provides loan forgiveness where sales of Title I commodities are used for development activities: this has the effect of making Title I sales gifts. Under the Humphrey Amendment to the Foreign Assistance Act of 1974, seventy percent of food aid in Title I must go to nations on a UN list of the poorest nations. The Humphrey Amendment was a reaction to Administration use of PL 480 as de facto assistance to Third World military allies. It led to expanded funds for PL 480, so that Presidents could still send aid to politically-preferred recipients while complying with the Amendment. Two billion dollars in food aid was provided under PL 480 in 1985, with 8.5 million metric tons of grain being exported. This figure was increased slightly in 1986 and 1987. Emergency shipments of food are also provided for: the United States has provided famine relief to Ethiopia but also sent emergency aid to El Salvador after an earthquake there.

Use of PL 480 has been criticized by food policy experts because of its use (other than rewarding Third World allies) in eliminating U.S. agricultural exports, replacing demand for domestic agricultural products with one for United States-style agricultural commodities. The danger is that U.S. surplus food shipments will make local farming diseconomic. Domestic producers will be unable to compete with U.S. free or subsidized products. This has to be added to the desire of Latin American governments to shift to cash crops for export, as well as the actions of the Guatemalan and Salvadoran governments in relocating populations, which has resulted in decreased agricultural production for domestic consumption. U.S. food shipments have facilitated both policies.

The ultimate effect of U.S. food shipments is to increase the dependency of the poorer nations in Latin America on the United States as a food supplier. This is not wholly unintentional: the United States competes with Brazil, Argentina, and Canada as a grain exporter, and it is not adverse to using its grain surplus and political leverage to take over a market. The negative effects of making Latin America dependent on the United States as a supplier include encouraging Latin American nations to shift to "cash crops" for export, with resultant displacements of small farmers and agricultural workers, retardation or abandonment of land reform policies, and dependency on world commodities markets for economic health. There also an assumption that U.S. agricultural products will be available at prices or on terms accessible to Latin American countries. Poorer countries which are import-dependent for food have heightened disparities in nutrition among different economic classes. During recessions, it becomes more difficult for middle class groups to meet nutritional needs but the primary effect is on low income groups, which plummet from meeting minimal requirements to extreme deprivations of those needs and starvation. In addition, not having to worry about domestic food needs causes governments to become less concerned about population problems.

A final set of solutions consists of technical development approaches, programs to expand Third World food production. Solutions in this area work at cross-purposes with food subsidies, unless food aid is being shipped in response to an emergency shortage, which is the exception, not the typical case. In the past, U.S. AID programs in the Third World have been generally well-regarded, providing technical training in soil conservation and expanding domestic agricultural production. The chief criticism of such programs is that they have tended to be short-term in duration, lasting three to six years where a ten-to-twenty year commitment would have been more realistic in meeting program goals.

The Reagan Administration's actions in this area have been counterproductive in two ways. First, it has pushed AID toward private sector, free enterprise programs. While such an emphasis may be desirable in some situations, agricultural development programs are more on the model of agricultural cooperatives and are administratively closer to public sector programs. AID also has a dearth of persons with private sector management experience, and the skills useful in those experiences can be argued to be of little value in a technical development context.

The Reagan Administration also has cut off funding to the UN International Fund for Agricultural Development. The culprit here may be the NIEO orientation of IFAD and the UN Food and Agriculture Organization. Both have attempted to create an international consensus among Third World nations on the prioritization of food self-sufficiency and the right to food of the poor in Third World nations. FAO is an example of an international organization which would like to have "vertical" power as a supranational organization, setting individual nation's food budgets, land uses, and allocations of development funds. It has generally been ignored by Third World nations, especially those in Africa, which have been intent on industrialization and urbanization and have been interested in FAO services only in times of food shortages. The Reagan Administration sees IFAD and UN FAO as conflicting with its private sector model of development, as well as getting in the way of its efforts at expanding exports of U.S. agricultural commodities.

The final "solution" to population increases is not a solution but an abdication of responsibility: outmigration, often to the United States. The new wave of illegal immigrants to the United States is as much from Guatemala and El Salvador as from Mexico. Honduras, Costa Rica, Panama, and Mexico also have experienced problems dealing with refugees and fear expanded conflict in Central America as increasing the number of refugees.

A different problem is posed by Cuba: it deals with internal dissent crime, and inability to deal with employment problems by occasionally permitting mass exoduses of its citizens. The "Marielista" emigration of 125,000 persons in 1980 was such an event: Cuba reached a tentative agreement with the United States in December 1984, under which it would take back the criminals and mental patients from the 1980 boatlift in exchange for the United States accepting the emigration of twenty thousand Cubans per year. The agreement was not concluded after the United States went ahead with the Radio Marti project. A new agreement has not been reached.

Refugees are the basis for the existence of the U.S. "Sanctuary" movement; they also lead to the argument about whether they are "political" or "economic" refugees. In one sense, they are political refugees, fleeing the civil wars and oppression of their governments. In another sense, political and economic refugees can be argued to be members of the same group: the standard of living Central American refugees seek to improve on, from this perspective, reflects the same or connected government policies. From the standpoint of the U.S. Immigration and Naturalization Service and the Department of Justice, a person is not a political refugee deserving of asylum unless his or her political or religious views mean that they would receive substantially different treatment at the hands of their government on their return. Hence, Soviet dissidents merit asylum but Salvadoran refugees do not. This result may have more to do with numbers than with ideology. Nicaraguan refugees have started to come to the United States in large numbers, and the United States has driven a hard bargain and not yet acceded to Cuban immigration, despite its repeated statements about the political oppression practiced in both countries. Haitians have always argued U.S. immigration policies to be racist, contrasting U.S. acceptance of Cuban refugees in 1980 (a large number of whom were black, however) with the Reagan Administration's reaching an accord with the Duvalier government to reduce the amount of Haitian "boat people" coming to the United States.

As Latin American population increases, so will emigration pressures. Efforts to decrease population growth, as well as to cause Latin American governments to be better able to deal with increased demands for jobs and adequate nutrition are necessary to reduce emigration. As the United States is already aware, it is the country of choice for Latin American emigration. Given the concentration of population increases in Mexico, U.S. assistance to Latin American countries is directly tied to future levels of emigration to the United States.

INTERNATIONAL DEBT

One commentator has written that there are two schools of thought
about the Central American economy: the optimists, who think the
current economy is a disaster, and the pessimists who think the
real disaster as yet to take occur. (See John Weeks, "The
Central American Economies in 1983 and 9184," in Hopkins, ed.,
Latin American and Caribbean Contemporary Record, vol. III,
1985.) Nearly all Latin American countries face serious debt
repayment problems. How they will deal with these problems will
have serious consequences for their national development, as well
as for their political stability. This section discusses reasons
for the debt problems of nations in the region, then examines
proposed solutions and the risks of those solutions.

Sources of the Problem

Latin America as a whole has been in a recession since 1979. All
nations in Latin America, with the exception of Panama, experienced declines in per capita income in 1982 and 1983. In part,
this reflected the worldwide economic recession, which had a
significant effect on export-dependent Latin American economies.
A number of Latin American nations, most notably Mexico, were
severely damaged by the decline in the world oil market. Mexico,
like a number of nations around the world, had gambled on prices
continuing to escalate and was highly leveraged, expecting to pay
back future debts as they came due with revenues from further
increases in oil prices. When oil tumbled in the early 1980's,
Mexico (and Venezuela, Colombia, and Brazil, to lesser extents)
found itself unable to pay back the interest on debts.
    However, even if the world economy were to experience
vigorous economic growth, it seems unlikely that Central America
would be able to take part in it. Central America's problems
have more to do with the ongoing political instability disrupting
its economies: the civil wars in El Salvador, Guatemala, the
U.S. embargo on trade with Nicaragua all have negative effects on
these economies which would not go away with the end of the Latin
American recession.
    Central America's economies also took a turn for the worse
in the late 1970's when the Central America Common Market (abbre-
viated sometimes as CACM or CAMCOM) ceased to be functional.
Begun in the early 1960's, CAMCOM encouraged intraregional
trading by reducing export duties among member nations. This had
the effect of creating regional economic cooperation, in addition
to guaranteeing markets for Central American manufacturers.
CAMCOM fell victim to long-standing internal frictions among its
members. The spark for this was probably the "football war"
between El Salvador and Honduran in 1969. Although CAMCOM still
exists, net intraregional trade has actually declined since 1980,
and all the CAMCOM nations had passed legislation by that date
abrogating their treaty commitments. Without CAMCOM, the Central
American nations are largely dependent on exports of "cash crops"

to the United States and Western Europe for capital earnings.

Although it may sound like good news that Central American nations have small amounts of foreign debt when compared with Mexico and Brazil, and have positive trade balances, this actually masks bad news. Given weak export markets for bananas and coffee, the Central American republics have been unable to finance significant loans from foreign banks, precluding them from accumulating debt. And since export earnings have been low, these countries have been unable to purchase much in the way of manufactured goods from the rest of the world, hence the positive trade balance figures.

The South American nations and Mexico are in a different position than the Central American states. The problem for them is an enormous external debt, variously estimated at between $370 and $400 billion. Eleven nations, known as the Cartagena Group, owe $337 billion. These nations are: Argentina, Bolivia, Brazil, Chile, Colombia, the Dominican Republic, Ecuador, Mexico, Peru, Uruguay, and Venezuela. Roughly seventy percent of this debt is owed to international commercial banks, forty percent to such banks located in the United States.

The debt problem can be viewed in two different ways: (1) will the debtor nations default on their payments and cause economic chaos in Western Europe, the United States and Japan as the banks collapse? or (2) will the repayment programs of the banks bleed the debtor nations dry, precluding economic growth and leading to revolution? A related matter is the austerity measures and internal economic reforms required of recipient nations by the International Monetary Fund, which can be viewed either as necessary to protect the lender or as violations of the economic sovereignty of the recipient.

The major criticisms of the Reagan Administration in this area have been that it has underestimated the seriousness of the problem and has had no strategy for dealing with it. The United States appeared to be surprised by the seriousness of Mexico's debt problems in 1982 when Mexico approached the United States for assistance. During the second term of the Reagan Presidency, Secretary of the Treasury James Baker has attempted to work out a debt rescheduling plan which would involve some accommodations by lenders and more loan funds to debtor nations: the Latin American response has been to ask for much more in the way of concessions and additional funds than had been anticipated by U.S. officials.

The Reagan Administration would prefer private sector responses here, as in other contexts. One Interamerican Development Bank proposal has been for banks or multinational enterprises to buy a portion of a nation's debt to international lenders, then resell the note to the country's central bank, with the requirement that the western bank or corporation invest some of the funds received within the country. This in effect refinances debt obligations, discounting them by the amount reinvested, which has the same effect as an additional foreign loan without a new set of debt repayment requirements. Some banks such as Citibank which have large outstanding loans to Latin

American nations have already begun to privately restructure debt obligations. The Reagan Administration has seen its role as being that of working out repayment obligations as a last resort, working out last-minute arrangements to avert disaster. It did this in 1982 with Mexico and Brazil, and again in 1984 with Argentina. These responses are essentially ad hoc.

Another solution, proposed by Peruvian President Alan Garcia in 1985, has been for Latin American nations to put a cap on their debt payments of ten percent of their export earnings. The Cartagena Group, named after a conference in Colombia in June 1984, has proposed a number of measures to reschedule debt payments. Twenty Latin American nations have advocated that their debt repayments be linked to growth in export earnings in some manner. The utility of this approach is that it preserves most export earnings to repay domestic producers and to finance internal development. It also operates as a disincentive to the United States and Western Europe to restrict Latin imports. The problems with this approach is that, with demand for exports weak and world prices for Latin American commodities low, ten percent of revenues falls well short of debt obligations, especially for the large debtors, Mexico, Brazil, and Argentina.

Another solution is to reduce rates of interest on outstanding debts. Many loan obligations by Latin American nations date from pre-Reagan Administration days, and have higher rates of interest attached to them than those currently available. A solution would be to remark these loans to current market rates. The justification for doing so would be that commercial banks are gaining the benefit of receiving payments set at inflationary rates while they are currently doing business in the much less inflationary atmosphere of the 1980's.

Another view, that of economist Larry Sjaastad in "Causes of and Remedies for the Debt Crisis in Latin America" in Michael Claudon, ed., World Debt Crisis: International Lending on Trial, 1986, is that solutions should ignore the size of a nation's debt and instead focus on the ratio between a nation's gross domestic product and the debt figure. From that perspective, the debts of Costa Rica, Chile, and Panama, while smaller in dollar amounts than those of Mexico, Argentina, Brazil, and Venezuela, are much less soluble because debt servicing requires greater percentages of gross domestic product. The former group of nations have debt amounts in excess of one hundred percent of gross domestic product, while the latter have debts equal to forty percent of their national incomes.

Even for nations with high debt: gross domestic product ratios, current repayment is a problem only because of high interest rates. At a ten percent rate of interest, a nation with debts equal to its gross domestic product would have to pay out ten percent of its national income in debt servicing alone. However, at a four percent interest rate, the amount of debt servicing would be the same as for nations with debt principal equal to forty percent of their gross domestic product at the higher rate of interest.

Nations with debt amounts equal to fifty percent of gross domestic product can handle repayments of these debts, even at the ten percent interest rate level, according to Sjaastad, if their governments run fiscal surpluses: unfortunately, Mexico, Argentina, and Brazil all have run large government budget deficits in recent years. Nations which must pay more than five percent of their gross domestic product on debt servicing, according to Sjaastad, need the equivalent of a world bankruptcy court.

In attempting to solve debt problems, three types of risks have to be considered. The first type of risk is that quid pro quos for United States and international assistance may produce domestic unrest. This has been a major factor in South American governments' reluctance to accept IMF and World Bank austerity measures as requirements for receiving additional loans to repay commercial debts. Food riots occurred in the Dominican Republic in April 1984 as a result of government price hikes on imported goods ordered as part of IMF-required austerity measures. While Mexico has accepted some austerity measures as part of deals in which the IMF has given it loans since 1982, the nature of these measures has been the subject of intense negotiation. Mexico is referred to as a "moral hazard" nation, which will be discussed further below. Its debts are so large that the IMF is reluctant to do anything which would lead to its defaulting on debts, resulting in favorable terms for Mexico.

Severe austerity measures have the practical effect of transferring sovereign authority over the administration of a country to the IMF. Haitian demonstrators once referred to the Interior Minister of the post-Duvalier government as the "puppy" of the IMF. Latin American leaders seeking IMF help must walk a fine line between sounding so amenable to populist concerns that they scare off international assistance and sounding so conciliatory to the IMF that populist reactions to austerity measures are fueled. There is a strong link between nationalism and opposition to IMF austerity programs in Brazil and Argentina in particular.

The second risk to be considered is the effect of credit availability on future development. The IADB in September 1986 warned that the recession in Latin America had been lengthened dangerously because of huge capital outflows to pay back debts: more than $100 billion in interest on debt has been paid by Latin American nations since the start of the decade. Measures which call for too high or too fast a repayment program would exacerbate this situation. This explains current U.S. reluctance to support tighter conditions on lending by the IMF. While the Reagan Administration is reluctant to be more accommodating to Latin American debtor nations than it has to be, as the U.S. economy slows down and the trade deficit mounts, the United States is unwilling to increase problems for debtor nations in gaining funds. However, protectionist trade measures and a weak U.S. economy may hamper Latin American recovery, even with additional IMF funding and rescheduled debt payments.

Finally, there is a "moral hazard" risk to debt solutions. Measures to reschedule Latin American nation debts on terms which are too easy on debtors can increase negligent or overly optimistic behavior by debtor nations. Although Latin American nations did not create many of the problems which currently are affecting them, they have been responsible for large government deficits, inefficiently-run state industries (Mexico's state-run oil corporation, Pemex, is sometimes given as an example of this), and grandiose building projects (such as the Brazilian nuclear reactor program discussed in Chapter Two).

A principal source of the problems of the major debtor nations, as described above, is that they assumed debts with 1970's outlooks on oil prices and inflation. While their behavior was arguably plausible at the time, they currently need to adopt very different outlooks: the worry of banks lending such countries additional funds is that they may still have 1970's-style aspirations and will be no more restrained than agreements require them to be. A key figure in debt repayment strategies is World Bank President Barber Conable, a former Republican Congressman from upstate New York, who has opposed suggestions of partial loan forgiveness to Cartagena Group nations. This makes sense from a "moral hazard" perspective, although it may also preclude economic growth, thereby also precluding loan repayment.

A related problem is "strategic behavior" on the part of debtor nations. This scenario poses the threat that Cartagena Group nations will bargain from the position that the alternative to accepting their terms in restructuring debt repayment proposals is no debt repayment at all: nearly all Latin American nations in fact interrupted their debt servicing payments in late 1982, which led to emergency loans engineered by the Reagan Administration to permit resumption of payments. Debtors have "bankruptcy power," the position of weakness, over their creditors. Although Latin American nations require additional funds to keep operating, they know they will get at least part of them, as international lenders know that they have no other prospect of securing debt repayment. IMF negotiations over debt restructuring have had to deal with avoiding the risk of making demands causing Latin American nations to cease negotiations (and payments on debts), while at the same time not making repayment conditions so lenient that they do not encourage reformed administration and development goals on the part of Latin American governments.

CIVILIAN VS. MILITARY GOVERNMENTS

A major trend in Latin America during the 1980's has been the transition from military to civilian rule. In some cases, such as Panama and Brazil, the military turned over the reins of government as part of a planned process. In other cases, such as Argentina, the military had ceased to provide effective govern-

ance, and was replaced by civilian leadership. This trend has
not been universal: the Pincohet regime remains in power in
Chile, despite long-term criticisms of both its human rights and
economic performance as a government.

It can be disputed whether these governmental changes
occurred because of, in spite of, or without regard to Reagan
Administration "constructive engagement" and "quiet diplomacy"
policies. The human rights community has been sharply critical
of the Reagan Administration for its toleration of restrictions
on civil liberties and institutionalized violence by military
regimes in Latin America. Supporters of the Administration,
consistent with the Administration's views on human rights, have
argued that maintaining a dialogue with military regimes is the
best way of curbing abuses of rights and easing the transition
toward democracy, while at the same time not increasing the risk
of leftist takeovers.

The key issue for debaters on the 1987-88 topic in this area
is the relationship between the form of government and the level
of political stability produced by it. Human rights practices
and other policies of Latin American governments, whether military or civilian, are relevant to topic analysis to the extent
that they are reflected in the effectiveness of those governments
to lead their countries. Sometimes the difference between
"military" and "civilian" rule is more semantic than substantive.
This section addresses the relationship between military and
civilian rule and democratic processes in Latin America. It
examines in particular the recent record of the governments in El
Salvador and Nicaragua, and then discusses roles the military
plays in civilian regimes.

Democracy in Central America

One illusion debaters should not be under is that the absence of
uniforms and the presence of elections makes a government democratic. The Somozas in Nicaragua held elections on occasion, and
even "President for Life" Jean-Claude Duvalier held plebiscites
on his performances. Both regimes received predictably unanimous
support even as their nations deteriorated. Factors to be
considered in appraising the degree of democracy of governments
are the responsiveness of governments to the problems facing
their countries, avenues open for criticism and for change in
government policies, and the respect for human dignities given by
the government, especially to minorities and the powerless. A
related set of factors stem from the "universal character"
discussion in the section on human rights. What should be the
role, if any, of the United States or the United Nations in
pressuring sovereign governments to modify their domestic practices? At one extreme is international concern about genocidal
practices by governments toward their citizens; at the other
extreme is the practice of governments, such as the United
States, in passing judgment on the wisdom and morality of the
policies of a government to which it has given assistance,

threatening to cut off aid if the recipient's conduct does not conform with the patron government's expectations.

El Salvador and Nicaragua provide two cases in which the manner in which the governments are characterized has a great effect on how observers perceive them and their policies. Both governments conducted elections in 1984. The United States condemned the Nicaraguan vote as a "farce," based on boycotts of the elections by Sandinista opponents, who had cited campaign restrictions and abuses by the government. Critics of the Administration's policies similarly charged that the Salvadoran elections excluded leftist opposition and so was not a true test of the sentiments of the people. Since 1984, both governments have been alternatively praised or condemned for their general practices, depending on the parties performing the appraisal.

It is an understatement to say that both the Duarte government in El Salvador and the Sandinista government, led by Daniel Ortega, face extreme difficulties. The Duarte government faces an economy which has been devastated by the effects of the world recession on its export-based economy. It also has had to deal with the guerrilla activities of the FMLN (named after Augustin Farabundo Marti, the founder of the Salvadoran Communist Party, who was executed after an Indian uprising in 1932). Duarte also faces internal opposition from the rightist ARENA party. Duarte was himself a victim of torture by the Army in the early 1970's and returned from exile in 1979 to lead his country. After a coup against the military government of General Carlos Humberto Romero in 1979, civilian caretaker regimes headed by Alvaro Magana and then Duarte presided over the country until the 1984 elections.

The Sandinistas came to power in 1979 with the ousting of Anastasio Somoza Debayle, who was later assassinated in Paraguay. During the period 1979-84 members of the military junta consolidated Sandinista control of Nicaragua. Several persons who departed the junta later became active in Contra and United Nicaraguan Opposition (UNO) activities. The junta members who have remained, including President Ortega, were members of the "Tercerista" faction of the FSLN. The Sandinistas (named after guerrilla leader Augosto Cesar Sandino, who fought against U.S. Marine occupiers in the 1920's and was murdered, probably by agent of Somoza's father in 1934. Somoza the elder, a National Guardsman, was installed in power on the departure of the Marines in 1933, and ruled Nicaragua until his own assassination in 1956) have had to deal with economic problems more severe than those in El Salvador. In addition to the decline in sugar prices, Nicaragua has had to deal with a cutoff in U.S. aid, followed by a reduction of ninety percent of the U.S. quota for sugar from Nicaragua, which was preparatory to a U.S. trade embargo being imposed in May 1985. The United States also has attempted to get the IADB to eliminate development funding to Nicaragua. And, almost since its inception, the government has had to deal with Contra opposition.

The records of the two governments have been clouded by the ideological lenses of observers and by the difficulty of gaining hard information. El Salvador does not have the kind of near-anarchy which prevailed in 1979-80. While Tutela Legal, the human rights monitoring office of the Roman Catholic Archdiocese of San Salvador has reported that the death squads are still active, they are not operating on the scale of 1979-80, when as many as one thousand persons per month were being executed, mainly by right-wing paramilitary organizations and the Army.

The difficulty for the Duarte regime is that it came to power on the strength of Duarte's personal popularity and promises to end the economic chaos afflicting the country. While the civil war has subsided, the economy has not improved. Duarte faces opposition from ARENA, which is critical of the openness of dissent, and from leftist groups impatient for jobs and land reform. His personal credibility may also have suffered as a result of concessions made in securing the release of his daughter from FMLN kidnappers.

In terms of human rights performance, Duarte has profited from the quelling of urban unrest in San Salvador and the shift in tactics of the FMLN to hit-and-run warfare from large-scale engagements. The former has decreased death squad responses, while the latter has decreased U.S. attention toward his country. Although the Reagan Administration has regularly certified El Salvador as having made significant progress in human rights, observers have pointed to a number of abuses. These are chiefly the effects of Operation Phoenix, under which civilians in guerrilla areas have been forcibly relocated or considered guerrilla sympathizers and been the subject of attack. Americas Watch has charged the military with massacres of civilians and bombings of towns, which the military has denied.

The other prong of human rights has been treatment of persons placed under arrest. El Salvador still operates under a state of siege (Decree 50) permitting the arbitrary arrest and detention of persons without cause. Detention for eight days prior to assistance of counsel is permitted. The danger for the Duarte government is that, if the economy does not improve, more public opposition will lead to more arrests, which will lead to more demonstrations, which may lead to increased death squad reprisals, creating a snowball effect. Amnesty International has charged that, although the FMLN has committed human rights abuses, the bulk of civil war deaths have been committed by the military. "Death squads" in El Salvador and other Latin American countries are usually composed of regular Army or National Police members acting under orders but in secret. While the right-wing groups in El Salvador conduct their own operations, human rights groups place the blame for most "disappearances" on the Army and the National Police.

In El Salvador, as in other Latin American countries, there is an uneasy truce between the military and a civilian government which has been critical of it. There is also a realization by each of its dependency on the other. A constraint on the military in its dealings with Duarte is the Reagan Administration's support of him; a constraint on Duarte is that such support is connected with Washington's perception that the state of the civil war has improved, which restricts the degree to which he can curtail Army abuses.

While Duarte has attempted to curb human rights violations by the military, sometimes by posting security force members to foreign diplomatic missions, his government is restricted by the power of the military in these actions. Americas Watch has charged that most arrests of Salvadoran Army members are for crimes committed against other members of the military. The number of the military tried for crimes against civilians has remained small (there were thirty-seven such prosecutions in 1985, the same as in 1982), despite the increase in the size of the military and its forced relocation programs in rural areas. The Army argues that this instead reflects the decreased unrest and improved military situation. However, few officers are ever charged with human rights abuses and two officers on a list of those linked with death squad activities presented to the government by Vice President Bush in December 1983 have since been promoted.

There is no such tension between the military and the elected leaders in Nicaragua, since the Sandinistas also control the armed forces, the Sandinista People's Army (EPS). Here the discussion is about restrictions on civil liberties imposed by a revolutionary government, both before and after elections took place in 1984. The primary restrictions are in four areas: freedom of the press, freedom of religion, relations with private business, and the treatment of Indians.

The FSLN consolidated its control over centers of political power after replacing the Somoza regime. One source of opposition was an independently-owned press, especially La Prensa of Managua, owned by the Chamorro family. Opposition to the Somoza regime galvanized around the killing of its owner, a leader of the liberal-moderate community. As the Sandinistas increasingly took over control of the society, La Prensa became more and more critical of the government. This led to restrictions on its publication and its eventual closing in 1986. Pedro Joaquin Chamorro now publishes an anti-Sandinista newspaper in Costa Rica and in 1987 was named to replace Adolfo Calero as a director of UNO. The Sandinistas can be criticized for their stifling of press freedoms, accusing La Prensa of publishing "counter-revolutionary propaganda." Conversely, the irony is that Somoza permitted La Prensa to survive for the Sandinistas to repress. Press censorship in Latin America has been pervasive: while deplorable, the Sandinistas have not acted in a manner unusual for a Latin American government.

Another area of friction has been religious freedom. The Sandinistas enjoyed the support of some Roman Catholic priests, part of the "liberation theology" movement. The Church was always anti-Somoza rather than pro-Sandinista. Since 1979, the government has moved against the Church in a fashion similar to its treatment of the press, criticizing the Church for impeding the revolution and expelling a bishop for making counterrevolutionary statements. It has also acted to suppress Protestant groups on the Atlantic Coast (Moravians, Jehovah's Witnesses, and others) as sects collaborating with the CIA. The Sandinistas have been less circumspect about dealing with Catholic opposition that have other Latin American governments. The issue is complicated by the "liberation theology" movement's support of the Sandinistas as a reform group, although this has declined (the Pope has also discouraged "liberation theology"). The same section of the Catholic Church has the enmity of other Latin American leaders, and for the same reason: the assassination of Salvadoran Archbishop Oscar Adulfo Romero in 1980 for his outspoken criticism of the military and the elites is a case in point.

A third area of conflict has been between the government and private business. The Reagan Administration had identified Nicaragua as a Communist state because of the takeovers of private business. While the government has claimed that the majority of the economy remains in private hands, it in fact has taken over the banking system and the control of foreign and domestic commerce, making ownership by private parties largely a formality. Much that has been done by the Sandinistas has been ideological in purpose, but it has also been in response to the departure of MNE's, such as Standard Brands (previously known as United Fruit Co.), the major producer of bananas in the country. One can also respond that Nicaragua has no greater a control of its economy than do many Third World nations.

The harshest criticisms by independent observers have been reserved for Sandinista treatment of the Indian population of the Atlantic Coast, the Miskitos but also the Sumus and Ramas tribes. These are groups which were ignored by the Somoza regime; the Sandinistas came to power with little or no Indian support. The Indians have been wary of Sandinista and Cuban literacy programs directed at them because of their heavy ideological content; Protestant missionaries have long been active in this part of Nicaragua, which has bred resistance to the Sandinistas by the Indians and suspicion about the Indians by the Sandinistas. The Indians have also been a major source of recruitment for the Contras, which has led to forced relocations of these tribes from regions bordering Honduras by the government. The Sandinistas have argued that they have been the first Nicaraguan government to attempt to bring social services of any kind to the Indians, and that the Indians have been the victims of atrocities by Contra groups operating from across the Honduran border. As in other Latin American countries, there is a certain amount of racism toward the Indians: the attraction of the Contras to them has to do with military pay as much as opposition to the Sandinistas.

It would be difficult to describe either the Salvarodan or the Nicaraguan government as fitting traditional American notions of democratic governments. Both have engaged in human rights abuses of some dimensions and both have restricted what Americans regard as fundamental political freedoms. Yet both probably enjoy support among the majority of their populations. The ultimate question is one of the interrelationship between the form of government and the degree of political stability produced.

Roles of the Military in Democratic Regimes

There are three different types of relationships between the military and nominally democratic, civilian governments in Latin America with implications for the level of political stability achieved by these governments.

First, there can be open conflict between the military and the civilian government over the conduct of counter-insurgency operations. Generally, civilian governments have attempted to avoid public displays of discord. One such incident did occur in January 1983 in El Salvador when a military commander refused orders transferring him to a diplomatic post and declared himself "in rebellion" against the Defense Ministry. The tendency has been for the civilian government to defer to military leaders in their conduct of counter-insurgency campaigns. This has been the source of criticism by liberal groups of Guatemalan President Vinicio Cerezo Arevalo, the first democratically-elected President of that nation since 1948. He took over after the rule of a series of military governments: while being elected on a mildly reformist platform, President Cerezo has not interfered with the "Model Villages" program of the military, which has the support of conservative elites in Guatemala.

A second relationship can be characterized as conflict over civilian policies critical of military human rights performance. This has been the case in Argentina, where the Alfonsin government has been conducting trials of members of the military for their involvement in the "disappearances" of members of the political opposition, including Communists. The Alfonsin government has been scored by human rights observers for the timidity with which it has approached the military and the leniency of the sentences meted out. At the same time, the government has been attacked by the military for the trials, justifying its past actions as having prevented a Communist takeover. In 1987, a military unit mutinied: the course of action taken by the government was to both negotiate with and oppose the rebels, calling on working-class support (with echoes of Juan Peron) to impress on the military that alternative power bases exist in Argentina. The government is in a position in which it politically cannot not have trials of the military. It came to power on the basis of cleaning up the abuses of the military. On the other hand, it cannot afford to have a sustained conflict with the military, which has charged that the trials are meant to distract the public from Argentina's economic woes.

Finally, the relationship between the military and the civilian government can be one in which "democracy" is a sham. Leftist writers in the United States have raised this charge against virtually all of the civilian governments in Latin America, but the charge appears most justified in the case of Panama. There General Omar Torrijos Herrera had prepared for a transition from military to civilian rule prior to his death in an airplane crash in August 1981. Although elections were held as scheduled in 1984, the effective leader of the government has remained General Noriega of the National Guard. Evidence later became public that the Guard had rigged the close election in 1984 and that the United States was probably aware of this. The opposition leader, Arnulfo Arias, was politically conservative but eighty-two years old at the time of the election, and ran on an anti-military platform. The nominal President, Nicolas Ardito Barletta, resigned in 1985, having lost both civilian and military support as the economy worsened. His resignation may also have been connected with the kidnapping and decapitation of a government critic, Dr. Hugo Spadafora, apparently by the National Guard.

U.S. SUPPORT OF THE CONTRAS

The central United States commitments to Latin America having an effect on political stability are its military assistance to the Central American republics, and its support of the Nicaraguan rebels, or Contras: the two are not unconnected. U.S. support of Contra guerrilla activity and CIA-conducted covert operations have altered United States approaches to Latin America in other contexts, refocusing U.S. relations with other countries in the region and affecting U.S. participation in international development organizations.

U.S. support of the Contras brings into conjunction different conceptions of human rights: opposition to the Sandinistas and to the Contras can be justified on the grounds of protecting human freedoms and the protection of the national rights to self-determination, free from outside interference. The human freedoms can be conceived of as either the protection of the peoples of Nicaragua and other countries in the region from Communist domination or the protection of the victims of Contra guerrilla attacks and ICA covert operations. The outside interference can be conceptualized as either Soviet-Cuban direction of the Nicaraguan state, or as United States violation of the Nicaraguans' right to determine their own political future.

This section recounts U.S. Contra support; it then discusses future U.S. policy options and their implications for Latin American political stability.

The United States and the Contras

When the Somoza government fell in 1979, some six thousand members of the Nicaraguan National Guard crossed the border into Honduras and Costa Rica to avoid possible reprisals by the Sandinistas. Several different groups have since opposed the Sandinistas, some which have been military, some political, some Somocistas (former members of the Guardia), and some disenchanted Sandinistas.

The major Contra group has been the Nicaraguan Democratic Front (FDN). Its civilian leader is Adolfo Calero, a Notre Dame graduate and Coca Cola executive once jailed by Somoza. The FDN started from a base of ex-National Guard members, the September 15th Legion: a number of its officers are former members, as is the military commander, Enrique Bermudez.

Other opposition groups have largely fallen by the wayside or been merged into the FDN. These have included the Democratic Revolutionary Alliance (ARDE), the other major military opposition to the Sandinistas. This group was organized by former Sandinista leader Eden Pastore (Commandante Zero) in 1982, and later joined by another former Sandinista junta leader, Alfonso Robelo. ARDE operated out of Costa Rica and dissociated itself from the FDN as a Somocista organization. Pastore was severely injured by a bomb blast which occurred while he was holding a press conference in southern Nicaragua in 1984. Robelo, a President of the Nicaraguan Industrial Association in pre-Sandinista days had been a leader of the Nicaraguan Democratic Movement (MDN), a party composed of businessmen, professionals, and industrialists opposed to Somoza. Robelo was an original member of the Sandinista junta but resigned in 1980, citing Cuban and Communist influences. He went into exile in 1982, joined ARDE in 1983, but left the group the following year. ARDE took credit for the bombing of the Managua airport, which was later revealed to have been conducted with the assistance of the CIA. ARDE no longer exists, although Robelo was later made a director of UNO.

The other opposition to the Sandinistas was political, primarily that of Arturo Cruz' Nicaragua Democratic Coordinate (DNC). Cruz was a member of the Group of 12, prominent Nicaraguans who opposed the Somozas at the behest of the Sandinistas. An economist, Cruz headed the Nicaraguan Central Bank after the Sandinistas took power, was a member of the junta and Ambassador to the United States until he resigned in December 1981 to protest Sandinista policies. After forming the DNC, he decided to pull out of the 1984 elections, contending that the FSLN would not permit a fair contest.

Outside of some splinter groups, the FDN is the only game in town: UNO's formation was encouraged by the U.S. State Department. With Robelo and Cruz added to UNO's directorate along with Calero, the Nicaraguan opposition had a broader appeal. The FDN's problem is its Somocista appearance: although most of the troops are too young to have been members of the Guardia, a number of the leaders were officers under Somoza. Robelo and Cruz had stronger bases of political support in Nicaragua, making the Nicaraguan opposition more attractive to Nicaraguans and to Congress. UNO has deteriorated with the resignation of Calero in February 1987. Since he heads the only fighting force (with Bermudez), Calero had resisted reaching compromise agreements with Cruz and Robelo. The FDN is the recipient of Congressional funds.

The Nicaraguan opposition was funded in 1979 and 1980 by wealthy Nicaraguan refugees in the United States and Central America: the Cuban exile community in Miami provided funds and training bases in Florida. In November 1982 the Reagan Administration admitted that it was supporting small-scale clandestine operations designed to harass but not overthrow the Sandinistas. At that time the Contras numbered between one and two thousand men, who were being trained by the CIA in Honduras in preparation for moving into Nicaragua in the spring of 1983.

In May 1983, the Congress agreed to provide $19 million in covert aid to the Contras. In September 1983, two light planes bombed the Managua airport; in December 1983, the port city of Corinto was attacked from the sea, with major oil and gasoline storage tanks set on fire. The following spring, the mining of Nicaraguan harbors, apparently with CIA assistance, was made public.

Congress cut off funding to the Contras under the Boland-Zablocki Amendment to the Foreign Assistance Appropriations Act in July 1983. Despite the Amendment, the Contras received $24 million in previously appropriated funds, which ran out in mid-1984. In addition, the Department of Defense transferred to the Contras "surplus aircraft"; there were also rumors that Cuban weapons confiscated during the Grenada campaign were transferred to the Contras. And, of course, recent revelations about Col. North's activities indicate that funds were being channeled through the National Security Agency and the CIA to the Contras or to CIA covert operations in the area. 1984 was also the year that CIA manuals intended for the Contras, "Psychological Operations in Guerrilla Warfare" and "The Freedom Fighter's Manual" were disclosed: the former suggested methods for "neutralizing" leaders of the police and state security officials, while the latter described methods of economic sabotage, with the goal of "paralyzing the military-industrial complex of the traitorous Marxist state."

In 1985, Congress resumed aid to the Contras, although this was to be restricted to $27 million in humanitarian aid, such as medicine, food, and clothing. The Government Accounting Office later reported that it had had difficulty in tracing the use of these funds, especially the close to sixty percent spent outside of the United States. The program was administered by the Nicaraguan Humanitarian Assistance Office of the Department of State, as Congress prohibited CIA-Defense Department involvement. "Irangate" revelations have included information that the aircraft used for the Humanitarian aid shipments were also used to transport arms purchased with funds received for arms sales to Iran.

In 1986, U.S. support to the Contras was increased to $100 million, $70 million in military aid, $30 million in nonlethal assistance. In addition, the 1986 action repealed the prohibition on CIA-DoD contact with the Contras. As of this writing, Congress was debating whether to release the last $40 million authorized but unspent under the 1986 appropriation. The President has indicated that he will ask for continued and increased funding for the Contras.

To this point, the Contras have accomplished little militarily, although they have grown in numbers to fifteen to eighteen thousand troops, and are expected to increase in size to twenty-five thousand with additional funding. The Sandinista Army also has grown in size. It also has received important Soviet military assistance. The Soviets have provided helicopters equipped with air-to-surface missiles, which have kept the contras from operating in open areas.

The Contras have become a major source of concern in Honduras, as they are now a close rival of the Honduran Army in size and strength. Operating from camps on the Honduran-Nicaraguan border, the Contras have displaced Honduran citizens, including coffee growers and ranchers, otherwise conservative supporters of the Suazo Cordaza government. The Contras have also become a rallying point for Marxist trade union groups in Honduras.

Future Options

The options open to the United States at this point are to continue funding to the Contras or to find some alternative approach for dealing with Nicaragua. A central problem for the United States is that the Reagan Administration has become a prisoner of its own rhetoric. It has repeatedly pronounced Nicaragua the linchpin in Soviet-Cuban adverturism on the North American continent. It has also stressed the depth of the U.S. commitment to the Contras, who President Reagan has likened to the Founding Fathers of the American Revolution. At this point, it would be difficult for the Reagan Administration, and future Administrations, to radically alter the course of American foreign policy.

Despite the revelations of apparent misconduct by the CIA and the NSA during the period of the Boland-Zablocki Amendment, it appears unlikely that Congress will abandon funding the Contras. The positions in Congress in 1986 were not pro-Contra versus anti-Contra, but "hard support" (military as well as non-military aid) versus "soft support" (non-military aid only). Although the President lost control of the Senate to the Democrats in 1986, several new Democrats support aid to the Contras; the ranking leadership on the Senate Select Committee on Intelligence changed from Senators Durenberger and Leahy to Senators Boren and Cohen, who are somewhat more sympathetic to the President's policies. An April 1986 New York Times-CBS News Poll revealed that by a two-to-one margin, Americans opposed military aid to the Contras. The same poll also revealed that, by a five-to-three margin, they felt that eliminating Communism from Latin America was important to U.S. security. The investment of United States prestige, feelings of moral obligations to the Contras, and the reluctance of Congressional Democrats to be blamed in the future by Republicans for their absence in resolve probably will guarantee future support of the Contras.

Saying that the United States will continue to support the Contras does not indicate the contours of future U.S. policy. The level of U.S. support probably will be increased, but it is unclear to what level and for how long. As was mentioned in Chapter Three, the possible dragging of Honduras into a conflict with Nicaragua would create expanded U.S. financial and military assistance commitments to the region and might possibly result in some direct U.S. military role.

All of this still does not indicate how the U.S.-Nicaraguan conflict will be resolved. It is unlikely that the Sandinistas will be able to eliminate the Contras, just as it is unlikely that, at current levels of support or anything like them, the Contras will be able to depose the Sandinistas.

With the Contadora negotiations apparently on hold, the Reagan Administration apparently sees support of the Contras as a means of gaining leverage for bilateral negotiations with the Contras. The United States attempted such negotiations in 1981, without success. The Contras are much more of a factor now, this argument would proceed, and the United States economic sanctions are having a greater effect. To this point, the Sandinistas have not altered their negotiating position from where it was in the Contadora talks in 1984.

Representative Stephen Solarz of New York has proposed that the Reagan Administration bargain support of the Contras for reductions in the size of the Nicaraguan Army, removal of Soviet bloc advisers, and a guarantee that the Sandinistas not support the FMLN or other insurgent groups in the area. These items are close to the provisions of the contradora draft treaty agreements, which the Reagan Administration considered unenforceable without adequate verification procedures, ones to which the Sandinistas would not agree.

The argument for increased support to the Contras is that it would place greater pressure on the Sandinistas and make the alternative of agreeing to on-site monitoring more attractive to them. The argument against increased funding of the Contras is that it carries with it only the guarantee of more and larger-scale funding, as well as a deepened commitment to continuation of such support.

BOOKS

American Association for the International Commission of Jurists, Human Rights and United States Foreign Policy: The First Decade, 1973–1983, New York, AAICJ, 1984.

Jeffrey W. Barrett, Impulse to Revolution in Latin America, New York, Praeger, 1985.

Vita Bite, The Genocide Convention, Washington, DC, Congressional Research Service/United States Library of Congress, 1980.

Jan Knippers Black, Sentinels of Empire: The United States and Latin American Militarism, New York, Greenwood Press, 1986.

Morris Blackman, William LeoGrande, and Kenneth Sharpe, editors, Confronting Revolution: Security Through Diplomacy in Central America, New York, Pantheon, 1986.

Cole Blasier, The Hovering Giant: United States Responses to Revolutionary Change in Latin America, 1980–1985, revised edition, Pittsburgh, U. of Pittsburgh Press, 1985.

Reed Brody, Contra Terror in Nicaragua. Report of a Fact-finding Mission: September 1984–January 1985, Boston, South End Press, 1985.

Thomas Buergenthal, Robert Norris and Dinah Shelton, Protecting Human Rights in the Americas: Selected Problems, Kehl, FGR, Engel, 1982.

E. Bradford Burns, Latin America: A Concise Interpretative History, Englewood Cliffs, New Jersey, Prentice Hall, 4th edition, 1986.

James L. Busey, Political Aspects of the Panama Canal, Tucson, University of Arizona, 1974.

Ronald H. Chilcote and Joel C. Edelstein, Latin America: Capital ist and Socialist Perspectives of Development and Under- development, Boulder, CO, Westview, 1986.

Joseph Cirincione, editor, Central American and the Western Alliance, New York, Holmes and Meier, 1985.

Michael P. Claudon, editor, World Debt Crisis: International Lending on Trial, Cambridge, Ballinger, 1986.

John F. Copper and Daniel S. Papp, editors, Communist Nations
    Military Assistance, Bouldern, CO, Westview, 1983.

Thomas O. Enders, Richard P. Mattione, Latin America: The Crisis
    of Debt and Growth, Washington, Brookings Institution, 1984.

Mark Falcoff, Small Countries, Large Issues: Studies in United
    States-Latin American Asymmetries, Washington, American
    Enterprise Institute, 1984.

David P. Forsythe, Human Rights and World Policies, Lincoln,
    University of Nebraska Press, 1983.

Raymond D. Gastil, Freedom in the World, Political Rights and
    Civil Liberties, Westport, CT, Greenwood Press, 1980.

Pradip K. Ghosh, editor, Developing Latin America: A Moderniza
    tion Perspective, Westport, CT, Greenwood, 1984.

Wolf Grabendorff and Riordan Roett, editors, Latin America,
    Western Europe, and the United States: Reevaluating the
    Atlantic Triangle, New York, Praeger, 1985.

Laurence E. Harrison, Underdevelopment is a State of Mind: the
    Latin American Case, Lanham, MD, Center for International
    Affairs, Harvard University and University Press of America, 1985.

J. Michael Hogan, The Panama Canal in American Politics: Domes
    tic Advocacy and the Evolution of Policy, Carbondale,
    Southern Illinois University Press, 1986.

Richard H. Immerman, The CIA in Guatemala: The Foreign Policy of
    Intervention, Austin, TX, University of Texas, 1982.

Edward L. King, Out of Step, Out of Line: United States Military
    Policy in Central America, Boston, Unitarian Universalist
    Service Committee, 1984.

Peter F. Klaren and Thomas J. Bossert, editors, Promise of
    Development: Theories of Change in Latin America, Boulder,
    CO, Westview, 1986.

Donald P. Kommers and Gilbert D. Loeschner, editors, Human Rights
    and American Foreign Policy, Notre Dame, University of Notre
    Dame Press, 1979.

Barry Levine, editor, The New Cuban Presence in the Caribbean,
    Boulder, CO, Westview, 1983.

Theodor Meron, Human Rights in International Law: Legal and
    Policy Issues, Oxford, Clarendon, 1984.

Harold Molineau, United States Policy Toward Latin America: From
    Regionalism to Globalism, Boulder, CO, Westview, 1986.

Ronaldo Munck, Politics and Dependency in the Third World: the
    Case of Latin America, Jordanstown, Ulster Polutechnic,
    1984.

Ved P. Nanda, James R. Scarritt and George W. Shepherd, Jr.,
    editors, Global Human Rights: Public Policies, Comparative
    Measures, and NGO Strategies, Boulder, CO, Westview, 1981.

David Nolan, The Ideology of the Sandinistas and the Nicaraguan
    Revolution, Coral Gables, University of Miami, 1984.

Michael Novak, Human Rights and the New Realism: Strategic
    Thinking in a New Age, New York, Freedom House, 1986.

Philip J. O'Brien, Dependency Revisited, Glasgow, University of
    Glasgow, 1984.

Jenny Pearce, Under the Eagle: United States Intervention in
    Central America and the Caribbean, London, Latin American
    Bureau, 1982.

Stan Persky, America, The Last Domino: United States Foreign
    Policy in Central America Under Reagan, Vancouver, BC, New
    Star Books, 1984.

Andrew J. Pierre, The Global Politics of Arms Sales, Princeton,
    NJ, Princeton University Press, 1982.

Andrew J. Pierre, editor, Third World Instability: Central
    America as a European-American Issue, New York, Council,
    Council on Foreign Relations, 1985.

B. G. Ramcharan, editor, The Right to Life in International Law,
    Boston, Martinus Niehoff, 1985.

B. G. Ramcharan, editor, International Law and Fact-Finding in
    the Field of Human Rights, Boston, Martinus Niehoff,. 1982.

Peter Rosset and John Vandermeer, The Nicaragua Reader: Docu
    ments of a Revolution Under Fire, New York, Grove Press,
    1983.

Paul B. Ryan, The Panama Canal Controversy: United States
    Diplomacy and Defense Interests, Stanford, Hoover Institu-
    tion, 1977.

Lars Schoultz, Human Rights and United States Policy Toward Latin
    America, Princeton, Princeton University Press, 1981.

Michael S. Teitelbau, Latin Migration North: the Problem for
    United States Foreign Policy, New York, Council on Foreign
    Relations, 1985.

C. Peter Timmer, Walter P. Falcon, and Scott R. Pearson, Food
    Policy Analysis, Baltimore, Johns Hopkins, 1983.

Jan Triska, editor, Dominant Powers and Subordinate States: the
    United States in Latin America and the Soveit Union in
    Eastern Europe, Durham, NC, Duke, 1986.

Augusto Varas, Militarization and the International Arms Race in
    Latin America, Boulder, CO, Westview, 1985.

R. J. Vincent, editor, Foreign Policy and Human Rights, Cam-
    bridge, Cambridge University Press, 1986.

Thomas W. Walker, editor, Nicaragua in Revolution, New York,
    Praeger, 1982.

Robert Wesson and Heraldo Munoz, editors, Latin American Views of
    United States Policy, New York, Praeger, 1986.

Howard J. Wiarda, Human Rights and United States Human Rights
    Policy, Washington, American Enterprise Institute, 1982.

Howard J. Wiarda, editor, Rift and Revolution: The Central
    American Imbroglio, Washington, American Enterprise
    Institute, 1984.

Bruce Wood, The Dismantling of the Good Neighbor Policy, Austin,
    TX, University of Texas, 1985.

Gary W. Wynia, The Politics of Latin American Development,
    Cambridge, Cambridge University Press, second edition, 1984.

                    PERIODICAL AND JOURNAL ARTICLES

Elliot Abrams, "Human Rights and the Refugee Crisis," Department
    of State Bulletin, September 1982, 43-45.

Robert Z. Aliber, "The Debt Cycle in Latin America," Journal of
    Interamerican Studies and World Affairs, v. 27 (Winter
    1985-86), 155-72.

Thomas P. Anderson, "Honduras in Transition," Current History, v.
    84 (March 1985), 114-117+.

Alan Angell, "Pinochet's Chile: the Beginning of the End?" World
    Today, v. 41 (February 1985), 27-30.

Marisa Arienza and Carols A. Mallmann, "Argentina on the Road to Democracy: Comparisons with Chile and Uruguay," <u>International Social Sciences Journal</u>, v. 37 (1985), 31-46.

Robert Armstrong, "Nicaragua: Sovereignty and Non-Alignment," <u>Report on the Americas</u>, v. 19 (May/June 1985), 15-21.

Edmar L. Bacha and Richard E. Feinberg, "The World Bank and Structural Adjustment in Latin America," <u>World Development</u>, v. 14 (March 1986), 333-346.

Joao Clemente Baena Soares, "A Different Perspective for the Financial Crisis in Latin America and the Caribbean," <u>Journal of Interamerican Studies and World Affairs</u>, v. 27 (Winter 1985-86), 9-20.

Werner Baer, "Growth with Inequality: the Cases of Brazil and Mexico," <u>Latin American Research Review</u>, v. 21 (1986), 197-207.

Bruce Michael Bagley and Juan Gabriel Tokatlian, "Colombian Foreign Policy in the 1980's: The Search for Leverage," <u>Journal of Interamerican Studies and World Affairs</u>, v. 27 (Fall 1985), 27-62.

Robert L. Bard, "The Right to Food," <u>Iowa Law Review</u>, v. 70 (1985), 1279-1291.

M. Cherif Bassiouni, "The Protection of 'Collective Victims' in International Law," <u>Human Rights Annual</u>, v. 2 (1985), 239-257.

Peter J. Beck, "The Future of the Falkland Islands: A Solution Made in Hong Kong?" <u>International Affairs</u>, v. 61 (Autumn 1985), 643-660.

Louis Rene Beres, "Ignoring International Law: U.S. Policy on Insurgency and Intervention in Central America," <u>Denver Journal of International Law and Policy</u>, v. 14 (1985), 76-86.

Ruben Berrios, "Relations between Nicaragua and the Socialist Countries," <u>Journal of Interamerican Studies and World Affairs</u>, v. 27 (Fall 1985), 111-139.

Jeffrey Blum and Ralph Steinhardt, "Federal Jurisdiction over International Human Rights Claims: the Alien Tort Claims Act After <u>Filartiga v. Pena-Iralda</u>", <u>Harvard International Law Journal</u>, v. 22 (1981), 53-113.

Edgardo Boeninger, "The Chilean Road to Democracy," <u>Foreign Affairs</u>, v. 84 (Spring 1986), 812-832.

Ahcene Boulesbaa, "An Analysis of the 1984 Draft Convention Against Torture and Other Cruel, Inhuman or Degrading Treatment or Punishment," Dickinson Journal of International Law, v. 4 (1986), 185-211.

Jennifer Bremer, "Comparative Advantage," Foreign Service Journal, July-August 1986, 21-28.

Philip L. Brock, "Financial Controls and Economic Liberalization in Latin America," Journal of Interamerican Studies and World Affairs, v. 27 (Winter 1985-86), 125-139.

David Bromwich, "Nicaragua, Civil Liberties and U.S. Policy," Dissent, v. 33 (Winter 1986), 14-15.

David Bromwich, "Reagan's Contempt for History," Dissent, v. 32 (Summer 1985), 265-268.

Alan Brudner, "The Domestic Enforcement of International Covenants on Human Rights: A Theoretical Framework," U. of Toronto Law Journal, v. 35 (1985), 219-254.

Abraham Brumberg, "Nicaragua: A Mixture of Shades: A First-Hand Report on Sandinista Politics," Dissent, v. 33 (Spring 1986), 173-178.

Abraham Brumberg, "Nicaragua: The Inner Struggle; Is There Still a Chance for Political Pluralism?" Dissent, v. 33 (Summer 1986), 294-303.

David Carleton and Michael Stohl, "The Foreign Policy of Human Rights: Rhetoric and Reality from Jimmy Carter to Ronald Reagan," Human Rights Quarterly, v. 7 (May 1985), 205-229.

Jorge G. Castaneda, "Don't Corner Mexico!" Foreign Policy, v. 60 (Fall 1985), 75-90.

Jorge G. Castaneda, "Mexico at the Brink," Foreign Affairs, v. 64 (Winter 1985-86), 287-303.

H. E. Chehabi, "Self-Determination, Territorial Integrity, and the Falkland Islands," Political Science Quarterly, v. 100 (Summer 1985), 215-225.

Noam Chomsky, "Intervention in Vietnam and Central America: Parallels and Differences," Monthly Review, v. 37 (September 1985), 1-29.

James D. Cochrane, "Perspectives on the Central American Crisis," International Organization, v. 39 (Autumn 1985), 755-777.

Benjamin J. Cohen, "International Debt and Linkage Strategies: Some Foreign Policy Implications for the United States,"

International Organization, v. 39 (Autumn 1985), 699–727.

Stephen B. Cohen, "Conditioning U.S. Security Assistance on Human Rights Practices," *American Journal of International Law*, v. 76 (April 1982), 246–279.

Forrest D. Colburn, "Nicaragua under Siege," *Current History*, v. 84 (March 1985), 105–108+.

David Cole, "Challenging Covert War: the Policies of the Political Question Doctrine," *Harvard Journal of Internatinal Law*, v. 26 (1985), 155–188.

Alberto R. Coll, "Functionalism and the Balance of Interests in the Law of the Sea: Cuba's Role," *American Journal of International Law*, v. 79 (October 1985), 891–911.

Jane L. Collins, "Smallholder Settlement of Tropical South America: the Social Causes of Ecological Destruction," *Human Organization*, v. 45 (spring 1986), 1–10.

Pamela Constable and Arturo Valenzuela, "Is Chile Next?" *Foreign Policy*, v. 63 (Summer 1986), 58–75.

Frank B. Cross and Cyril V. Smith, "The Reagan Administration's Nonproliferation Nonpolicy," *Catholic University Law Review*, v. 33 (Spring 1984), 633–665.

Lloyd N. Cutler, "The Right to Intervene," *Foreign Affairs*, v. 64 (1985), 96–112.

Erica-Irene Daes, "Native People's Rights," *Cahiers de Droits*, v. 64 (1985), 123–133.

Roland Dallas, "South Atlantic Solutions," *World Today*, v. 41 (November 1985), 193–194.

Manfred A. Dauses, "The Protection of Fundamental Rights in the Community Legal Order," *European Law Review*, v. 10 (1985), 398–419.

Carmen Diana Deere, et. al., "The Peasantry and the Development of Sandinista Agrarian Policy, 1979–1984," *Latin America Research Review*, v. 20 (1985), 75–109.

Juan M. Del Aguila, "Central American Vulnerability to Soviet/Cuban Penetration," *Journal of Interamerican Studies and World Affairs*, v. 27 (Summer 1985), 77–97.

Juan M. Del Aguila, "Cuba's Revolution After Twenty-Five Years," *Current History*, v. 84 (March 1985), 122–126+.

Jorge I. Dominguez, "Cuba: Charismatic Communism," Problems of Communism, v. 34 (September-October 1985), 102-107.

Jorge I. Dominguez, "Cuba in the 1980's," Foreign Affairs, v. 65 (Fall 1986), 118-135.

Jack Donnelly, "International Human Rights: A Regime Analysis," International Organization, v. 40 (1986), 599-642.

Gerhard Drekunja-Kornat, "The Rise of Latin America's Foreign Policy: Between Hegemony and Autonomy," Latin American Research Review, v. 21 (1986), 238-245.

Richard Drifte, "Japan's Growing Arms Production and the American Connection," Atlantic Community Quarterly, v. 24 (Spring 1986), 67-72.

W. Raymond Duncan, "Castro and Gorbachev: Politics of Accommodation," Problems of Communism, v. 35 (March-April 1986), 45-57.

Esperanza Duran, "Latin America's External Debt: The Limits of Regional Cooperation," World Today, v. 42 (May 1986), 84-88.

Esperanza Duran, "Mexico: Economic Realism and Political Efficiency," World Today, v. 41 (May 1985), 96-99.

Marc Edelman, "Lifelines: Nicaragua and the Socialist Countries," Report on the Americas, v. 19 (May-June 1985), 33-56.

D. M. Edwards, "International Legal Aspects of Safeguards and the Nonproliferation of Nuclear Weapons," International and Comparative Law Quarterly, v. 33 (1984), 1-21.

"Effective Enforcement of the Law of Nations: A Proposed International Human Rights Organization," California Western International Law Journal, v. 15 (1985).

Robert K. Evanson, "Soviet Political Uses of Trade with Latin America," Journal of Interamerican Studies and World Affairs, v. 27 (Summer 1985), 97-127.

Mark Falcoff, "Central America: A View from Washington," Orbis, v. 28 (Winter 1985), 665-672.

Mark Falcoff, "Chile: The Dilemma for U.S. Foreign Policy," Foreign Affairs, v. 64 (Spring 1986), 833-848.

Tom J. Farer, "Contadora: The Hidden Agenda," Foreign Policy, v. 59 (Summer 1985), 59-73.

David Lewis Feldman, "The United States Role in the Malvinas Crisis, 1982: Misguidance and Misperception in Argentina's Decision to Go to War," Journal of Interamerican Studies and World Affairs, v. 27 (Summer 1985), 1-22.

Elizabeth G. Ferris, "Interests, Influence and Inter-American Relations," Latin American Research Review, v. 21 (1986), 208-219.

Elizabeth G. Ferris, "The Political Impact of Refugees," World Today, v. 41 (May 1985), 100-101.

Amy Finkelstein, "Brazil, the United States and Nuclear Nonproliferation: American Foreign Policy at the Crossroads," Fletcher Forum, v. 7 (Summer 1983), 277-311.

E. V. K. Fitzgerald, "Agrarian Reform as a Model of Accumulation: the Case of Nicaragua Since 1979," Journal of Development Studies, v. 22 (October 1985), 208-226.

Thomas Fleiner-Gerstner and Michael A. Mayer, "New Developments in Humanitarian Law: A Challenge to the Concept of Sovereignty," International and Comparative Law Quarterly, v. 34 (1985), 267-283.

Carl P. Florez, "United States Policies and Strategies to Control Foreign Production of Marijuana and Cocaine: Peru, Bolivia and Colombia," Police Studies, v. 18 (Summer 1985), 84-92.

David P. Forsythe, "The United States and Human Rights," Political Science Quarterly, v. 100 (Summer 1985), 249-269.

Francis Fukuyama, "Gorbachev and the Third World," Foreign Affairs, v. 64 (1986), 715-731.

Jose Z. Garcia, "El Salvador: Legitimizing the Government," Current History, v. 84 (March 9185), 101-104+.

Richard N. Gardner, "U.S. Termination of the Compulsory Jurisdiction of the International Court of Justice," Columbia Journal of Transnational Law, v. 29 (1986), 973-983.

Jeffrey E. Garten, "Gunboat Economics," Foreign Affairs, v. 63 (1985), 538-559.

Bryant Garth, "Aggressive Smugness: the United States and International Human Rights," American Journal of Comparative Law, vol. 34 (1986), supplement, 411-426.

John Gerassi, "Pluralism vs. Centralism in Nicaragua: The Sandinistas Under Attack," Policy, v. 5 (1985), 77-94.

Heliodoro Gonzalez, "Latin America at the UN: the Gathering
    Storm," Inter-American Economic Affairs, v. 39 (Autumn
    1985), 11-25.

Louis Harrell and Dale Fischer, "The 1982 Mexican Peso Devalua-
    tion and Border Area Employment," Monthly Labor Review, v.
    108 (October 1985), 25-32.

Edward S. Herman and James Petras, "Resurgent Democracy: Rhetor-
    ic and Reality," New Left Review, November-December 1985,
    83-98.

John Hickey, "The Debt Crisis: the Misleading Statements of the
    Export-Import Bank," Inter-American Economic Affairs, v. 39
    (Autumn 1985), 37-44.

Keith Highet, "Litigation Implications of the United States
    Withdrawal from the Nicaraguan Case," American Journal of
    International Law, v. 79 (October 1985), 992-1005.

Paul L. Hoffman and Linda Willett Brackins, "The Elimination of
    Torture: International and Domestic Developments," Interna-
    tional Lawyer, v. 19 (1985), 1351-1364.

Ian A. Hunter, "When Human Rights Become Wrongs," University of
    Western Ontario Law Review, v. 23 (1985), 197-204.

"International Court of Justice Case Concerning Military and
    Paramilitary Activities in and Against United States,"
    Harvard Journal of International Law, v. 26 (1985), 622-629.

"International Human Rights Symposium," Whittier Law Review, v. 7
    (1985), 663-826.

"International Protection of Fundamental Freedoms and Human
    Rights: The Convention Against Torture and Other Cruel,
    Inhuman or Degrading Torture or Punishment," ASILS Inter-
    national Law Journal, v. 8 (1984), 67-101.

Miles Kahler, "Politics and International Debt: Explaining the
    Crisis," International Organization, v. 39 (Summer 1985),
    357-382.

Robert R. Kaufman, "Democratic and Authoritarian Responses to the
    International Debt Issue: Argentina, Brazil, and Mexico,"
    International Organization, v. 39 (Summer 1985), 473-503.

Penn Kemble and Arturo Cruz, "How the Nicaraguan Resistance Can
    Win," Commentary (December 1986), 19-29.

Eldon Kenworthy, "United States Policy in Central America: A Choice Denied," Current History, v. 84 (March 1985), 97-100+.

Jeane Kirkpatrick, "Establishing a Viable Human Rights Policy," World Affairs, v. 143 (Spring 1981), 323-334.

Jeane Kirkpatrick, "Our Cuban Misadventures," Atlantic Community Quarterly, v. 24 (Summer 1986), 155-156.

Klaus Knorr, "Burden-sharing in NATO: Aspects of U.S. Policy," Orbis, v. 29 (1985), 517-536.

A. David Knox, "Resuming Growth in Latin America," Finance and Development, v. 22 (September 1985), 15-18.

Lawrence J. Korb, "DoD Assistance in the War on Drugs," Police Chief, v. 52 (October 1985), 57-58+.

Clifford Krauss, "Revolution in Central America?" Foreign Affairs, v. 65 (1987), 564-581.

John G. Laquerre, "From Slavery to Nationalism," Social and Economic Studies, v. 34 (1985), 283-309.

Jack A. LeCuyer, "Burden Sharing: Has the Term Outlived its Usefulness?" Atlantic Community Quarterly, v. 24 (Spring 1986), 63-65.

Rensselaer W. Lee, III, "The Latin American Drug Connection," Foreign Policy, v. 61 (Winter 1985-86), 142-159.

Christian Leipert, "Social Costs of Economic Growth," Journal of Economic Issues, v. 20 (March 1986), 109-131.

William LeoGrande, "The United States and Latin America," Current History, v. 85 (January 1986), 1-4+.

Michael Levitin, "The Law of Force and the Force of Law: Grenada, the Falklands, and Humanitarian Intervention," Harvard Journal of International Law, v. 27 (1986), 621-657.

Richard B. Lillich, "The Paris Minimum Standards of Human Rights Norms in a State of Emergency," American Journal of International Law, v. 79 (1985), 1072-1081.

Jennie K. Lincoln, "Neutrality Costa Rican Style," Current History, v. 84 (March 1985), 118-121+.

W. Lissner, "Development in the Caribbean," American Journal of Economic Sociology, v. 45 (April 1986), 255-256.

Abraham F. Lowenthal, "Threat and Opportunity in the Americas," Foreign Affairs, v. 64 (1985), 539-561.

J. Michael Luhan, "AIFLD's Salvadoran Labor Wars: A Painful
    Record of Political Arm-Twisting," Dissent, v. 33 (Summer
    1986), 340-350.

Anthony P. Maingot, "Coming to Terms with the 'Improbable'
    Revolution," Journal of American Studies and World Affairs,
    v. 27 (Fall 1985), 177-190.

David R. Mares, "Explaining Choice of Development Strategies:
    Suggestions from Mexico, 1970-1982," International Organiza-
    tion, v. 39 (Autumn 1985), 667-697.

John Markoff and Silvio R. Duncan Baretta, "What We Don't Know
    About the Coups: Observations on Recent South American
    Politics," Armed Forces and Society, v. 12 (Winter 1986),
    207-235.

John D. Martz, "Counterpoint and Concatenation in the Caribbean:
    the Substance and Style of Foreign Policy," Latin American
    Research Review, v. 21 (1986), 161-172.

T. David Mason, "Land Reform and the Breakdown of Clientelist
    Politics in El Salvador," Comparative Political Studies, 18
    (January 1986), 487-516.

Robert Matthews, "The Limits of Friendship: Nicaragua and the
    West," Report on the Americas, v. 19 (May-June 1985), 22-32.

Theodor Meron, "On a Hierarchy of International Human Rights,"
    American Journal of International Law, v. 80 (1986), 1-23.

Alois Mertes, "Europe's Role in Central America: A West German
    Christian-Democratic View," Atlantic Community Quarterly, v.
    23 (Spring 1985), 87-98.

Richard Millett, "Guatemala: Progress and Paralysis," Current
    History, v. 84 (March 1985), 109-113.

John N. Moore, "The Miskitu National Question in Nicaragua:
    Background to a Misunderstanding," Science and Society, v.
    50 (Summer 1986), 132-147.

John N. Moore, "The Secret War in Central America and the Failure
    of World Order," American Journal of International Law, v.
    80 (1986), 43-127.

Joshua Muravchik, "The Nicaragua Debate," Foreign Affairs, v. 65
    (Winter 1986-87), 366-382.

Ved P. Nanda, "Development as an Emerging Human Right Under
    International Law," Denver Journal of International Law and
    Policy, v. 13 (1984-85), 161-179.

Ved. P. Nanda, "The Right to Development Under International Law--Challenges Ahead," California Western International Law Journal, v. 15 (1985), 431-440.

Richard W. Nelson, "International Law and U.S. Withholding of Payments to International Organizations," American Journal of International Law, v. 80 (October 1986), 973-983.

"Nicaragua vs. the United States before the International Court of Justice," World Affairs, v. 148 (Summer 1985), 3-70.

Miguel Obando y Bravo, "Nicaragua: the Sandinistas Have 'Gagged and Bound' U.S.," Atlantic Community Quarterly, v. 24 (Summer 1986), 103-106.

Frank Orlando and Simon Teitel, "Latin America's External Debt Problem: Debt-Servicing Strategies Compatible with Long-Term Economic Growth," Economic Development and Cultural Change, v. 34 (April 1986), 641-671.

Guillermo Ortiz and Jaime Serra-Pache, "A Note on the Burden of the Mexican Foreign Debt," Journal of Development Economics, v. 21 (April 1986), 111-129.

Robert A. Pastor, "Explaining U.S. Policy Toward the Caribbean Basin: Fixed and Emerging Images," World Politics, v. 38 (April 1986), 483-515.

Mario Payeras, "The Guatemalan Army and U.S. Policy in Central America," Monthly Review, v. 37 (March 1986), 14-20.

Deborah Perluss, J. F. Hartman, "Temporary Refuge: Emergence of a Customary Norm," Virginia Journal of International Law, v. 26 (1986), 551-626.

"Perspectives on the New Law of the Sea," American Journal of International Law, v. 79 (October 1985), 871-991.

George Philip, "The Nicaraguan Conflict: Politics and Propaganda," World Today, v. 41 (December 1985), 222-224.

David Pion-Berlin, "Theories on Political Repression in Latin America: Conventional Wisdom and an Alternative," PS, v. 19 (Winter 1986), 49-56.

H. J. Pollard, "The Erosion of Agriculture in an Oil Economy: the Case of Export Crop Production in Trinidad," World Development, v. 13 (July 1985), 19-35.

Alejandro Portes and Alèx Stepick, "Unwelcome Immigrants: the Labor Market Experiences of 1980 (Mariel) Cuban and Haitian Refugees in South Florica," American Sociological Review, 50 (August 1985), 493-514.

Susan Kaufman Purcell, "Demystifying Contadora," Foreign Affairs, v. 64 (Fall 1985), 74-95.

Michael Radu, "The Origins and Evolution of the Nicaraguan Insurgencies, 1979-1985," Orbis, v. 29 (Winter 1986) 821-840.

Pedro Ramet and Fernando Lopez-Alves, "Moscow and the Revolutionary Left in Latin America," Orbis, v. 28 (Summer 1984), 341-363.

Linda L. Reif, "Seizing Control: Latin American Military Motives, Capabilities, and Risks," Armed Forces and Society, v. 10 (Summer 1984), 563-582.

W. Michael Reisman, "Has the International Court of Justice Exceeded its Jurisdiction," American Journal of International Law, v. 80 (1986), 128-134.

Jose Luis Restrepo, "Latin America: An Assessment of the Past and a Search for the Future," Inter-American Economic Affairs, v. 39 (Winter 1985), 3-26.

Edme Dominguez Reyes, "Soviet Relations with Central America, the Caribbean and Members of the Contadora Group," Annals of the American Academy of Political and Social Sciences, v. 481 (September 1985), 147-158.

Gordon Richards, "Stabilization Crises and the Breakdown of Military Authoritarianism in Latin America," Comparative Political Studies, v. 18 (January 1986), 449-485.

Michael Richards, "Cosmopolitan World View and Counterinsurgency in Guatemala," Anthropology Quarterly, v. 58 (July 1985), 90-107.

Bill Richardson, "Hispanic American Concerns," Foreign Policy, v. 50 (Fall 1985), 30-39.

Selwyn Riley, "Campaign Against Torture," New Zealand Law Journal, v. 1985 (1985), 297-299.

Alfonso Robelo, "The Nicaraguan Democratic Struggle: Our Unfinished Revolution," Atlantic Community Quarterly, v. 23 (Fall 1985), 269-274.

Kenneth K. Roberts, "Democracy and the Dependent Capitalist State in Latin America," Monthly Review, v. 37 (October 1985), 12-26.

Davis R. Robinson, "The Treaty of Tlatelolco and the United States: A Latin American Nuclear Free Zone," American Journal of International Law, v. 64 (April 1970), 282-309.

William I. Robinson and Kent Norsworthy, "Nicaragua: the Stra-
    tegy of Counterrevolution," Monthly Review, v. 37 (December
    1985), 11-24.

David F. Ronfeldt, "Rethinking the Monroe Doctrine," Orbis, v. 28
    (Winter 1985), 684-696.

Peter I. Rose, "The Politics and Morality of U.S. Refugee
    Policy," Center Magazine, v. 18 (September-October 1985),
    2-13.

Jay Rosenthal, "Legal and Political Considerations of the United
    States' Ratification of the Genocide Convention," Antioch
    Law Journal, v. 3 (1985), 117-144.

James P. Rowles, "'Secret Wars', Self-Defense and the Charter--A
    Reply to Professor Moore," American Journal of International
    Law, v. 80 (July 1986), 568-583.

J. Mark Ruhl, "The Honduran Agrarian Reform Movement under Suazao
    Cordova, 1982-85:   An Assessment," Inter-American Economic
    Affairs, v. 39 (Autumn 1985), 63-80.

Rigoberto P. Rush, "Armed Intervention on the Pretext of Counter-
    ing a Mythical Threat," World Marxist Review, v. 28 (July
    1985), 24-30.

Carlos Santiago Nino, "The Human Rights Policy of Argentine
    Constitutional   Government: a   Reply,"   Yale   Journal   of
    International Law, v. 11 (1985), 217-230.

Oscar Schachter, "The Legality of Pro-Democratic Invasion,"
    American Journal of International Law, v. 78 (July 1984),
    645-649.

Hugh Schwartz, "The Industrial Sector and the Debt Crisis in
    Latin America," Journal of Interamerican Studies and World
    Affairs, v. 27 (Winter 1985-86), 95-110.

Martin J. Scurrah, "Military Reformism in Peru: Opening the
    Pandora's Box," Latin American Research Review, v. 21
    (1986), 244-257.

Aaron Segal, "Caribbean Realities," Current History, v. 84 (March
    1985), 127-130+.

Peter Shearman, "The Soviet Union and Grenada Under the New Jewel
    Movement," International Affairs, v. 61 (Autumn 1985),
    661-673.

Jerome Slater and Terry Nardin, "Nonintervention and Human
    Rights," Journal of Politics, v. 48 (February 1986), 86-96.

Gerald Smith and George Rathjens, "Reassessing the Nuclear Nonproliferation Treaty," Foreign Affairs, v. 59 (Spring 1981), 875-894.

Stephen J. Solarz, "When to Intervene," Forgien Policy, v. 63 (Summer 1986), 20-39.

Pierre Spitz, "The Right to Food in Historical Perspective," Food Policy, v. 10 (November 1985), 306-316.

Stephen C. Stamos, Jr., "Energy and Development in Latin America," Latin American Research Review, v. 21 (1985), 188-201.

Michael Stohl, David Carleton and Steven E. Johnson, "Human Rights and U.S. Foreign Assistance from Nixon to Carter," Journal of Peace Research, v. 21 (1984), 215-226.

Dale Story, "Policy Cycles in Mexican Presidential Policies," Latin American Research Review, v. 20 (1985), 139-161.

Leonard Sullivan, "Allied Burden Sharing: Another View," Atlantic Community Quarterly, v. 24 (Spring 1986), 73-79.

"Symposium of the 1977 Geneva Protocols," Akron Law Review, v. 19 (Spring 1986), 521-577.

Gabriel Szekely, "Recent Findings and Research Suggestions on Oil and Mexico's Development Process," Latin American Research Review, v. 20 (1985), 235-246.

Jerzy Sztucki, "Intervention under Article 63 of the International Court of Justice Statute in the Phase of Preliminary Proceedings: the 'Salvadoran Incident'," American Journal of International Law, v. 79 (October 1985), 992-1005.

Fernando Teson, "International Human Rights and Cultural Relativism," Virginia Journal of International Law, v. 25 (1985), 869-898.

"The Fine Line Between the Enforcement of Human Rights Agreements and the Violation of National Sovereignty: the Case of the Soviet Dissidents," Loyola Journal of International and Comparative Law Journal, v. 7 (1984), 323-350.

"The State Department's Analysis of the Debt Problem," Inter-American Economic Affairs, v. 39 (Winter 1985), 79-82.

"The United States Action in Grenada," American Journal of International Law, v. 78 (January 1984), 131-175.

"The United States Position on Chile," Inter-American Economic Affairs, v. 39 (Autumn 1985), 81-85.

"The United States Position on Peru," Inter-American Economic Affairs, v. 39 (Autumn 1985), 86-98.

Katarina Tomasevski, "Human Rights: the Right to Food," Iowa Law Review, v. 70 (1985), 1321-1328.

Guillermo Ungo, "What Prevents a Settlement of the Salvadoran Conflict," World Marxist Review, v. 29 (April 1986), 100-105.

"United States Nicaraguan Policy," Center Magazine, v. 18 (November-December 1985), 2-8.

Raul Valdes Vivo, "Central America: the Clash of Two Policies," World Marxist Review, v. 28 (July 1985), 77-83.

Jiri Valenta, "Nicaragua: Soviet-Cuban Pawn or Non-aligned Country," Journal of Interamerican Studies and World Affairs, v. 27 (Fall 1985), 163-175.

Jiri Valenta and Virginia Valenta, "Sandinistas in Power," Problems of Communism, v. 34 (September-October 1985), 1-28.

Cyrus R. Vance, "The Human Rights Imperative," Foreign Policy, v. 63 (Summer 1986), 3-19.

Harry E. Vanden and Waltrand Queiser Morales, "Nicaraguan Relations with the Nonaligned Movement," Journal of Interamerican Studies and World Affairs, 27 (Fall 1985), 141-161.

Ernest Van den Haag, "The Business of American Foreign Policy," Foreign Affairs, v. 64 (1985), 113-129.

David Weissbrodt, "The Three 'Theme' Special Rapporterus of the UN Commission on Human Rights," American Journal of International Law, v. 80 (1986), 685-699.

Leslier Raissman Wellbaum, "International Human Rights Claims After Tel-Oren v. Libyan Arab Republic: Swan Song for the Legal Lohengrin?" Hastings International and Comparative Law Review, v. 9 (1985), 107-147.

Phillip A. Wellons, "International Debt: the Behavior of Banks in a Politicized Environment," International Organization, v. 38 (Summer 1985), 441-471.

GOVERNMENT PUBLICATIONS

Congressional Hearings and Reports

Administration Proposal for Counter-Terrorism Assistance for
Central America, Hearings, Committee on Foreign Relations,
Senate, November 1985. Y4 F76/2: S.hrg 99-623.

Agency for International Development Oversight, Hearings, Committee on Foreign Relations, Senate, April 1986, Y4 F76/2: S.
hrg 99-782.

DoD's Foreign Military Sales Program, Hearings, Legislative and
National Security Subcommittee of the Committee on Government Operations, House, March 1986. Y4 G74/7: D 36/22.

Economic Summit: Latin Debt and the Baker Plan, Hearings,
Committee on Foreign Relations, Senate, May 1986. Y4 F76/2:
S. hrg 99/889.

Foreign Assistance and Related Appropriations Bill, 1987,
Hearings, Committee on Appropriations, Senate. Y1:1/5:
99:443.

Human Rights and Political Developments in Panama, Hearings,
Subcommittees on Human Rights and International Organizations and on Western Hemisphere Affairs, Committee on
Foreign Affairs, House, April and July 1986. Y4.F76/1:H
88/42.

Investigation of United States Assistance to the Nicaraguan
Contras, Hearings, Subcommittee on Western Affairs, Committee on Foreign Affairs, House, March 1986. Y4:F76/1: In
8/69 v.1.

Investigation of U.S. Assistance to the Nicaraguan Contras,
Subcommittee on Western Hemisphere Affairs, Committee on
Foreign Affairs, House, April-June 1986. Y4 F76/1: In 8/69
v.2.

Joint Resolution Relating to the Additional Authorization and
Assistance Requested by the President: Adverse Conference
Report, Committees on Appropriations, Foreign Affairs and
Armed Services, and Permanent Senate Select Committee on
Intelligence. Y1.1/8:99-483 pt.1.

Joint Resolution Relating to Central America Pursuant to the
International Security and Development Cooperation Act of
1985: report together with additional and dissenting views,
Committees on Appropriations, Foreign Affairs and Armed
Services, and Permanent Senate Select Committee on Intelli-
gence. Y1.1./8:99-483, pt.3.

Review of Export Initiatives in the Food Security Act of 1985,
Subcommittee on Departmental Operations, Research, and
Foreign Agriculture, Committee on Agriculture, House, April
1986. Y4.Ag 8/1:99-28.

Review of the International Lending Supervision Act of 1983,
Subcommittee on International Finance and Monetary Policy,
Committee on Banking, Housing, and Urban Affairs, Senate,
June 1986. Y4.B 22/3: S.hrg. 99-811.

Review of the President's Report on Assistance to the Nicaraguan
Opposition, Hearings, Subcommittee on Western Hemisphere
Affairs, Committee on Foreign Affairs, December 1985. Y4
F76/: N51/21.

Review of the UN Commission on Human Rights, Hearings, Subcom-
mittee on Human Rights and International Organizations,
Committee on Foreign Affairs, House, June 1986. Y4 F76/1:
H88/41.

The Air War and Political Developments in El Salvador, Hearings,
Subcommittee on Western Hemisphere Affairs, Committee on
Foreign Affairs, House, May 1986, Y4 F76/1: Sa 3/9.

The Situation in Central America, Hearings, Senate Foreign
Relations Committee, April 1985. Y4 F76/2: S. hrg. 99-471.

Third World Debt Legislation, Hearings, Subcommittee on Inter-
national Development Institutions and Finance, Committee on
Banking, Finance, and Urban Affairs, House, March 1986. Y4
B22/1: 99-74.

Trends in Foreign Aid, 1977-86, Report Prepared by Congressional
Research Service for the Select Committee on Hunger, House,
1986. Y4 H89: F76/977-86.

United States Food Assistance and the Food Security Act of 1986,
International Task Force of the Select Committee on Hunger,
House, July 1986. Y4 H89:99-20.

United States Human Rights Policy, Hearings, Subcommittee on
Human Rights and International Organizations, Committee on
Foreign Affairs, House, February 1986. Y4 F76/1: H88/40.

United States Policy Toward Nicaragua: Aid to Nicaraguan Resistance Proposal, Hearings, Committee on Foreign Relations,
Senate, February-March 1986. Y4 F76/2: S.hrg. 99-645.

Other Publications

An Analysis of the President's Budgetary Proposal for FY 1986,
Congressional Budget Office, February 1985.

Annual Report of the Council of Economic Advisors, CEA, January
    1987.

Budget of the United States Government for FY 1988, Office of
    Management and Budget, January 1987.

Has Trade Protection Revitalized Domestic Industries, Congres-
    sional Budget Office, November 1986.

United States Contributions to International Organizations,
    Report to the Congress for the year 1985, Department of
    State, October 1986.

United States Participation in the United Nations for 1985,
    Department of State, October 1986.

World Population and Fertility Planning Technologies, Office of
    Technology Assessment, February 1982.

APPENDIX: Bibliographic and Research Note

Most of the materials included in the bibliography were obtained
through Social Sciences Index or Public Affairs Information
Service. Another index which will be useful on the 1987–88 topic
is Index to Legal Periodicals: international law journals
contain articles on treaties and international conventions of
themselves relevant to the topic, but also include discussions of
the substance of U.S. Latin American policy, particularly human
rights policy which will be useful sources of evidence.

Two international law publications of special value on the
1987–88 topic are Human Rights Quarterly and the American Journal
of International Law. Human Rights Quarterly provides theoretical articles about human rights, including the right to development, as well as survey articles on current human rights practices. The American Journal of International Law, published by
the American Society for International Law, in addition to
containing articles of interest on the topic, contains a number
of regular features of value to research. These include a
section entitled "Contemporary Practice of the United States
Relating to International Law," which is compiled by the Office
of the Legal Advisor of the Department of State and includes a
digest of current treaties, agreements, and exchanges between the
United States and other nations. The same publication also
includes a "Current Developments" section and an index to the
current issue of International Legal Materials, a State Department publication which reports both agreements to which the
United States is a party, as well as other international and
multilateral agreements. In addition, most law school international law review publications include comment sections on
current developments: international law review publications are
generally less available in law libraries than general subject
law reviews; American Journal of International Law and Harvard
Journal of International Law are probably the most widely available.

There are several other publications of use in following
recent developments or building research bibliographies. One is
a publication entitled Human Rights Internet Law Reporter (1338 G
Street, SE, Washington, DC 20003). This publication provides an
overview of activities and developments within the human rights
community, abstracts current publications on human rights, and
presents materials of groups investigating and reporting on human
rights situations throughout the world.

Several "annual" publications are of value. First, both
Foreign Affairs and Current History have issues devoted to
"roundups" of world affairs. In addition to being time-specific
and area-specific, these articles tend to be written in a more
journalistic style than in a research publication format: this
makes them more useful for novice research and for "quick and
dirty" country-by-country research and background analysis.
Foreign Affairs also contains a "chronology" section in a year-
end issue which indexes noteworthy events on a region-by-region
basis during the year.

There have been a number of current periodical articles about the bias of some sources, mainly about the Reagan Administration's support of the Contras, but with accusations being raised against both opponents and proponents of Administration policies. A central figure in this controversy is Robert S. Leiken of the Carnegie Endowment for International Peace. A sampler of such articles: Time, April 2, 1986, 48-49; Nation, March 15, 1986, 639, May 10, 1986, 294-295, and September 6, 1986, 164-165; and America, May 24, 1986, 432-434, and October 25, 1986, 218-219.

Finally, some introductory readings. There are a number of standard works in the history of U.S. Latin American affairs, most of which get bogged down between the Spanish-American War and the Good Neighbor Policy: the Molineau, Blackman, et.al., and Blasier books in the bibliography are more oriented toward U.S. policy since 1960. The Rosset and Vandermeer text, while now somewhat dated, provides a balanced collection of materials on the Sandinistas and U.S. policy toward Nicaragua. Lastly, Human Rights Quarterly, v. 6 (1984), has an excellent introductory article entitled "Human Rights" at pages 257-283, by Burns Weston of the University of Iowa Law School.

APPENDIX: 1983 NATIONAL DEBATE TOURNAMENT
FINAL DEBATE*

Edited by John K. Boaz

The Thirty-Seventh National Debate Tournament, sponsored by the American Forensic Association and the Ford Motor Company Fund, was held at The Colorado College in Colorado Springs, Colorado, on March 30-April 2, 1983.[1]   The sixty-two participating teams debated the 1982-83 intercollegiate debate proposition: "Resolved: That all United States military intervention into the internal affairs of any foreign nation or nations in the Western Hemisphere should be prohibited."

Eight preliminary and four elimination rounds, all using cross-examination debate format, resulted in this final debate[2] between the University of Kansas and Dartmouth College. Representing Kansas on the affirmative were Rodger Payne and Mark Gidley, and representing Dartmouth on the negative were Robin Jacobsohn and Thomas Lyon.   Judges awarded the decision to the affirmative team from Kansas.[3]   Critiques of the debate by the final round judges follow this transcript.   The test of the debate follows:[4]

FIRST AFFIRMATIVE CONSTRUCTIVE: RODGER PAYNE, KANSAS

On behalf of the University of Kansas, Mark and I want to express our sincere thanks to our fine coaching staff over the past four years, especially Dr. Parson, including the short-bald guy, the KU debaters, especially Paul, David, and Jerry, and our pleasure of debating in the 1983 NDT final round.[5]   We'd also like to thank Mike Hicks and Bill Holmes.

Cuba's proximity to the United States is unfortunately only reflected in geographic terms.

For reasons to be outlined below, Mark and I are Resolved: That all military intervention into the internal affairs of any foreign nation or nations of the Western Hemisphere should be prohibited.   Before offering the affirmative examples of the

---

*"1983 National Debate Tournament Final Debate: Should the United States Military Intervention into the Internal Affairs of any Foreign Nation or Nations in the Western Hemisphere be Prohibited."   *Journal of the American Forensic Association*, Summer 1983, pp. 23-61.

resolution, we submit observation (1):   Inherency.   (A)   Current
American-Cuban policies are antagonistic.   We begin our description of inherency by stating the obvious.   U.S.-Cuban relations
are unfriendly.   Professor Sergio Roca of Adelphi University
wrote in February of 1983, "Under the Reagan Administration,
United States policy toward Cuba has become uncompromisingly
tough, if not openly hostile."[6]   The motive for American policy
is also easily identified.   The Reagan Presidency accuses Cuba of
international militarism.   William LeoGrande, Director of Political Science at American University, explained this form of
military intervention in Spring 1982:   "The Reagan administration
has, from the outset, taken a hard line on Cuba, in part because
of Cuban assistance to revolutionaries in Central America.   The
administration has imposed new sanctions, including tightening
the economic embargo, and is attempting to re-isolate Cuba within
the hemisphere."[7]

(B)   Hard-line policies are not optimal.   American policy
toward Cuba is not likely to succeed as LeoGrande summarized in
Spring of 82:   "As unveiled thus far the Reagan administration's
policy options hold nothing new or innovative.   The rising war of
words, the renewed effort to isolate Cuban diplomatically, and
the tightening of the economic embargo are sanctions refurbished
from the 1960s.[8]   Having failed then, they are no more likely to
succeed today."[8]   Moreover, the U.S. position promotes tension.
As Michael Kryzanci, Associate Professor of Political Science at
Bridgewater State College wrote in 1982, "The present administration seems unwilling to negotiate with Cuba and is fostering a
heightened state of hostility between the two countries."[9]

The U.S. government with appropriate consultation with
allies will implement the following examples of the resolution
within six months:

Provision (I):   All U.S. military intervention into the
internal affairs of any foreign nation or nations of the Western
Hemisphere shall be prohibited.   Maximum enforcement for Provision I, except as delineated for Cuba in Provision II, will be a
fine of one United States dollar.   Normal democratic procedures
will be guaranteed.

Provision (II):   A. U.S. military intervention into the
internal affairs of Cuba will be prohibited, as outlined in the
following subpoints: (A)   All U.S. military personnel and
equipment at the military base on Guantanamo Bay will be with-
drawn.   (B) American trade and travel sanctions against Cuba will
be terminated.   (C) All unrequested U.S. military operations on
the island of Cuba will be prohibited.   All paramilitary attempts
to overthrow the current Cuban government will be prohibited.
(D) The radio station commonly identified as "Radio Marti" will
be prohibited.   (E) Enforcement for Provision II will be through
normal democratic procedures, which will include increased
communication between governments to assure compliance.   Appropriate penalties, up to and including fines and/or imprisonment
will be guaranteed for plan violators.   Government and private
options for future recommendation including but not limited to
alternative solutions, alternative causalities, and cost bene-

fits. (F) Any necessary funding will be appropriated through
normal budgetary processes. Affirmative speeches will be used to
clarify what we mean.

Advantage (I): Kansas prevents racial tensions. (A) Cuban
immigration is coming. Unfortunately, hard-line policies increase immigration. As LeoGrande says in '82, "Cuba can now
strike back in ways that it could not before; Castro could
unleash ... Cuban refugees from Mariel."[10] Dominguez said in
'81, "Havana has signaled that it is ready to open the gates
again" [to allow Cubans to emigrate].[11] The scale of such
immigration was noted by LeoGrande in 1982. He said, "The flow
of tens of thousands of exiles [from Cuba] could be resumed at
any time."[12] T. B. Miller said in '81, "When allowed to do so,
Cubans emigrate in their [sic] scores of thousands."[13] McColm
and Maier said in '81, "According to exile leaders currently ...,
as many as one million to three million Cubans might be involved
in a second boatlift."[14]

(B) Immigration promotes societal disorder. This was
empirically documented by Business Week in June of 1980: "The
massive influx of Cubans in recent weeks has focused the attention of the nation on a problem too long ignored. If a solution
is not found soon, the nation is heading for social and economic
explosions that will make the recent fiery riots in Miami --
touched off by a criminal case verdict but attributable in part
to ethnic competition for jobs -- look like a Boy Scout's camp-
fire."[15] The chances of new tensions are even greater today. As
Newsweek indicated in January of '83, "'Miami has not changed
much since 1980,' said black state Sen. Carrie Meak. 'It's still
capable of blowing up at any time.'"[16] Steven Mumford said in
'81, "In these pressures [from massive immigration into U.S.] lie
the dangers of widespread terrorism, crime against persons and
property at a higher rate than now believed possible, and ultimately, societal disintegration. In comparison, the possibility
of a conventional armed attack from the Soviet Union becomes a
threat of lesser importance."[17] Masotti said in '69, "But before
the militant leaders push the Negro community beyond the point of
no return, we must do some sober thinking about the consequences
of such a confrontation. American society itself would be the
ultimate loser. We would become the captives of fear and hate of
a magnitude which would make Nazi Germany and apartheid South
Africa seem like meccas for civil libertarians."[18]

(C) The affirmative solves. William LeoGrande said in
Spring of '82, "A realistic assessment of the advantages to the
United States or pursuing a strategy of gradual engagement with
Cuba shows that limited gains, particularly on bilateral issues,
are fairly certain ... Such gains may not be impressive, but
they are nevertheless superior to the results achieved over the
past two decades by a policy of hostility."[19] The New York Times
said December 1980, "[Castro] ... said Cuba was ready to work
toward a 'reasonable and constructive agreement' on Cuban emigration to the United States."[20]

Advantage (II): Kansas prevents a U.S.-Cuban war. (A)
Military confrontation is assured. After twenty years of hard-

line policies, the threat of direct military action against Cuba has never loomed so large. The Council on Hemispheric Affairs [COHA] reported this on November 4, 1981: "COHA has learned that high on the agenda is the serious consideration of military actions against Cuba."[21] While some may scoff at such a possibility, the threat is real, as Flora Lewis wrote in May 1982: "A Canadian parliamentary commission that studied the area's urgent problems for nearly a year concluded that 'potentially the most dangerous threat to security in these regions [is] the growing confrontation between the United States and Cuba.'"[22] A second manifestation of the hard line is the threat of naval blockade against Cuba. As The Philadelphia Inquirer editorialized in February '81, "There is a clear danger that the U.S. will move to blockade Cuba."[23] The Quarterly Economic Review of Cuba, Dominican Republic, Haiti and Puerto Rico assessed this risk in the fourth quarter of '81: State Department counselor Robert MacFarlane said, "[T]here was a strong possibility that the Reagan administration might go through with its election threat of creating an interAmerican naval force to cordon off Central America from shipments of arms from Cuba. Practically, such a maneuver would have to escalate into a more comprehensive naval blockade."[24] While the risk from hard-line policies is already great, a number of even more haunting aspects of U.S. policies trouble us. Initially note that the Reagan administration is building a case that the '62 Missile Crisis agreement has been abrogated. This could trigger a U.S. military response. William Safire noted in February '82, "[T]he U.S. is building a case that the 1962 Khrushchev-Kennedy agreement removing offensive weaponry from Cuba has been abrogated by Moscow. This would mean that the U.S. is no longer bound to refrain from using force against that Soviet base."[25] Further, Reagan's preoccupation with Cuban subversion throughout Central America might cause the administration to go to the source. Professor Gonzalez of UCLA explained in the Fall of '82, "If left unchecked, the latent security threat presently posed by Cuban-Soviet activities in the Caribbean Basin could grow to such a degree that Washington would have to employ a military solution for the Cuba problem as in the 1962 missile crisis."[26] This threat seems to grow day by day, as the recent Reagan focus on El Salvador indicates. Carl Rowan wrote on March 10th of '83, "The idea [of a U.S. move against Cuba] seems less preposterous as this administration pours forth more and more rhetoric portraying Cuba as the great communist subverter in this hemisphere."[27]

(B) American actions are disastrous. First, note that an invasion would cost countless American lives--as Lynn Darrell Bender of Inter-American University wrote in '81: "On that occasion [Cuban Missile Crisis], former Secretary of Defense McNamara estimated that an invading force of U.S. troops would have had to expect 40-50,000 casualties. Today the far better equipped and trained Cuban forces would be even more effective."[28] Another problem with such an intervention is the threat of regional warfare--as the Council on Hemispheric Affairs reported November 4th, '81: "U.S. moves against Cuba would inevitably trigger a violent response from the Castro government which could easily escalate into regionalized warfare."[29]   Such regionalization is not the only threat of escalation, however. An invasion would surely be met with a Soviet response.   Professor Dominguez of Harvard explains the reasoning in 1979: "The presence of Soviet advisors, equipment, and some ships in Cuba serves as a 'trip wire.'"[30]   LeoGrande concluded in Spring '82, "[A]n invasion would provoke an immediate confrontation with the Soviet Union."[31]   Moreover, a blockade would also invite Soviet confrontation as Lynn-Darrell Bender said in '81: [Naval blockade] "employment would carry the great risk of engaging the Soviet Union in a direct confrontation."[32]   The impact of such a confrontation with the Soviet Union seems obvious. For the sake of argument, however, one can examine the predicted effects of such actions during the Cuban Missile Crisis of '62.   Edgar O'Ballance described the crisis in September of '78 as having "nearly sparked off World War III."[33]   In fact, Charles Krauthammer wrote in April '82, "When did we come closest to nuclear war in the last 36 years?   In October 1962."[34]   The risk seems even greater today as Dr. Kolkowicz argued January '82: "[T]he Soviets may believe 'no more Cubas ...' I'm referring to the Cuban missile crisis where we humiliated them. The no-more-Cuba syndrome is very powerful, particularly in the military/defense circles of the Soviet Union. They will not again blink first if confronted by us."[35]   Senator Weicker noted in April '82, "[M]ilitarily we could go ahead and squash Cuba ... If we did ... we would lose not only this hemisphere but probably the whole world."[36]

(C) Kansas solves. By banning the actions described, we clearly solve this harm. Human Events reported December 11th '82: Lowenthal "stressed that one of the real worries is that we might blunder into a global war with the Soviet Union over the area [of Central America]. To avoid this kind of catastrophe, we 'should immediately take steps, therefore, to reassure the Soviet Union that our government will continue to respect Cuba's territorial integrity.'"[37]   Moreover, by ending the trade embargo, we ease the tensions that cause war as the Christian Century reported May 5th '82: "[Reagan] could display his ability to tamp down war fears. All he needs to do is lift the trade embargo and establish normal relations with a neighbor 90 miles to the south."[38]

Advantage (III): Kansas improves the Cuban way of life.

(A) Cuba is repressive. Representative Baltasar Corrada explains the general situation in July of 1977: "The people of Cuba are currently submitted to personal persecutions, continuous harassment and a police state vigilance. Indiscriminate mass arrests, without legitimate cause and without evident purpose, are commonplace and daily occurrences which have become, due to their frequency, acceptable and normal."[39]   The State Department elaborated further in February of '81: "Cuba is a totalitarian Marxist-Leninist state. Under the 1976 constitution, the government may restrict any right or freedom when exercised in opposition to the state."[40]   Finally, please note that Cuba has one of the worst human rights records in the world as Irving Horowitz, Professor of Political Science at Rutgers wrote in '81: "Similarly, Congressman Harold Hollenbeck ... constantly draws attention to the fact that Cuba is one of the biggest violators of human rights in the world."[41]

(B) Kansas solves. First, please note that it is current hard-line policies that cause [Cuban] repression as Lowenthal of Brookings Institution said in April '81: "Washington's previous bursts of hostility may have helped Castro consolidate his hold in Havana and given him a plausible pretext for harsh repression."[42]   Finally, we note that a policy of negotiating with Cuba allows the United States to gain leverage to deal with this problem. Carmelo Mesa-Lago of the Center for Latin American Studies wrote in '78, "If it [U.S.] decides to take the initiative and does not neglect the interests of the Cuban people at the bargaining table, it may induce the slow transformation of the current centralist-dogmatic and Soviet-dependent Cuban regime into a more democratic and independent socialist system."[43]

Kansas feels the best policy towards Cuba is a friendly one. Vote affirmative. Vote for Kansas.

CROSS-EXAMINATION: THOMAS LYON QUESTIONING PAYNE

Lyon: OK. It will be implemented within six months. When do we know that it has been passed? Payne: What do you mean? Lyon: That is, when do we know that we are going to implement the policy? Payne: Well, sometime within the next six months the U.S. government implements our plan--or at least should implement our plan. Lyon: Now what does the "U.S. government" mean? Payne: I mean obviously the United States government never takes action on Kansas' affirmative.

Lyon: Right. So, what does "the U.S. government" mean? Payne: Well, there are a number of different channels that that could be. I mean that could mean that the President does this through executive order. That could mean that the Congress does this with the President voting for it or vetoing and overriding.

Lyon: Who decides? Payne: I mean, that's something that we don't feel that can be debated accurately, because it's obviously impossible to tell. We only say that the United States government should adopt this policy. Lyon: OK. Can it be that--that simply the President decides not to intervene? Payne: No--Lyon: I mean there does have to be a prohibition, right? Payne: That's true. Lyon: So it prevents into the future? Payne: Right. We forbid by legislation. This is the legislation--Lyon: OK. Payne: --or executive order which is the equivalent.

Lyon: All right. How, how is Radio Marti and lifting the trade embargo military intervention? Payne: Well, I'll do Radio Marti first. There's a number of reasons. First of all, there's a lot of evidence that indicates it could spark a war. Also, the

Department of Defense is building this, and it's obviously intervening in their internal affairs. The trade embargo is an act of war. It was imposed for military reasons. Lyon: OK. So any acts of hostility which might lead to war are bound by the plan then? Payne: That's not true. Lyons: Well, then how is Radio Marti intervention? Payne: Well, the Department of Defense has this radio station in South Florida--Lyon: Right. Payne: --that's going to broadcast. Lyon: And you say it's military--Oh, then it's because it's the Department of Defense does it? Payne: That's a very good reason. Lyon: So, if someone else did it, would it be military intervention? Payne: The Radio Marti we're banning is the government radio station built by the Department of Defense and, you know, spreading military propaganda.

Lyon: OK. All right now, if this is legislation, and we assume this is enforced upon the President? Payne: Well, the President could be the one who implements--as I indicated this could be executive order. Lyon: But you agree it is--Oh, so it's not legislation any more, it's executive order? Payne: Well, I said executive order is legislation's equivalent.

Lyon: All right. Do you assume attitude change? Payne: I don't think you have to assume attitude change. We should convince these five judges that they should vote for our proposal.

Lyon: I see. Now, that means we can't consider--How is it a prohibition if it's simply a decision not to--to go in? Payne: Well, this is by legislation. Our definition of prohibition--Lyon: OK. So, if it is by legislation--Payne: --is to forbid by legislation. Executive order is the same thing. Lyon: So, if it is executive order, then do we assume that the President has changed his mind about going into Cuba? Payne: Well, given the inherency evidence that--that would probably have to be an assumption, but as I said, we just--the United States government. Lyons: Wouldn't that be an assumption? Payne: If it were executive order, that means the Reagan administration probably had--would have had to change its mind--Lyon: I see. Payne: --but we don't necessarily think that that's the way this plan would be proposed or adopted. Lyon: So, it is possible that your plan is an executive order, and Congress is opposed to the policy? Payne: Well, I think this is, you know, really irrelevant, since we're convincing these five judges to vote for our plan.

FIRST NEGATIVE CONSTRUCTIVE: ROBIN JACOBSOHN, DARTMOUTH

On behalf of Dartmouth College, Tom and I would like to express our gratitude to Al Johnson, Mike Hazen, and their staffs for this great National Debate Tournament. We would also like to thank Herb, Ken, Steve, Ike, Karen, and all the other Dartmouth debaters at home and abroad; and I'd also like to thank my brother, Mark, and Dusty. Tom and I would like to dedicate this

round to Lenny and Mark, the only team in this room to go undefeated and two pretty terrific guys. Without their help and
sacrifice in more ways than one we would not be here.[44]

Disad[vantage]: Rose tint my world. (A) subpoint: Europe
opposes U.S. hard-line. Griffith of MIT [Massachusetts Institute
of Technology] says in '83, "[B]y 1982 the assessments of the
governments in Washington and in Western Europe of Soviet policy
and the Soviet threat to NATO differed sharply. For Reagan,
detente, always a fraud, was dead; the Soviet threat was much
greater ... Western Europe's main aim, in contrast, was to
maintain itself as an island of detente."[45]

(B) subpoint: U.S. hard-line in Central America divides the
alliance. Leiken, CSIS [Center for Strategic and International
Studies], in '82: "U.S. military actions in Central America ...
[would serve] to heighten pacifist and neutralist tendencies in
... Europe and further dividing the Alliance."[46] Sanders,
Columbia, in '82: "[The Reagan] administration's ideological
hostility toward the Soviet Union ... has done something to the
NATO alliance that the Soviet Union has not been able to do for
all these years--tear the alliance to the seams."[47]

(C) subpoint: NATO is on the brink of collapse. Senator
Nunn says in '82, "The North Atlantic Treaty Organization today
faces multiple problems which if left unresolved, could destroy
the Alliance as a credible collective security organization."[48]

(D) subpoint is to, first impact: NATO collapse averts
World War III through Finlandization. (1) NATO collapse assures
Finlandization. Pilat at the CRS [Congressional Research Ser-
vice] says in '82, "[A] deeper and more abiding effect might
emerge [from allied disagreement], ... a reduction in the power
and cohesion of the Atlantic Alliance, and even the Finlandization of Europe."[49] This is subpoint (2): Finlandization
prevents World War III. Sloan, CRS, in '82: [The authors
Beilenson and Cohen] "have recently argued that, 'To remain so
entangled is to invite a Soviet nuclear strike against the United
States in any war that starts in Europe--to risk our national
survival. We can survive without the Western Alliance, even if
the Europeans elect to accommodate to the Soviet Union rather
than provide for their own defense. But nuclear war can kill
us.'"[50] Of course, this war is highly probable as Novak says in
'82: "Another great European war could break out before this
century's end."[51]

This is the (E) subpoint, second impact: NATO collapse
averts World War III through preventing TNF [theatre nuclear
forces] deployment. Subpoint (1): Decreased NATO cohesion stops
TNF deployment. Record of the IFPA [Institute for Foreign Policy
Analysis, Inc.] says in '81, "[F]ull implementation of the
decision to deploy 572 new long-range theatre nuclear missiles
... is justifiably regarded as an acid test of political cohesion
within the Alliance."[52] This is subpoint (2): Increases the
risk of war. [Unintelligible] says in '80, The deployment in
Europe of American tactical cruise missiles [unintelligible]
missiles [unintelligible] is likely to enhance NATO's perception
of the [unintelligible] nuclear war. Modernizing will not make

the threat any more credible, but it might increase the probability of a nuclear war in Europe.[53]
    Caseside. First contention (Observation I). (A) subpoint
talks about our antagonistic policy toward Cuba. Evidence here
proving the link in the disad describing our unchanging hard-line
attitude toward Cuba. (B) subpoint says, this is not optimal.
First subpoint (1): There is no impact to the hostility and the
particular ones that are different from the 1AC [first affirmative constructive] evidence will be dealt with later on. Second
argument (2): Hard-line is [unintelligible] to maintain the
effect it is having on the alliance now. Third argument (3) is
as soon as you can topically eliminate the economic embargo which
is not military intervention. Study for the Washington Center
for Foreign Policy Research, Johns Hopkins in '65: "This section
will deal with all types of nonmilitary alignments ... They, too,
are instruments with which to combat common adversaries though by
economic, psychological, or diplomatic 'warfare' only."[54]
    This is racial tensions. First advantage (I) Number (1):
Preparation to release them does not mean that Castro will
actually do so. Thus, I'd indicate, what would cause him to
actually do so? (2) Trouble is the U.S. can merely tighten the
borders and prevent them from coming in. (3) Third argument is
soft-line actually caused the Mariel incident. At the turn,
Gonzalez of UCLA [University of California at Los Angeles] says
in '82, "[A] by-product of the thaw," with Carter, "was the
return of tens of thousands of Cuban exiles to their homeland on
brief visits, which in turn precipitated the surge of political
unrest that suddenly confronted the regime in 1979-80, and which
ended with the mass exodus of 125,00 Cubans in the 1980 'Freedom
Flotilla'"--which was Mariel. "Indirectly, therefore, U.S.
policy contributed to developments that had significant impact
within Cuba by allowing the return of the exiles."[55] That caused
political unrest within Cuba which caused Castro to send them
back. More evidence from the Miami Herald in '83: "... [I]llegal
boatlifts, in which a Cuba can dump its unwanted onto an obliging
neighbor, remain a threat because the fundamental blunders made
by President Carter out of misplaced humanitarian motives are
likely to be repeated by successive U.S. Presidents who haven't
done their homework."[56] Reagan has.
    This is the fourth argument: (4) Exile backlash. The
hard-line exile rightists who have left Cuba will actually
backlash and cause terrorism in the U.S. As Casal says in '79,
"As the United States and Cuba move toward normalization of
relations, an increase in the violent activities of groups toward
the extreme right of the exile political spectrum can be expected
... Their dangerousness and, at the very least, their nuisance
value cannot be over-emphasized."[57] Casal says, "Faced with the
prospect of a change in U.S. policy toward Cuba, the most conservative elements in the Cuban community reacted with verbal and
physical terrorism."[58]
    This is the fifth argument: (5) Assumes that U.S. invasion
actually would occur. Will not be proven. Argued below.
    Sixth subpoint: (6) His impact evidence is from Mariel in

'80. They were eventually absorbed into the Florida community. Disproves any harms.

Seventh response: (7) Assumes increased relations which will not occur. Ambler Moss, Former U.S. Ambassador to Panama, says in October '82, "[B]oth the Carter and Reagan administrations have seriously tested [their chances of accommodation with Cuba and] found no possibility of success."[59]

Second advantage (II). (A) subpoint talks about invasion. (1) Evidence only proves rhetorical threats not that we'll actually follow through. None of it does so. Subpoint (2): Evidence is also incredibly old. Most of it is in '81 or early '82. Changes in the political conditions and the U.S.-Cuban relations have made it different. Third argument: (3) U.S. won't undertake military action. Gonzalez [sic], UCLA and Rand, says in '82: These Cuban defense preparations may seem overdrawn, gives the implausibility for an actual U.S. military assault on Cuba.[60] (4) Political barriers preclude. New York Times March '83: "DeConcini asked Shultz what he thought about using force to stop aid to the insurgents, a plan once given serious thought by Shultz's predecessor, ... Haig ..., who also advocated going 'to the source,' [Shultz] said wryly that it was 'difficult enough' to get the committee to approve the current level of 55 American military 'trainers' in El Salvador, 'let alone one military adviser, let alone ... American troops, so I don't sense any great political mood for us to conduct an armed U.S. force there."[61]

This is the next argument: (5) Only threats to Castro. Gonzalez [sic] in '82: "No doubt the principal aim of these threats is to intimidate Cuba into reducing its support for revolutionary movements abroad, and perhaps even reducing its general activism in foreign affairs."[62]

Next response is (6) risk of Soviet nukes deter. Dominguez of Harvard in '78: "Since 1960 the Soviet nuclear shield has been one factor deterring a United States attack on Cuba, somewhat shakily in 1960 and more firmly after 1970."

The next argument: (7) Cuban defense capability deters. They read evidence from Dominguez saying it would cause loss of American lives. That is why Dominguez concludes we would not go in. He says in '79 that "This 'bee-sting' capability may well be too high a price for any U.S. government to pay in the foreseeable future."[64] He continues, "Cuban force structure is probably sufficient to deter an invasion of the island."[65]

The next argument: (8) Cuba's third world leadership role deters. LeoGrande, American University, '82: "Cuba has sought similar prominence," as Tito, in the third world, "as protection from attack by the United States or abandonment by the Soviet Union ... [B]y creating a constituency in the Third World, Cuba could ... raise the diplomatic cost to both superpowers for policies unfavorable to Cuba."[66]

The last response is (9) no blockade. Boston Globe March '83: "After lengthy internal deliberation, the buildup of enormous U.S. public apprehension and submission of a secret plan by Haig to impose a sea blockade of Cuba, this approach was rejected by Reagan as too risky."[67]

Oh, I'm sorry, the final action is--are (10) no covert action. Washington Post '83: "Congressional sources said recently those plans ...," covert, paramilitary against Cuba, "were never executed after meeting with stiff Congressional opposition."[68]

Final response: (11) Some near term probability has to be given. Otherwise, you don't know if the Soviets would respond in the future. Maybe they'd get bogged down even more into Poland or someplace and would not be able to respond, or the U.S. administration might not do so, or that Cuba would not respond. Has to get some near term probability.

On the (B) subpoint, number (1): Lives lost assumes a full scale invasion which is only one of the scenarios they gave above.

Subpoint (2). Regionalization assumes that we fail to overthrow Cuba and others in the hemisphere support Castro. That is not proven either.

Third response: (3) Soviets would back down. This is Whalen in '82: The Soviets will exploit their opportunities to keep as long as possible but when confronted by genuine American resolve the Soviets quite likely will abandon Cuba as they [unintelligible] twenty years ago. And in the absence of massive Soviet support the Castro regime would quickly collapse."[69]

This is subpoint (4): Use arms as a substitute for action. U.S. News in '81: "The belief is that because Moscow will not confront the U.S. over Cuba, it is giving Castro the weapons to fight on his own."[70]

(5). No defense commitment. Cuba in the World '79: "The USSR has long posed as the protector of Cuba, trying to give the impression that Soviet armed forces would rush to Cuba's defense if she were attacked by the United States. Yet the USSR has been careful not to commit herself formally to do so, and Cuba's exclusion from the Warsaw pact is not an accident."[71]   (6): Cubans out to prove. St. Louis Post Dispatch, July '82: Cubans have reason to doubt that their protector would actually protect them should the tough-talking right-winger in the White House vent American frustrations on Cuba.[72]   (7): Conventional strength is the key to deterrence. Thus, a disad, since you need conventional force availability to deter crisis escalation. Rusk, McNamara, Ball, Gilpatric say in '82: "The decisive military element in the resolution of the ['62] crisis was our clearly available and applicable superiority in conventional weapons within the area of the crisis. U.S. naval forces, quickly deployable for the blockade of offensive weapons that was sensibly termed a quarantine, and the availability of U.S. ground and air forces sufficient to execute an invasion if necessary, made the difference."[74]   (8): Soviets won't confront us in Latin America. South Mag says in '82: "Realizing the strong geo-political position of the U.S., Moscow would be content to see the U.S. hold in Latin America diminished and loosened. But even with this limited goal, the Soviet Union is not terribly active

.... Moscow applauds the struggle, but would not intervene. It is prepared to guarantee that the only interventions in Latin America would come from the U.S., as so often in the past."[74] (9) They would only do it with proxies. South Magazine continues: The Soviet Union "is content to provide limited support to revolutionary elements in the region. The belief is that history is on the side of the revolutionary struggle."[75]

The last response here is that (10) it would actually shift to the Middle East, if we don't go into Cuba. (a) subpoint: Western Hemisphere precludes Middle East intervention. Leiken, CSIS, '81: "U.S. military actions in Central America would ... bog down the U.S. politically and perhaps militarily in the Caribbean Basin thus robbing us of freedom of action elsewhere."[76] Montgomery, Oklahoma State, in '80: "That study" [by the Library of Congress] "concluded that successful operation of ground forces in the Persian Gulf would depend on the absence of U.S. involvement anywhere else at the same time .... One consequent scenario far from the Gulf but affecting plans for forwarding of supplies and manpower from the U.S. to those waters pits the U.S. against Russian interests in the Caribbean and Central America."[77]

(b) subpoint: Middle East intervention is likely. First, (1) is general reasons. ((a)) subpoint is this is the RDF [Rapid Deployment Force] mind set. Klare says in '81: "[T]he RDF is an army in search of a war. And the chances of finding a war must be considered exceptionally high."[78] ((b)) subpoint is alternative subverted: MERIP [Middle East Research & Information Project] Reports in '83: "[T]he availability of a rapid deployment force will make it much easier for the U.S. to intervene militarily in a situation it might otherwise have had to resolve by political or diplomatic means. It thus makes it more rather than less likely that Washington's interventionary impulse will translate into armed actions."[79]

This is subpoint ((2)): Regional instability. ((a)) MERIP Reports in '83: "The propensity to see Soviet subversion and Soviet proxies behind any local upheaval, ... make it difficult to rule out military measures against local Soviet allies and interests in the area [Persian Gulf]. Indeed, the possibility of such an intervention against Iran must be considered quite high."[80] This is subpoint ((b)): Perceived Soviet threat. Klare says in '81, The RDF preemptive strategy "obviously suggest a 'hair-trigger' stance in which American forces would be sent overseas at the first sign of a crisis .... It doesn't take much imagination to recognize that such a 'first strike' posture could prove a shortcut to catastrophe. It might, in some cases, force the 'other guy' to back down--but it might just as easily result in a major conflagration that could otherwise have been prevented."[81] Subpoint (c) is the impact: First is (1) regional escalation. Shapley in '80: "[T]he Mideast-Persian Gulf area is bristling with international even tribal conflicts, and the Middle East nations are as heavily armed as NATO."[82] Subpoint (2): Soviet response escalates. Grayson in '82: "Should this country attempt to introduce major combat units into Afghanistan

and Iran, for example, Moscow would fear their possible utiliza-
tion against Soviet territory and conclude that the risk of
reacting militarily was less than if it did not respond."[83]
Subpoint (3): [unintelligible] in Latin America. Klare in '80:
"So long as the R.D.F. is confined to military backwaters like
Central America or the Caribbean, the greatest danger we would
have to face is a nasty guerrilla war and worldwide condemnation
like that produced by the Soviet invasion of Afghanistan, but if
forces are sent to the Middle East or other highly armed regions,
we may find ourselves in a quagmire that will make Vietnam look
like a mud puddle."[84]

On repression, last advantage. (1): No problem in Cuba.
John Davis says in '83, "I expected an atmosphere of political
control, if not coercion. I could not have been more wrong."[85]
Dominguez, Harvard, '78: "Stable authoritarian rule does not
require continual repression, and repressive acts are relatively
rare in contemporary Cuba."[86] Subpoint (2): Media bias exagger-
ates abuse. Davis in '83: "The expectation that I would find
Cubans poor and fearful made me aware of how easy it is to be
seduced by the American press. I have visited many Caribbean
nations and the standard of living for the average Cuban is, at
the very least, the equal of the best of them."[87] Third response
is (3) the evidence above takes out. [Unintelligible] Fourth
response is (4) Turnaround. Evidence comes from Dadrian in '76:
"Given the magnitude and precedent setting character of the crime
of genocide, external deterence is of paramount import."[88] He
continues: Moreover, the fact of non-interference can tempt and
may even embolden other groups inclined toward, or bent on
destroying their own minorities as a matter of following up
precedents."[89]

Underview, "Any"--"Every." (A) subpoint: Grammatically
means "every." (1) In affirmative sentences "any" means "every."
Words and Phrases in '57: "'Any' in affirmative sentences is
equivalent to 'every' or 'all.'"[90] The topic is clearly an
affirmative sentence. It uses the words "resolved" and "should
be prohibited." (2) In implied negative sentences "any" means
"every." Century Dictionary and Encyclopedia says, "When any is
preceded by a negative, expressed or implied, the two are together equivalent to an emphatic negative, 'none at all,' 'not
even one': as, there has never been any doubt about that."[91]

(B) subpoint: There is no ambiguity. Pennsylvania Casualty
v. Elkins says, "The adjective 'any,' in effect, is equivalent
to every. It serves to enlarge the scope of the phrase 'any
employee,' as used in the exclusion clause of the policy, so as
to clearly negative the idea that it was used in a restrictive
sense ... That such is the significance of 'any,' as ordinarily
used and popularly understood, is attested to by all standard
dictionaries. There is no need for resort to technical rules of
interpretation or construction."[92]

Our position on the Middle East is pretty much that there is
going to be intervention one way or the other, and it would be
better to have it in Cuba, since Middle East has worst risks.

CROSS-EXAMINATION: PAYNE QUESTIONING JACOBSOHN

Payne: I may be wrong, but doesn't the plan repeat the resolution word for word? Jacobsohn: Yes, it does. Payne: Do you want to explain to me how we don't meet "any" and "all"? Jacobsohn: Well, the plan has differential enforcement provisions. Payne: What does that mean? Why does that matter? Jacobsohn: Well, it means that, since you don't enforce the same for one, then it's not a prohibition at all. Payne: What's your definition of a prohibition? Jacobsohn: Prohibition is to establish--to prevent. Payne: Do you think topicality should be judged by effects? Jacobsohn: I'm not sure.

Payne: Let's talk about this disadvantage on Europe. Now, the link is--Jacobsohn: I mean that wasn't the end of my definition. I take it you don't want to hear the rest. Payne: Whatever. Jacobsohn: OK. Payne: The link. Leiken says, if we intervene in Central America, then it would increase pacifism in Europe. Right? Jacobsohn: No, it talks about our current hard-line. Payne: Just the current hard-line? Jacobsohn: Yeh. Payne: Could I see the Leiken evidence, please? Jacobsohn: Sure. Payne: Now, I know it wasn't in the card that you read, but in that same sentence he talks about Japan. Right? Jacobsohn: Um, I didn't research it. I honestly don't know. Payne: All right. Is this from Washington Quarterly? Jacobsohn: You'll have to wait 'til I find it. Payne: All right. Jacobsohn: All right.

Payne: The Finlandization impact. Now, your argument is they're going to Finlandize now, and you are going to prevent that? The present system prevents that? Jacobsohn: The argument is that NATO is on the brink, that our hard-line would cause NATO to collapse, and then it would Finlandize, which would be good. Finlandization would be good. It would stop a war. Payne: So we need to have the hard-line to cause Finlandization? Jacobsohn: Again Cuba to break up NATO to cause Finlandization and for TNFs.

Payne: Is West German proliferation good? Jacobsohn: Well, I guess it depends on what perspective you're looking at it from. [laughter] Payne: Let's say from the Soviet perspective. Jacobsohn: Well, it probably would have good results in the long run. Payne: Good results in the long run. I see. Jacobsohn: I mean, you know, that's hard to say. I mean you can argue it both ways.

Payne: TNFs. Now, these are the TNFs, I assume, that are supposed to be starting to be deployed December 1983. Jacobsohn: I believe that's the day. I mean they're the same missiles. Payne: Same missiles. All right. They don't increase our credibility, but they do cause Europe to have a greater chance of war? Jacobsohn: Right. Payne: What is that? Jacobsohn: Because it gets the Soviets upset. Payne: So the Soviets don't like nuclear weapons so close to them in Europe? Jacobsohn: I imagine that has part--you know--a great deal to do with it. Payne: Can you tell me what difference it makes whether the Europeans have American nuclear weapons? Is there any difference between American nuclear weapons and, say, German nuclear weapons? Jacobsohn: Yeh. Payne: What is that? Jacobsohn: Well, I mean, make the argument, because we haven't talked about West German prolif. Payne: I know, I'm just saying, should—should you know, this occur, would there be any difference? Jacobsohn: Well, I would imagine the fact that West Germany is closer to them and that they've had a different relationship might make a difference. Payne: But we're going to deploy these TNFs in Germany. Right? Jacobsohn: Well, that's one place, but they'll be under U.S. control. Payne: All right.

Payne: Could   I   see   this   Leiken   evidence,   please? Jacobsohn: Sure. That's—third card. I mean, you're right, it blips, so I don't—

SECOND AFFIRMATIVE CONSTRUCTIVE: MARK GIDLEY, KANSAS

At the end of this debate you have to decide whether there is a good option to intervene into Cuba. We would indicate that that's an indefensible option. In terms of the (A) subpoint, they indicate that we are poised at the brink right now. The evidence in '82 doesn't assume any recent changes. (B) subpoint, they indicate the hard-line causes. First, the evidence comes from Leiken in '82. Evidence doesn't indicate that they think it would cause pacifism or other things the Reagan hard-line could cause. (C) subpoint, they indicate brink now. The evidence comes from Nunn in 1982. He indicates a number of problems, indicating NATO would smash up for many reasons. (D1) subpoint, in terms of Finlandization. First argument is, of course, it would take more. (2) The 1AC—!NC [first negative constructive] doesn't indicate what the time frame is in terms of Finlandization. (E) argument, in terms of World War III, (1) subpoint, they indicate decreased NATO cohesion now. First argument here is (1) there is no link evidence. The evidence she reads indicates that the Pershing II missile crisis is merely an acid test. There is no evidence which indicates we're on the brink now. (E2) argument, she indicates that they would attack and be a war, but (2) the evidence indicates no explanation.

(F) Underviews to the argument. We indicate (1) evidence does not assume co—of course co-election indicates NATO is strong now.

Second argument is (2) does not assume TNF talks. We would indicate TNF talks take out the link.

Third argument is (3) does not prove that pacifism will be effective, doesn't indicate what the pacifists will win in West Germany.

Fourth argument is (4) turnaround. West German prolif. (a) subpoint, of course, decrease in the alliance will decrease in the alliance will decrease West German prolif. Will increase West German prolif as Fisher indicates in 1975: "[A] strong alliance policy I think is the viable alternative to the pressures in Germany that might want to go nuclear."[94] Evidence comes from Dunn who indicates in 1982, "West German confidence in the NATO alliance and the U.S. nuclear umbrella will remain critical to minimizing its incentives to acquire nuclear weapons."[95]

(b) subpoint: It would cause World War III if they acquired. As Lefever indicates in 1979, "As Henry Kissinger said, 'Germany cannot have a nuclear capability, because if it did the Russians would go to war.'"[96] Fisher indicated in 1975, "I think if they (West Germany) went independent in nuclear capability it would be the greatest threat to peace."[97]

Fifth argument is, of course, (5) the evidence indicates in terms of the above impact risk that the NATO war may occur by the year 2000. Of course the case was for the immediate.

Sixth argument is, of course, (6) the hard-line is already decreasing now. Reagan's already decreased the intervention policy into Nicaragua. The Congress has done that through the Bohland amendment.

Seventh argument is, (7) his rhetoric has decreased now. Evidence comes from the New York Times in January of 1983: "The Reagan administration, once given to tough statements about the need to confront insurgencies in Central America, has softened its tone."[98] Boston Globe indicates in March of 1983: "Enders .... has toned down his rhetoric since the departure of his patron, Alexander M. Haig."[99]

Eighth argument, of course, is (8) the plan can be done credibly by Reagan. Evidence comes from Christian Century in May of 1982: "The time would seem appropriate to lift the trade embargo ... [T]he Reagan administration is well known to be strongly anticommunist. No charges of 'appeasement' threaten this government."[100]

Argument number nine is, of course, (9) there would be no war. Several reasons. (a) subpoint is terrain would prevent war. Evidence comes from Center for Defense Information in 1980: "In terms of terrain alone, any Warsaw Pact aggression against the West would be fraught with obstacles, hazards and high risks."[101]

(b) subpoint is fear of naval blockade of Europe will deter Soviets. Dyer indicates in '77, "Assuming that a Soviet rush to the English Channel would have overrun NATO and 250,000 American troops .... American troops .... America might well use its naval forces to reduce the flow of oil. An occupied Western Europe without sufficient oil could turn out to be more of a liability than a benefit to the USSR."[102]

(c) subpoint is Warsaw Pact forces are not reliable. As Gelb indicates in 1980, "[H]ow can they [the Soviets] count on their Eastern European allies when Romania refuses to permit Warsaw Pact exercises on its territory, will not let Soviet troops cross its borders, and voted against Moscow on Afghanistan in the United Nations General Assembly?"[103] Kaplan indicates in '75, "The political reliability of the Czechoslovak and Polish divisions, at least for offensive warfare, is doubtful."[104]

(d) subpoint is NATO invasion is on balance too risky. As Boston Study Group indicates in '79, "[P]olitically and militarily, a war in Central Europe looks very improbably. The stakes of such a gamble are too high and the chance of winning too low to warrant such adventurism on the part of either side."[105] Indicating we are stable now.

Topicality argument. First argument is (1) affirmative standards. (a) subpoint, of course, the affirmative has the right to define terms. She indicates no definitions there. (b) subpoint is there is no violation. The plan does the entire resolution. (c) subpoint she indicates no ambiguity. Of course, she must not have debated on the topic. This has been debated by everyone.

Now, underviews. We would indicate that we do prohibit. First argument is (1) prohibit means to forbid. As the Oxford English Dictionary indicated in 1969, "Prohibit ... l.trans. To forbid (an action or thing) by or as by a command or statute."[106]

Second (2) prohibition requires only a specified offense and penalty. Of course, the plan does this at the one dollar level. As Andrews v. Goodman indicates, ordinarily we content ourselves by defining a crime and prescribing the penalty therefore. This means that the offense is prohibited.

Third argument is (3) any other standard of prevention, etc., would require an effects assessment. She makes no position, hence there is no argument.

Fourth argument is (4) Nineteenth Amendment prohibited the sale and use of alcohol, but allowed Congress to determine the enforcement levels. Nineteenth Amendment from the United States Constitution from a textbook it indicates: "Section 1 .... (T)he manufacture, sale ... of intoxicating liquors ... is hereby prohibited. Section 2. The Congress and the several States shall have concurrent power to enforce this article by appropriate legislation."[107]"

Fifth argument is (5) no affirmative would win. If you must prove one hundred percent solvency, it would be impossible to ever prove.

Back to the top of the case. We indicate (A) antagonism now. She indicates disadvantage, which we take out. (B) subpoint, not optimal. She grants the evidence from LeoGrande which indicates it's never been beneficial. Granted.

In terms of the third argument, she indicates (B3) topicality. First argument is there's no standards, there's no topicality argument, et cetera.

Second argument is embargo is military intervention. By definition embargo is an act of war as Webster's indicates in 1970: "Embargo ...[A] government order prohibiting the entry or departure of commercial ships at its ports, esp. as a war measure."[108]

Third argument is we limit. This interpretation does not legitimize all economic sanctions, merely those which are militarily motivated and which are complete embargoes.

Fourth argument is embargo is opposed for military reasons. The perception is made clear as Saul Landau indicates in '82: "Mr. Castro claims that the embargo is an act of war."[109]"

Fifth argument is we should be able to make new answers is an undeveloped argument.

First advantage: (I) We indicate racism. (A) subpoint: Hard-line causes refugees. She indicates, (1), Castro is not prepared. The evidence indicates he could do it at any time. Second, she talks about (2) tighten the borders. Right, with a blockade or an invasion. That's the only way to tighten. Third argument is (3) she indicates hard-line deters. First argument is it apparently is effective. Our evidence indicates that despite the hard-line they are ready to go now.

Second argument is Carter did not decrease. In other words, Carter never decreased the hard-line they are ready to go now. Dominguez indicates in 1978, "[E]vents in the United States, such as the beginning of the primary election season in the Republican Party in 1975 and the protracted discussion of the Panama Canal Treaties, led both the Ford and Carter Administrations to slow down their efforts to change U.S. policies toward Cuba, and may have persuaded the Cuban leadership that opportunities to gain influence in Africa were preferable then to a remote and unlikely improvement in relations with the United States,"[110] taking out the Carter example which her evidence refers to.

Third argument is doesn't assume Reagan. We indicate he could do the plan credibly.

Fourth argument is our hard-line is ineffective in stopping the refugees. Loescher and Scanlon indicate in 1981, "The current US threat that another illegal flow of Cuban refugees will be regarded as an 'act of war' may have stemmed the tide, but it cannot be expected to hold it back indefinitely,"[111] indicating they will come soon.

Fifth argument is hard-line actually increases the refugees. [unintelligible] Scanlon and Loescher indicate in 1981, "Geographical approximately, a large and vocal Cuban-American community, opposition to the Castro regime, and economic hardship in Cuba are all factors promoting refugee flow,"[112] indicating that the hard-line is actually perverse.

Finally, independently, the plan solves. The evidence is in the 1AC, the (C) subpoint. Independently, the emigration issues can be resolved as LeoGrande indicates in 1980: "It would be much easier for us to arrange some sort of orderly evacuation of refugees from Cuba if we had normal relations."[113] Now, in terms of the fourth argument, she indicates (4) exile backlash. First argument here is hard-line actually increases the exiles. Lovler indicates in 1981, "The Administration's rhetoric has infused the Cuban exiles with a new boldness."[114] Second argument is evidence indicates that they are made now indicating empirically denying any impact. Third argument is there is no impact from the Casal evidence. Her evidence here is terrible. She indicates fifth, (5) cause, that's in the 1AC. Sixth argument, she indicates, (6) Mariel, empirically denied. Note the evidence indicates the future will equal war, and we are on the brink now. Seventh argument, she indicates, (7) no increase. Yes, but it will come in the future.

(B) subpoint, social disorder, is granted. The Masotti evidence indicates that we need sober thinking, indeed a radical takeover would be catastrophic. He continues in '69, "But even this might be a relatively minor consequence." [i.e., loss of freedoms]." In a mood of rage and hate, the balance of power in this nation might very well shift into the reckless hands of those who would disrupt the precarious balance of peace between the nuclear powers and plunge the whole world into nuclear holocaust."[115]

(C) subpoint. Solvency is independent of the hard-line. We indicate that we can negotiate over the issues. It's granted.

Second advantage. (II) In terms of U.S.-Cuban war, first she indicates (1) evidence is rhetorical. First, please extend the 1AC's scenarios. We indicate three paths to war: The escalation of the current hard-line policies; weakening of the '62 missile crisis agreement; and finally retaliation for Cuban subversion. All are granted by the first negative.

Second argument is independently, Radio Marti will spark war. _Congressional Quarterly Weekly Report_ indicated in 1982, "[Representative] Harkin said ... some administration officials hope to use Radio Marti to incite a confrontation with ... Cuba."[116]

Third argument is the Symms amendment will lead to war as Dodd indicates in '82: "[T]his [Symms] resolution resurrects the ... Gulf of Tonkin resolution by giving the President ... a blank check to undertake whatever military action [against Cuba] he deems appropriate without obtaining a declaration of war."[117]

Fourth argument is as long as we have the hard-line, war is inevitable. Weicker indicates in '82, "[S]ooner or later, if we allow that vacuum to continue, there will be some sort of military confrontation and blood will be shed on both sides."[118]

She indicates (2) the evidence is old. Then we read March '83 evidence on the case. She says (3) the United States will not go. We indicated in the future scenarios will cause. (4) She talks about political barriers. They may check now but not in the future. Second, they are public statements indicating, of course, there's no threat--on hard-line now taking out our arguments up above. Fifth, she indicates (5) intimidate. No. the 1AC indicates we will do it in the future. Sixth argument, she indicates (6) nukes deter. No, we indicate that the past is irrelevant. That's talking about past. Her evidence is old. Seventh argument, she talks about (7) a loss of American lives. No, Dominguez is outdated. We indicate that they are willing to escalate now. And towards the eighth argument (8) third world. No, the evidence indicates that the Third World will backlash, not that they would be any sort of a [unintelligible] check. Ninth argument (9) in terms of blockade, we indicate risk in the 1AC. (10) Covert we do not claim. The eleventh argument, she indicates (11) near term. Our 1AC indicates Mideast near. She grants them all.

(B) subpoint, on disaster. First overview is U.S. invasion equals invasion of Poland. A. subpoint U.S. invasion of Cuba causes Soviet invasion of Poland. That's what COHA indicated in November of '81: "The most likely result of a Reagan gambit is Cuba ... would be to provide a ready-made ... justification for Soviet intervention in Poland."[119]   B. subpoint: Invasion of

Poland means nuclear war Wicker. in 1981: "If ... Soviet forces
have to be called into Poland ..., [such developments] would pose
real dangers of East-West conflict."[120]
   First, the answer. She indicates [unintelligibly] (1) full
scale. Taken out above. We indicate (2 and 3) the Soviets would
back down. No, there will be a collapse of Cuba. We indicate
they would fight to the death. Fourth argument, (4) on substitute. No, we indicate they would go in. Second argument is Cuba
is already covered by the Soviet nuclear umbrella Robbins said in
'82, "Cuba's basic security is guaranteed by the Soviet nuclear
umbrella."[121] Fifth argument is she indicates (5) that they--the
repression would be checked. The Cuba in the World evidence she
reads here is old. Sixth argument: (6) Cuba doubts. It's
irrelevant to whether it would happen or not. Seventh argument,
(7) disadvantage in terms of conventional military. No, of
course, we are not superior. Her evidence is talking about '62.
Eighth argument, she says (8) Soviets not in Latin America. One,
evidence is generic. Second, does not assume U.S. attack.
Tenth argument (10) shift to the Middle East. First, of course,
attack equals nuclear war. Proven up above, Second a new CMC
[Cuban Missile Crisis] would be much worse. Anderson indicates
in 1982, "[I]f a similar situation did develop," [like the Cuban
missile crisis]" the risks of escalation would be much higher
today because we do not have the militarily superiority that we
enjoyed 20 years ago."[122] Second argument is (b) Middle East
war. We would have to draw down in the Middle East as LeoGrande
indicates in 1982. "To occupy the island of Cuba would require
the United States to strip every other theatre of operations,
including Western Europe and the Persian Gulf."[123] Third argument is no reason you would not increase forces through the
draft. Fourth argument is does not prove that Reagan wants to go
in. Fifth argument is, of course, the Soviets should stay out by
her own evidence. Sixth argument: It's empirically denied.
Should go in now. Seventh argument is no reason to go in. The
Israelis are already winning, and it is not assumed by her
evidence.
   Down below in terms of the Klare evidence, we would indicate, first argument: Turnaround. We would indicate we prevent
Mideast war. National Security Record indicates in '81, "[T]he
Soviet Union had repeatedly threatened to seize West Berlin if
the United States intervened in Cuba. Such a reaction could
still take place against Berlin or in the Middle East,"[124]
indicating Soviet response would be [unintelligible]. Second in
terms of the Klare evidence she reads down on the three subpoint,
it doesn't assume invasion of Cuba.
   Third advantage: (III) Way of life. She indicates: (1) No
problem. Of course, we indicate: All liberties. (2 and 3) she
talks about media bias, but our evidence does not come from the
media. Four, she talks about the (4) turnaround. One, we
indicate a hard-line increases aggression. That's the Lowenthal
evidence under the B. (C) subpoint. Also, MesaLago indicates
independently we would guarantee their liberties through decreasing the hard-line. Hence, we indicate the hard-line isn't a
repressive.

Now, I think this debate will be crystal clear. The risk of nuclear war in this region would be disastrous, and, of course, we would prevent it. One final argument here would be that we end escalation over the scenario. LeoGrande indicates in 1982, "[A]n improvement in U.S.-Cuban relations would eliminate Cuba as a potential flashpoint of superpower confrontation."[125] Fontaine in '75: "[R]enewed relations would remove a point of tension between the two superpowers."[126] I think this debate will be crystal clear on these strategic issues. We indicate immediate risk of invasion. She grants all the scenarios. How is she expecting to win? It's beyond me.

CROSS-EXAMINATION: JACOBSOHN QUESTIONING GIDLEY

Jacobsohn: Can you go through your answers on shift in the Middle East? Gidley: Sure. Jacobsohn: Just start, and go down. Gidley: My numbering may be off. Just a sec[ond]. The first argument is that if we attack, it's immediate nuclear war up above. Jacobsohn: OK. Gidley: I think the second argument is Reagan could get increase through a draft. OK. I think that's the second argument. [Someone]: No, Gidley: No? Then, the second argument must be draw down in the Middle East. [Someone]: No, that's the third. The second--Jacobsohn: Missile crisis cause escalation, right? Gidley: Oh, the Anderson card from the Cuban missile crisis; you're correct. Jacobsohn: OK. Three is? Gidley: Drawn down. Jacobsohn: Four is Gidley: Prove Reagan wants to go in the Middle East. Jacobsohn: Are you sure that wasn't draft? Gidley: That might be draft. [Laughter] Jacobsohn: Five? Not prove something? Gidley: Not prove that the Soviets would attack. Your evidence on escalation would take out. Jacobsohn: Oh, OK, but you proved the Soviets would attack in the Middle East, right? Gidley: Over Cuba. We don't indicate anything about the Middle East. Our evidence merely--Jacobsohn: They go into the Middle East over Cuba, right? Gidley: We indicate that they Soviets might aggress, yes. Jacobsohn: OK. Sixth--Gidley: Empirically denied. Should do it now, if Reagan has the motivation now. Jacobsohn: Oh, Reagan should go in. OK. Gidley: And the seventh argument is, it doesn't assume Israel which is whooping up on everyone in the region. Jacobsohn: What? Gidley: Israel--We don't need to go in. Israel is killing everyone that we would want to kill. [Laughter] Jacobsohn: OK. Gidley: We may hear from the Jewish lobby tomorrow, but--Jacobsohn: Two turnarounds. Prevent mideast war. Gidley: Right. Jacobsohn: Something about West Berlin? Gidley: Yes. The evidence says that if we go for Cuba they would retaliate either in West Berlin or the Middle East. Jacobsohn: So they would be willing to go into Europe then? Gidley: Under--ah--you know--extreme provocation. Jacobsohn: Well, what kind of a provocation would it require? Gidley: We indicate loss of an ally. The total loss

of Cuba. Jacobsohn: Can I see the evidence that says it's loss
of an ally that would cause them to--Gidley: <u>National Security
Record</u> says that if, you know, they lose Cuba, they go in.
Jacobsohn: Right. OK. I need to see all this evidence. And
the last thing you said was not Cuban invasion. What? Gidley:
Doesn't assume Cuban invasion. The Klare evidence that compares
isn't assuming a Cuban invasion, because a lot of people don't
foresee that. Jacobsohn: Oh, I see.

Jacobsohn: Now, the Masotti evidence on riots is talking
about nationwide racial riots, correct? And this back in the last
'60s. Gidley: That's when he wrote his book. Jacobsohn:
Right, and that's what he assumed, right? Gidley: Yes, nationwide riots. Jacobsohn: Where do you prove that it's going
anywhere beyond Southern Florida? Gidley: We indicate that
riots could snowball. We indicate massive social tensions, the
B. subpoint. Jacobsohn: OK. It snowballs in Northern Florida.
What evidence proves it'll get anywhere beyond that? Gidley:
Well, the recent instance that the racial tensions are poised
now. They're on the brink now. They would snowball. Jacobsohn:
OK. Gidley: Even if they don't, it could be regional.

Jacobsohn: I'm anxious to see all the evidence on hard-line
and causing Mariel. Gidley: Pardon. Yeh. Jacobsohn: OK?
Gidley: Uh, huh.

Jacobsohn: Now, you read March '83 evidence on the invasion
scenario. That's the evidence from Roca saying--Gidley: Carol
Rowan. Jacobsohn: Saying what? Gidley: Rowan says that if
subversion continues, we'll go in. Jacobsohn: Subversion. What
does that mean? Gidley: The Cubans trying to support or overthrow governments. Jacobsohn: Oh. I see. When is this going
to occur? Gidley: Pardon. Jacobsohn: When? Gidley: Just any
time during the 1980's. It's a risk now. Jacobsohn: OK.
Gidley:--'cause they're obviously intervening in Cuba and Nicaragua. Jacobsohn: Carter didn't--Gidley: Well, not in Cuba.
Jacobsohn: Carter didn't--slow down--hard-line fails to stop
hard-line increases. Gidley: OK. Hard-line is effective is
that top card. Jacobsohn: Um, hum. Gidley: Only card.
Immigration issues can be solved. There's cards before that I
think. Just sec[ond]. Hard-line increases is about that.
Jacobsohn: Um, I need also from Tom, Warsaw Pact prevents war.
Gidley: Yeh.

SECOND NEGATIVE CONSTRUCTIVE: THOMAS LYON, DARTMOUTH

On the (Disadvantage IA) point, in terms of Europe opposes U.S.
hard-line, he says in '82, there've been recent changes. First
of all what changes have there been? He does not specify, does
not give you any idea. Secondly, they still don't like hard-
line. This is <u>Boston Globe</u> in March 15, 1983: "The role played
and the positions taken by our European allies in the struggle
for democracy in Central America and the Caribbean have been
disappointing,"[127] quoting Fred Ikle. I would argue thirdly, and

this is that they threw U.S. hard-line against Cuba. Flora Lewis says in '82. "[T]hreats and warnings [to Cuba], ... this bombastic domestic dialog resounds around the world. It is frightening friends."[128] More evidence from Tad Szule--says in '81 that, "As to the major focus of the Reagan get-tough policy, the concentration on El Salvador and Cuba, there is a growing consensus in the international diplomatic community that such a stance is dangerous."[129] <u>Time</u> says in '82, "[T]he complexities of the real world, in which bellicose anti-Soviet rhetoric sometimes frightens U.S. allies more than it does the leaders in the Kremlin,"[130] and that from an article on Cuba. Thus, proving that they still fear it, there is a division in the alliance right now.

Now, in terms of (B) on U.S. hard-line divides the alliance. He says, Leiken is not pacifism, says there are other things, but I would argue that other things are secondary. This is Freedman of London in '82: "Anti-America and neutralist sentiments would be disappear if the LRTNF [long-range theatre-nuclear force] program were abandoned, because they reflect deep-rooted concerns about the hawkish trend in U.S. foreign policy over a range of issues, including the management of relations with the Soviet Union and the responses to sundry Third World crises, from El Salvador to the Middle East."[131] Reston says in February of '83 that, "The main thing is not the number of missiles on both sides--even if they agreed to cut their arsenals in half, both superpowers would still have enough weapons to destroy the other--but on holding the alliance together."[132] Thus, these other problems that NATO has are secondary, and belongs to the one symbolic action, can cause NATO to come back together. Also, extend the standards card that says it is tearing the alliance at the seams right now, that hard-line is enough to cause that.

Now, (C) NATO on brink. First of all, he says, other problems. Above I show that is not significant, that it is not the crucial thing, and we also say the one symbolic action will be enough. Extend the Nunn card. The Summer of '82 says, will destroy the alliance. This more evidence comes from Joffe of Woodrow Wilson Center in '83: "In the end, the larger lesson for both Europe and the United States was as trite as it was profound: unless they restore a sense of balance and moderation to their mutual affairs, unless they resist the growing temptations of neutralism. and unilateralism, the most benign alliance in history will continue to unravel."[133] Hogberg says in December of '82 that tempers are rising on both sides of the Atlantic. Political positions are hardening. Relations between the U.S. and its allies in Western Europe are at an all-time low.[134] Thus, we are on the brink of collapse.

I would argue secondly. The one symbolic action alone can save them. Williams says in October of '82 that "one of the most valuable features of detente was that it involved a transformation in the superpower relationship: the intermittent and tenuous co-operation to manage crises that had been a characteristic of the Cold War was superceded by more extensive cooperation to prevent or avoid confrontations. Recognition of this, and an attempt by the Reagan Administration--if only by some kind of symbolic action--to consolidate it would ... receive widespread approbation in Western Europe. It would make the Europeans feel that the United States is beginning to realize that attempts to isolate Moscow, economically, politically and strategically, could be counter-productive."[135]

I would argue three: Past is not prologue for NATO solidarity. Freedman says of London in '82: "[T]he North Atlantic Treaty Organization has survived a stormy three decades in international affairs and many internal arguments. Nevertheless there are elements of the current situation that distinguish it from previous crises."[136]

Now, on (D): First, full impact. He says, 1NC, no time frame. First, it says that they would move slowly. Thus, there is no war likely. Russians would simply increase pressure. That is the whole idea behind Finlandization. I would argue secondly, most recent evidence agrees. This is from Wall Street Journal in March of '83: "[A] U.S. troop pullout could lead to further accommodation of the Soviets by Western Europe ... with the threat of Western Europe's 'Finlandization.'"[137] Finlandization means that it is over the long terms, means that there is no war in the short term.

The second point is dropped, prevents World War III. He only says decreased cohesion, now so other things are not important, and secondly, a war is likely. Christian Science Monitor says in November of '82, "But what is the single most likely way in which a nuclear war might start? The most likely scenario, and the one to be found in most studies of how a third world war might start and might then escalate into a nuclear weapons exchange, begins with a Soviet offensive aimed at the NATO front on the north German plain."[138] Myers says in '82, "The upshot of the policy shift to counterforce has made nuclear war a distinct possibility and has made that traditional tactical battleground, Europe, the most likely place for the war to happen ... After 35 years of carefully nurtured peace and economic recovery, Europe is ripe for another war. History bears this out. One need only look at the previous centuries of recurrent cycles of war, recovery, rearmament and war again to realize that it is high time for Europe to get on with her destiny."[139] Myers says in '82, "Unfortunately for Europe, her next war will be her last. Nuclear weapons will finally break the historical cycle; recovery will be next to impossible ... A Saharan Europe will not inspire must of a renaissance."[140]

Now, on (E): Prevent TNF. He drops this. He says, no explanation. Well, the explanation is that a weakening of NATO will stop TNF. TNF is bad. I would argue the reason it is is because it leads to launch on warning [LOW]. Workers Vanguard, a very good source from Steve Mancuso, says in February of '83, [TNF] "would force the Soviet Union to go to a hair-trigger 'launch-on-warning'" strategy to protect its retaliatory power. The introduction of these Pershing and the small, highly accurate cruise missiles will bring the world a large step closer to nuclear holocaust."[141] Barnaby, a more reliable source, is the

card that Robin reads, Says it will ... enhance NATO's perceptions of the winnability and "not make the threat any more
credible."[142]   Paine continues of FAS in '80, "[T]he deployment
of flexible, low yield, highly accurate nuclear weapons such as
the Pershing II will heighten, rather than lessen, the dangers of
nuclear war, by tempting decision-makers in a crisis to pursue
illusory nuclear 'options' when none, in fact, exist."[143]   It
sends them the hair-trigger, because they are counter-force
weapons which is what the Soviets ...
    Another set of responses. First, he says, pull. Simply
asserts, and it will not make any difference. Boston Globe says
in March of '83, "So NATO and the Reagan Administration have
their German vote of confidence ... The Year of the Euromissiles
has passed its first crisis, but there will be other danger
points ahead."[144]   Goldman of Harvard says in March of '83, "We
would be fooling ourselves if we assumed that West German and
American interests will coalesce easily. And we would be grossly
misreading Bonn's attitude if we take for granted that it will
warmly endorse any and all American initiatives." [--"Any" and
"all," um--] "Despite the current emphasis on bilateral harmony,
there is a substantial potential for disagreement and conflict on
issues."[145]
    In terms of two, he says, no TNF, because there will be
talks. First of all, there will be no agreement. Griffith says
in February of '83, "Thus, with the Soviet-U.S. Geneva negotiations on intermediate nuclear forces (INF) stalled, deployment in
West Germany (and in Great Britain and Italy) of INF by late 1983
seems likely."[146]   Secondly, it would not be in time. Alterman
says in March of '83, "Even if Reagan were fully committed to
arms control--and had hidden this by exposing every major agreement proposed by a U.S. President in the past twenty years--it
would be extremely difficult to hammer out an agreement by
December when deployment of the missiles is scheduled to
begin."[147]
    Now, on three, he says, (F3) not prove that pacifism has any
effect. First of all, it is not the link. The link is the
argument that NATO will break up now, that the symbolic U.S.
action will protect them. That is what stops the TNFs. But I
would argue, secondly, and this is that we do have a link to this
as well. Freedman of London says in '82, "These points [anti-
nuclear movement in Europe] are all relevant, but the real clue
to what has happened may be found in the fourth explanation--that
much of what has happened [demonstrations] is a response to the
hawkish trend in U.S. foreign policy, which has exacerbated all
of these other factors," and "alarmed the Western European
public."[148]   However, we need an event to get this movement.
Myers says in March of '82 that "Each country will probably need
some event or series of events to arouse its people; and in each
country there will be those who know best how to galvanize their
populations."[149]   And, of course, this hard-line action is what
can accomplish that.
    Now, in terms of (F4). He talks about West Germany. He
says, (a) decrease alliance is critical, and (b) they will cause

World War III. First of all, German and Japanese proliferation meet Soviet ABM [Anti-Ballistic Missile]. This is Dunn of Hudson Institute in '80: "Japanese and West German acquisition of nuclear weapons would probably produce great pressures on the Soviet leadership to renegotiate--or, barring that, even abrogate--the 1972 [missile treaty]."[150] Dunn says in '79, "If the emergency of lesser nuclear powers had not done so, West German and Japanese acquisition of nuclear weapons could create strong incentives for the Soviet Union to call for renegotiation of the 1972 ABM Treaty."[151]

Secondly, this will resolve their fears. Coffey, a professor of international affairs Pittsburgh, says in '69, ABMs "might ease, if not end, concern that an embattled West Germany might launch a nuclear strike, a move which, however unlikely it may seem to the West, is a continuing preoccupation of the Soviet authorities."[152]

Three, it would be far more stable. High Frontier study says in December '82, On the purely military strategic side, we would be moving away from the unstable world of terror balance to one of Assured Survival--a much more stable condition.[153]

Four, it would increase uncertainty and increase deterrence. Strategic Review says in '81, "Defenses have always been designed to cost the attacker time and to weaken him. The best defense is one which deters the enemy from attacking at all, and that could be accomplished by a significant spaceborn defense against Soviet missiles."[154]

Five is it means no first strike. High Frontier says in December '82, a point defense for U.S. ICBM silos which, within two or three years, at a cost less than that of superhardening, can destroy any confidence the Soviets might have in a first strike against our deterrent.[155] Now, of course, what this means is that whole case is taken out. To the extent that we have ABMs, no U.S.-Soviet escalation, and no U.S.-Soviet war on that level.

Now, in terms of (F4b). He says, to cause World War III. Reads a card from Kissinger. He talks about me reading blurb cards. This card gives no explanation, and it makes no sense whatsoever as to why the Soviets would attack.

Now, I want to distinguish the West German nukes versus TNF nukes. First of all, the West German nuclear force would be counter-valve rather than counter-force. That is, it would be targeted against cities. It would not be accurate enough to be counter-force. The Soviets would opt [unintelligible] these against attack versus TNF which is counter-force and is seen as a first strike strategy.

Secondly, the West Germany is not the threat of TNF, TNF is tied to U.S. aggression, and lead to all out attack which German prolif would only lead to protective measures.

Three, if TNF and West German prolif both lead to Soviet ABMs, we still take escalation in our case.

Four, the TNF leads to launch-on-warning. Now, the West German forces are our counter-force, thus, they do not have to do that. Thus, there would be different Soviet responses to these two different systems.

Now, how much time? [Timekeeper replies, two and a half.] Two and a half. OK. Fine. He says, (F5) evidence impact by the year 2000. First of all, no, it would occur soon. That is the evidence I read above that says it would cause preempt. This is Herbert Scoville says in December '82, "In Europe ... we are proposing to deploy weapons which, rather than deterring Soviet aggression, are likely to provoke a nuclear strike in the earliest moments of any serious confrontation on that continent."[156]

I would argue, secondly, they will go to launch-on-warning. This is above as well as <u>Washington Post</u> says in November '82, "Political observers here believe that, apart from their propaganda aims, the Soviets would, in fact, adopt [LOW] ... as a preliminary and relatively cheap response."[157] Thus, the war can occur soon with TNFs.

On sixth, he says, (F6) hard-line decreases now. First of all, it did not do anything. This is the Nicaragua amendment. <u>Miami Herald</u> says in December of '82, "The Senate killed two amendments Saturday that would have barred U.S. funding."[158] But same source says, "Dodd said the Moynihan-Chaffee amendment had so many loopholes that a truck could drive through them."[159] <u>Time</u> says in January '83, "The provision [of the House Bill] specifically renews a ban on any American-supported military activities designed to overthrow the Sandinista government in Nicaragua. The CIA has been arming bands of anti-Sandinista rebels based in Honduras. But the White House insists that it has been complying with this restriction and will continue to do so."[160]

Now, on seven, he says, (F7) rhetoric is decreasing now. First of all, I would argue that there is not a very big rhetoric change. <u>Progressive</u> says is February of '83, "[W]hile Shultz may have modified the language somewhat, Reagan has not shifted from his original Alexander Haigian assertion that the line against communism was to be drawn in Latin America."[161] Secondly, their case denies. They say in February of '83 that we still have this hard-line against Cuba. Thirdly, of course, his evidence is not specific.

In terms of eight, he says, (F8) credibility by Reagan can still have action. First of all, I show that one symbolic action by Reagan will be enough, and that will be enough to save NATO. His argument on credibility of anti-Soviet action does not take into account my link. I would argue, secondly, it does not assume the whole hemisphere which I will win is what they have to do on "any"-"every".

In terms of nine, he says, (F9) no war. Of course on case he argues that Russia will be attacked. Thus, it denies this argument. (F9a) He says, we stray because of terrain. First of all, does not assume the TNF. Secondly, it only means that they are not conventional forces, but that could mean a nuclear war. (F9b) He says, fear of naval blockade. First of, it does not assume that they think they can win. On (F9c), he says, Warsaw Pact. Only means they cannot go in conventionally. You still can have nuclear attack. (F9d) She says, on balance it is too risky, but, of course, we proved increases tensions recently. How much? [Timekeeper"replies, one, ten.] One, ten. OK. That's enough for "any"-"every." He calls it a blip. Now it's a bigger blip. First of all, he says, affirmative has right to define. But not to destroy grammar, however, because the affirmatives then could simply define the affirmative topic as nuclear power and run my favorite case. (b) Of course, he says, no violation because of the whole topic. But if that's true then they get the whole DAs [disadvantages], if they are willing to debate it. On (c), he says, only a blip argument. But we expanded it--well, Robin explains well how it is a grammatical rule in terms of meaning a clear and unambiguous. He says, debated by everyone. Only proves that debaters do not understand grammar, not even John Barrett.[162]

In terms of his specific response, he says, (2) prohibition requires only a specified penalty. First of all, answers to dollar enforcement are that they cannot pull the enforcement out of enforcing every nation. Either enforcement is part of prohibition and affirmative does not prohibit intervention into any nation or nations, or enforcement is not part of prohibition in which case their enforcement was extra-topical, and they're left with no enforcement whatsoever. He says, at least, is (3) any other prevent efforts. But first of all, why the effects that? He does not explain. Second, the definition of prohibition assumes the effects, because prohibition means to effectively eliminate. And, of course, you can decrease power of labor unions--was an effects topic. That was justified. Now, the rest on (4) prohibit sale of alcohol and no affirmative win solvency are all based on this enforcement argument which we win--I hope anyway [Laughter].

CROSS-EXAMINATION: GIDLEY QUESTIONING LYON

Gidley: OK. On your extensions on the C. subpoint, the third answer is only need one symbolic act right? Lyon: Right. Gidley: that's the evidence from Williams? Lyon: Right. Gidley: Could I see that card? Which card is that? Lyon: that's Williams. Gidley: Thank you. Now, can I see all the cards on ABMs are good? ABMs only come about when West German prolif comes, right? Obviously, its a response. Lyon: Right. Gidley: Once the West Germans proliferate, then they begin to negotiate the ABM treaty, right? Lyon: Or when it looks imminent. I mean obviously the West Germans building nukes will not be--I don't think will be a convert thing. Gidley: Why not? Lyon: Well, because it would require--I mean, West Germany is a--Gidley West Germany is a developed country, you know they have scientists. Why can't they do it secretly? We built our bomb secretly. Lyon: Because West Germany would do it in order to show their deterrence. Thus, they would want to do it publicly.

Gidley: OK. Lyon: Now, let's see this is first, second and they they're numbered. I think I only went up to five, right? Gidley: Yeh.
    Gidley: How long does it take to renegotiate the ABM treaty? Lyon: How long? It wouldn't take long. I mean, we just say to the Soviets. They'd say we want to abbrogate it. We'd say OK. Gidley: OK. Lyon: And we--Gidley: Only takes one symbolic act, right? Lyon: Yeh. Gidley: OK. Now, your evidence down below on--Lyon: [unintelligible]. Gidley: Right, which Williams says.
    Gidley: Decrease rhetoric. Your first answer is no rhetoric change, right? Could I see that card? That's February '83, right? Lyons: Right. Gidley: OK. Your third answer is evidence not specific, right? Lyon: Right. Gidley: Now, up on the Bohland Amendment, now, are any of the cards you read on the Bohland Amendment allied perception? Lyon. No. Gidley: You must talk about the Bohland as ineffective, you don't prove that they perceive it that way? Lyon: Well, it proves that the loopholes were big enough for a truck to drive through. It seems they'd be able to see that, even from Europe. Gidley: But all they need is a symbol, right? Lyon: Well Gidley: It doesn't have to be correct, it just has to be a symbol. Lyon: No, because this is not a symbolic action by the Reagan Administration to have Congress pass--an emasculated bill. Gidley: The Reagan Administration spurred this amendment.
    Gidley" "Any"-"every." Lyon: OK. Here's the rhetoric change card. It's the bottom one. Gidley: OK. Thanks.

FIRST NEGATIVE REBUTTAL: ROBIN JACOBSOHN, DARTMOUTH

He says (Advantage II Al) pull scenarios. All of those are outdated. He says, Radio Marti. Only indicates confrontation, not war. Symms Amendment only allows a person, doesn't require him to go in. And the hard-line only says confrontation from the Weicker evidence. Does not say what kind it will be. Please extend the fourth argument. (4) Political barriers preclude. He says, not in the future. Says won't even allow fifty-five military advisors. And it goes on to the indefinite future. Says there's no political support. He says, those are public statements. No, just saying there is no support now. Not that if it was necessary in the future. We would not do so. Thus, I've taken out the disad. Fifth response, (5) only threats to Castro. He says, do in the future. Not serious in the intent. This, will not do now, or in the future as well. Sixth response, (6) Soviet nukes. He says, past irrelevant. It says, continue to deter. There is no reason it would be any different now. They still would [unintelligible] to get a Soviet nuclear confrontation. Civil defense. (7) Cuban defense capability. He only says, outdated. No answer here. It says, even the small capability would prevent the U.S. from going in, and that's their

Dominguez evidence. The eighth response, (8) Cuban third world role. He says, Latin America would backlash. Does not say that. Only says, it deters the superpowers from moving in. Now, please go down to save them. The last response is they have to have some probability. None in the near term is given.

On the (B) subpoint on Soviet invasion. Please group. Evidence here is perfectly old. Does not assume the Soviets would abandon Cuba. Second R response, the Soviets would abandon Cuba. Second R response, the Soviets not want to go in. Valenta says in '81, "For the Soviet Politburo, however, an invasion [of Poland] was, and perhaps still is, the last and least wanted solution of the Polish crisis."[163] Three, of course, assumes any nation which we will take out above. Now the third response I made, Soviets would back down. There is no answer here. Whalen says, they will abandon them altogether, meaning they would not respond in Berlin, Poland, or elsewhere, because they do not care. Wells says in '82, Despite the formidable military build-up, the Soviets are no more willing today than they were in '72[164] to engage in thermonuclear war with the U.S. over Cuba. Bailer says in '82, "[I]n view of current Soviet military capacities, the death-watch in the Kremlin [which obviously now is over] and the Soviet fears of Reagan, the Soviets would react chiefly with rhetoric--[Thus, not going anywhere else--that's my addition]--and threatening gestures should the US move against Cuba.[165] The fourth response, use arms as a substitute. Green-field--will not go in--an extension here. He says, covered by umbrella, but there's no commitment, and it is not be luck as the evidence says. The sixth response, Cubans quit. This is '82 evidence, not old.

Now please go down to (10) Middle East. First he says, attack gets the [unintelligible], that's taken out above. He says, the missile crisis causes escalation. First, plan does not solve that, and the Soviets put missiles in Cuba, the U.S. would respond, and the plan prevents response in Cuba, just go directly against the Soviets. Second, assumes Soviet response, taken out above. His third response, strip other theatres. First, assumes a full scale invasion. Second, it proves the disad that we can't go into the Middle East if we do go into Cuba. There is no impact to this. Soviets [unintelligible] in the Middle East. [unintelligible]. Four, increase forces with the draft. Of course, does not prove it would occur or would be adequate. Second, political bog down makes this irrelevant. We would not be able to go for political reasons as well as for physical ones. Three, manpower is not the problem; it is logistics. Army says in '82, "In effect, a RDF mission would strain U.S. logistical capabilities; the simultaneous execution of a NATO defense and a RDF mission is beyond the present capacity of U.S. forces."[166] Fifth response, not prove Soviets would attack. All the--in response to the U.S., because they perceive U.S. invasion in the Middle East as a threat to them. That's the evidence on the (B3) subpoint which he drops. Sixth, he says empirically Reagan as a voter. But he cannot do both. Political and physical bog down. That's the thesis of the disad. Seventh, he says, no reason,

because of Israel. If we're [unintelligible] to the scenarios in
the INC, RDF mind set, alternatives are subverted. Those are all
conceded.

Now, his two turns at the bottom. First, he says, go into
West Berlin. First, that's the only Soviet threat not [unin-
telligible] will do Bailer evidence I read above from [unin-
telligible] says they will only react with rhetoric. Two,
evidence is old. Not true now. We will abandon Cuba [unin-
telligible]. The last thing he says is not some Cuban invasion
that the risks of way, says all Latin America. I think that is
both.

On (Advantage III A) repression, he says, all [intelligible]
arms is from '83, saying there is no problem now. Media bias
means that when it gets reported back to the U.S., it is all
against bias. His third response is hard-line increases aggression. That is taken out by the hard-line caused crackdown in
Cuba. There is no answer to that. And he says, guarantee
liberties which decreased hard-line, and knowing the [unin-
telligible] the threat deter genocide. I think that's a turn.

Racial tensions. First, response, it's only preparation.
He says, he can go in at any time, but there's no proof that he
will. Second response, U.S. contains borders. He says, they
would do a blockade, but we did it [unintelligible]. We don't
have to tighten around Cuba. We can tighten the Florida immigration controls. Third response, [unintelligible]. We don't have
to tighten around Cuba. We can tighten the Florida immigration
controls. Third response, [unintelligible] Mariel. He says,
hard-line fails, but the evidence proves that you cannot stop
refugees. It says, we're going with several; we cannot hold
back. Second, he says, Carter did not increase hard-line. But
he did not do enough. That doesn't deny that slow soft-line
Carter did was responsible for the refugees, because he did take
some economic measures which were soft-line, even if he was not
totally soft-line. He says, now the [unintelligible]. He says,
hard-line fails to solve and is taken out above. His fifth
response is hard-line increased refugees. First, there is not
argues against him. None of these things are things they can
solve. Talks about geographical proximity, vocal Cuban community, and economic problems. Second, it is a turnaround,
because they increase the vocalness of the anti-Cuban hard-
liners, the right wing people. This evidence proves that there
would be an increase of refugees that turns back.

His sixth response, LeoGrande proves [unintelligible]. All
he says, it would be more orderly, that the impact evidence comes
from large numbers coming in. That's not taking at their solvency. Fair, it's not a backlash. He says, hard-line increases
itself. Only encourages those who exist who act against Cuba.
But if they, take a soft-line, they get mad at us and backlash
against us instead. [unintelligible] would not allow us to
withstand the existence of the Cuban regime. Five, assumes U.S.
invasion is true. Sixth response, impact evidence. He says,
will cause a future war, but not if you absorb these people, and
Mariel proved we did in Florida. Now, this Masotti card is

ridiculous. National black riots in '69. Not now. No proof of ripple anywhere beyond Northern Florida. The seventh response which I didn't mean to miss. He says, will in the future. Misses the argument, and assumes increased relations. The card I read says, you can't increase relations. And all the solvency evidence talks about negotiations and Castro agreeing with us which he concedes you can't increase relations. And all the solvency evidence talks about negotiations and Castro agreeing with us which he concedes you can't solve. But those cards he reads turns the advantage back on him. And Middle East, you know, once the Soviets react only with rhetoric, we get a clear turn. The risks there are worse.

FIRST AFFIRMATIVE REBUTTAL: MARK GIDLEY, KANSAS

I think we'll win on the risk of intervention. In terms of the topicality argument, group his answers together in terms of prohibit. First, we do the entire resolution which is granted by the gentleman. Second, the enforcement level is irrelevant. We indicate one dollar fine and other enforcement elsewhere. Third argument is all we have to do is specify the penalty and pro-hibit. We indicate two definitions of prohibit, all granted. Fourth argument is we indicate Nineteenth Amendment example which is granted. Fifth argument is, of course, we indicate that we have the right to define terms. He says, not grammatical, but, of course, we still get to be able to set the boundary. He doesn't indicate grammar violation because he does not have enough time.

Soviets disad (Disadvantage IA), second extension at the very top. He indicates, the second answer is that Europe does not like now. Evidence is very generic; indicates that Europe doesn't like general U.S. policies. Third argument is, he indicates Cuban threats. First two cards talk about frighten U.S. allies, but doesn't say anything about threatening the cohesion of the alliance, etc.

(B) Down below, in terms of other things triggering, he says, other things will be secondary, etc., but the evidence there he reads is too strong. It indicates that it takes out the disadvantage, because our policy is a major disappointment to them.

(C) subpoint, in terms of brink. He extends Nunn evidence, etc., but the Nunn evidence indicates many problems could trig-ger. Second argument is the 2NC evidence is general here, it just indicates that tempers are rising. Third argument is Williams evidence is affirmative. First argument, Bohland Amendment is the symbol Williams wants. Second argument is doesn't indicate that Cuba would be enough.

(D) In terms of the Finlandization—he says, slowly—but that indicates the case would not win. In terms of war being likely, of course, we indicate [unintelligible] down below.

(E) In terms of the TNFs, he indicates weakening NATO equals TNFs. Not the evidence read in 1NC equals only to acid test.

In terms of hair-trigger, we would indicate direct escalation outweighs. Co--He indicates, asserts, no difference, <u>Boston Globe</u>, March '83. First, we indicate other danger points. It will be equal test.

In terms of TNFs, group together, we indicate, of course, the missiles could be decreased in the future, or in other words, it's all irreparable. Moreover, his evidence indicates there will be many tests. That's the <u>Boston Globe</u> evidence March '83 indicating that this disad will be on the brink forever. In terms of the third argument, no prove pacifism. Group his answers together. First the evidence does not link here. Just says the events will arouse. Fourth argument, turnaround to West German prolif.

(F) He indicates, in terms of ABMs, turnaround. Several arguments here. First argument is there would be some time lag. He doesn't indicate when this would occur. Second argument is, of course, the ABM harms outweigh. As Pugwash Symposium indicates in '69, "Most authorities feel that the arguments against the deployment of ABM systems completely outweigh the arguments for such deployment."[167] Third argument is it causes an arms race. As Spanier and Uslander indicate in '78, "The strongest opposition to an ABM came from McNamara. Along with Secretary of State Rusk and the ACDA, he felt that an American decision to deploy an ABM would also mean a spiraling and costly arms race that would also destroy all chances for stabilization of the American-Soviet deterrent balance."[168] Moreover, if he accident risk, of course, that would mean the arms race would increase literally. Fourth argument is it would cause a preemptive strike as Kruzel indicates in '81: "No one doubts that such a transition could be an extremely dangerous process. If one nation saw its assured destruction capability being eroded by an adversary's deployment of BMD [Ballistic Missile Defense], it might be tempted to launch a preemptive attack before the adversary's system became operations."[169] Finally, I would indicate, on balance, peace would be destroyed. UPI [United Press International] indicates in 1981, "Any revival of a US anti-ballistic missile program could endanger peace and upset the delicate balance of power that has prevented nuclear war."[170]

(F) He indicates in terms of two, resolve Soviet fears. No it doesn't indicate this. Third answer, more stable. Evidence comes from [unintelligible]. Fourth argument, increase deterrence. Of course we have the same risk as the present system. Do not need the increase. Fifth argument, he says, no first strike. No, doesn't assume the transition which we would have had. In terms of the argument, he grants the argument basically. He says, evidence is old, but Kissinger does explain it to be the number one threat.

Down below, the contradiction, he says, West German doesn't equal counter-value. Asserts this. Could be counter-value. Second argument, he says, West German not threat. No, could be threats in population centers as well as missiles. Third argument in terms of TNFs, will not take out the case, but there would be delay, hence we would solve the case advantage. Fourth argument is not counterforce beaten up above. Fifth argument, we indicate case risk by 2000. All he reads is LOW risk, and he reads no impact. In terms of the sixth argument, hard-line decreasing now. He says, did not now. No evidence. Is not equal. European perception is terrible. Second, of course, we indicate any one symbol, and, of course, it could be that. Seventh argument, decreasing rhetoric. Group it together. We indicate March of '83 evidence there. Down below in terms of the eighth argument, we indicate no credibility. In terms of the restraints, pull B. and C. subpoint as the answers there are terrible.

Turn now to the case. In terms of (observation I) the overview and the inherency, we indicate it's not optimal, and it's granted. In terms of (Advantage I) the first advantage, go to the third answer, where he indicates turnaround hard-line. We indicate, first, the scenario is now. Second, we indicate Carter was not soft. Third, Reagan is not soft. We indicate that on the plan side. Fourth argument is hard-line is worse. The evidence indicates there that it did cause, and, of course, it is assuming the present system. Fifth argument, we solve. Sixth argument is the hard-line turnaround. She just merely asserts that the hard-liners would be worse.

On exiles, first, please extend the evidence from the 2AC, evidence indicates hard-liners will be increased. Second, there is no impact to exiles, which he grants. Down below in terms of Mariel empirically, we indicate they were not absorbed. In terms of the Masotti evidence, we indicate that there is some chance of a nuclear war here. Second, in terms of solvency evidence, the evidence indicates it would be easy. [Unintelligible] Pull through first the scenarios. Second, some risk with Radio Marti. And third line that it is inevitable that that evidence is granted. In terms of [unintelligible] restraints, two through four, of course, we indicate future. Also Shultz public statements.

In terms of (Advantage IIA6) Soviet nukes deter, our evidence doesn't talk about future. Also, future American lives doesn't indicate deterrence. And third world, the same argument applies.

Down below on the (B) subpoint. She indicates (1) lives equal full scale. First, her evidence is old, and we indicate they would. Second, they are allied now. Third, a Cuban missile crisis would be worse today. Fourth argument is they would be humiliated. The 1AC evidence rationale is granted. Fifth argument in terms of Whalen, he is biased, he advocates a response.

(10) Shift to the Middle East. She indicates nuclear war equal attack. No, we indicate would not be absolute. CMC equals risk. Fourth argument, draft, she talks about logistics, but doesn't improve Reagan perception. Sixth argument, empirically denied. Cannot do both. Seventh argument, Israel. Answer is terrible. Doesn't equal scenario, but there is no chance. First

answer, we indicate turnaround. Soviets would respond elsewhere.
Group it together. We indicate, first, the Soviets would respond. Bailer and Stepan indicate in 1982, "[A] Soviet reaction
to another US blockade of Cuba or to mining of its ports would,
in our view, come in Europe or the Middle East rather than in
this hemisphere."[171] We indicated in terms of two, our evidence
from Klare does not assume Cuba. We indicate all Latin America.

Third advantage (Advantage III) First, we indicate the
hard-line is force. Second argument is we indicate that the
soft-line is the best policy. That's the evidence on the B.
subpoint which she cannot grant.

(F) In underview here we would indicate Western prolif is
the worst risk. Please examine the evidence. The evidence
outweighs.

Now, at no point do the—I think they win anything close to
a disadvantage. On the case side we clearly turn, because when
the United States does intervene in Cuba both—there will be a
Middle Eastern war as well as an escalated nuclear war. The only
other argument is the TNF argument which is taken out by any
symbol, and the Bohland Amendment was plenty that.

SECOND NEGATIVE REBUTTAL: THOMAS LYON, DARTMOUTH

In terms of the (Disadvantage 1A) point on Europe opposes U.S.
hard-line. He says, evidence is only there. Of course, the
evidence is specific to whole hemisphere, and Cuba is certainly
part of that. Secondly, all evidence in 1NC is dropped. It is
still good, and three below drops the argument that in February
of '83 there was no change right now. Of course, four, the
Allies arguments. That obviously includes NATO. The A. point is
enough to win on this.

In terms of (B) on U.S. hard-line. He says, evidence takes
out the disadvantage. No, it means that the inevitable breakup
is won below. But, this is that all the problems are not as
important as the terms of U.S. hard-line.

Now, in terms of (C) NATO on brink. First of all, he
extends many [unintelligible] on general evidence, but general
evidence is all we need. We show that other problems are not as
significant, and one symbolic action is enough. He says, Bohland
would be enough to cause it. First of all, no, I say that a
truck can drive through this. Obviously, it is totally emascu-
lated. It has no effect whatsoever. Secondly, it is not Reagan
policy. It is only Congressional policy, and we show that it is
Reagan Administration that makes the difference. Thirdly, it is
only not overthrow the government. It does—and the White House
card that I read from _Time_ in '83 says, it makes no difference,
the policies. Four, I read a card about from March of '83 that
says that they still pay U.S. hard-line. Means even after
Bohland Amendment. They feel the U.S. is hard-line. And five,

of course, I win on "any"-"every" that they will have to cover the whole hemisphere.

(D) Now, in terms of the impact on Finlandization. He says, [unintelligible] outweighs. No, it only means that there will be no war whatsoever. But he drops the argument that Finlandization will prevent World War III from occurring. He says only acid test and prevents TNF. But, first of all, it means that no alliance will decrease TNF. Since we win a total breakup of the alliance, how can they have TNF missiles? We do not have to win evidence on this. And he drops all the evidence; says war is likely in the future.

(E) In terms of TNF is bad. He says, does not extend the impact. But I showed leads to launch-on-warning. That would increase accidental war. I think that is the <u>Worker's Vanguard</u> evidence. Now, in terms of co-response. He says, they'll be test. But this action alone will save. It is with TNF negotiations, but the evidence does not occur in time, that evidence is dropped from '83. He says on prove, no link advance, but, of course, yes, they oppose the hard-line action. This stirs up the protest. The evidence is all clear.

(Advantage III) Now, on (F4), in terms of West Germany specifically. He says, ABM harms our way. It is a blurb card, does not explain anything whatsoever. In terms of arms races, first of all, it decreases. <u>Washington Times</u> in '83: "Defending America need not threaten the Soviets. It will give them more incentive to negotiate an over-all reduction in offensive weaponry."[172] Kahn of Hudson says in '69, "[B]ecause the defense is large, even if one side or another cheated by a factor of two in, say, the number of missiles, it would no necessarily make a great deal of difference."[173] I would argue, secondly, would decrease war. Burt says in <u>New York Times</u> in '80, "In view of backers of the new nuclear strategy, an anti-missile system could strengthen deterrence by increasing Soviet doubts over whether a first strike against American land-based missiles could be successful."[174] And he drops the argument that we would renegotiate the treaty making all these pre-emptive strikes arguments and destabilizing arguments untrue.

Now, in terms of what he says, West Germany is the number one priority, for that does not assume that it will lead us to Soviet ABMs, and we read evidence says it takes out all their fears. He only asserted that West Germany is countered by you, but I explain what is true. It is a small, and of course, would not be as accurate. TNFs would be increasingly destabilizing. On five, evidence impact, he said that TNF leads to pre-emption. That will occur next year. On hard-line increasing now, he says, now your perceptions. Above I argued that a truck could drive through it, and that it would have overall hemispheric reaction with "any"-"every." The rhetoric is decreasing now. Extend the February '83 evidence. Says, it does not our policy, and the March '83 evidence says, Europe still ates hard-line. In terms of credibility by Reagan, we show that one symbolic action can save them, and it is that savings of them that will cost the disadvantage. In terms of nine of the war, he drops all of his arguments talking about conventional attack. Can simply assume nuclear attack. I think we win that clearly. They have no evidence on this.

OK. Now, in terms of the second contention. (Advantage IIA) Group (1). First of all, all the scenarios are outdated. Enough for the direct U.S. invasion or blockade. Secondly, the political barriers show no sign of receding, but don't deny that we can act if there's a need. For the five that it is only threats; the six, the Soviet nukes deter; and the seventh, the Cuban defense also deters. On Poland specifically, first of all,--proves that it is--we only react with rhetoric. Secondly, the Soviets won't go in.

Why hasn't it changed in a year. And thirdly, of course, it assumes an invasion which will obviously take out. Now pull three, back down, and for arms as a substitute. He only indicates Whalen, extorting other evidence, and no proof that he is biased.

(II B10) Now, on Mideast shift. First of all, the Cuban attack leads to war. That is all taken out above. And secondly, the CMC [unintelligible]. Now, the plan doesn't solve. It would just shift to a direct Jewish response against the Soviet, plus it assumes intervention. On three, strip other theatres. It is dropped. Assumes full invasion. He drops the DA [disadvantage] that that's theirs to trade off. And, of course, there's no impact. The Soviets are only responding to U.S.

In terms of four on the draft. First of all, there's no proof that it will occur or that is is adequate. Secondly, the political bog down. It's totally irrelevant. And three, the logistics prevents regardless of manpower. That is dropped as well.

In terms of six, what Reagan would do now. What he can do both political and physical bog down prevents him. In terms of seven on Israel, he goes to one of these [intelligible] for intervention which are independent, the mind set, alternative, subverted, and others.

On the turn that Soviets go elsewhere, first of all, the 1AR evidence shows there is no Soviet response to Cuba. Secondly, he always says, the others are possible. And three, the problem by [unintelligible] say the Soviets only respond with rhetoric. They will not respond with attack.

In terms of (Advantage I) the first advantage, he drops the number two that says nothing in SALT. And on, three, that Carter's not soft enough, be decreased some and it caused Mariel. That is dropped. Pull all answers on hard-line causes which turn the advantage their evidence proves. That there's no turn on exile backlash. The plan forces the shift to backlash against the United States, and pull seven as well that assumes increase in relations which they can't do.

Now, (Advantage III) the third advantage, just pull that deter genocide, and that there's no problem because of media bias, which they also drop. On "any"--"every", first of all, grant that it is tied to the resolution and that enforcement is irrelevant. Thus, what you mean is that you assume that they implement throughout the entire hemisphere and enforcement makes no difference to this, thus, you assume that Reagan takes an action against the whole hemisphere. Now, I think this feeds the link very closely, because all we've done at the most is Nicaraguan action which is not the President, it's Congress. It's not perceived, because a truck could drive through it, but you've now got a plan that covers the whole hemisphere, giving me the link clearly to NATO.

Now, I think we win Mideast shift. We turn all the advantages. Hell--I mean heck--I wish I were as good as Lenny,[175] but I hope that I've debated well enough.

SECOND AFFIRMATIVE REBUTTAL: RODGER PAYNE, KANSAS

"Any"-"every" is not very important as a topicality argument. [Laughter] (Disadvantage I) Please go to (F) the turnaround on West German proliferation. Overview on this: none of his evidence says that West German proliferation does not provoke war. His evidence does say that it would cause the Soviets to go to ABM, but it doesn't say that it solves all tensions or anything like that. It is totally over-claimed if he asserts that, because none of this evidence does. It does say that ABM is good, etc., but there is no timeframe on any of this stuff, or when this happens, or anything.

The first answer: Time lag. There is no 2NR answer. Our argument here is that it will take some time to deploy ABMs. The Soviets can't just wake up the day after West Germany makes the bomb and say, ah, we'll just do ABMs. No problem. Our evidence in the 2AC says, West Germany prolif causes the Soviets retaliation and it's the greatest threat to European war which means it outweighs all of his TNF stuff and everything like that which there is no timeframe on up above, and in this clearly outweighs.

The second argument is the harms outweigh. He says, the evidence is blurb, but it's from the Pugwash Symposium in 1969 which says that most experts agree that the harms of ABM outweigh the good. I think that evidence is not--it might be blurby, but its Symposium evidence that assesses all of these political scientists' beliefs.

The third argument: Arms race. He says, one, decreases the arms race. This is simply not true. Evidence comes from <u>Denver Post</u> in March 1983: "But [Senator] Hart ... contended that the Reagan plan could lead to a 'new kind' of arms race."[176] Secondly, it increases the chance of nuclear war. Evidence comes from John Steinbruner in November '81: "If we attempt to do it unilaterally (by withdrawing from the current ABM treaty), it promises to be a thoroughgoing disaster, creating a sense of confrontation far more serious than we have now."[177] John Quirt says in '81, "Critics like Jimmy Carter's Defense Secretary, Harold Brown, ... counter that a new push for missile defense would do the opposite, igniting an uncontrollable arms race that

could increase the likelihood of nuclear war."[178]   Moreover, it's
the greatest threat to peace.   Evidence comes from Wolf in 1980:
"If carried out [a Pentagon revival of the ABM program], such a
step would bring the world closer to the possibility of nuclear
war than any act contemplated by either the United States or the
Soviet Union since the decision to develop the hydrogen bomb."[179]
And that's pretty important, since our evidence on the case side
said the Cuban missile crisis was the closest act, and it nearly
sparked World War III which means that ABM would do the exact
same thing.   He also says that they get renegotiation, and so
they decrease it, because they decrease the chance of war.   First
of all, it's taken out by all the above evidence.   It says, it
increases nuclear war.   Secondly, none of this evidence assumes
that the West Germans have the bomb.   All of his cards on ABM do
not assume the West Germans have the bomb.   It might be true that
ABMs would be good, but none of it says, if West Germany had the
bomb.

Preemptive strike is granted.   He says, renegotiation takes
this out, but our evidence says that it's during deployment, when
you're trying to make it operational that it will cause one side
to launch a preemptive strike which makes his argument largely
irrelevant.   Even we do negotiate, and both agree to deploy, one
side could build it faster and preemptively strike.

Now, number one threat.   He says, does not assume ABM, but
none of his evidence assumes West Germany prolif, and our cards
do say that if West Germany gets it, it's the greatest threat to
peace.   More evidence comes from Passin in '77:   "[M]ore than
anything else, it is hard to imagine the Soviet Union standing by
and allowing Germany to become her nuclear rival.   Since a
nuclear arsenal is not built overnight, the Soviet Union would be
in a position to interfere with every stage of such a development."[180]   Calder says in '79, "If West Germany makes the bomb it
may be the end of the world, in the near-literal sense of nuclear
war.   As noted in the previous chapter, such a move would enrage
the Soviet Union and it is one of the very few imaginable events
that could set the Soviet tanks rolling into Western Europe and
into the nuclear war promised by NATO."[181]   Field Marshall Lord
Michael Carver says in '82, "If anything could be calculated to
bring about a war in Europe, it would be Russian reaction to the
prospect of West Germany acquiring its own nuclear weapons."[182]
More evidence.   Will come very fast as Calder said in '80: "West
Germany might make its own nuclear weapons within a matter of
days and that, as we have seen, could precipitate the big war in
Europe."[183]   Now, I think we've just got 'em cold on this.

Now, I was going to go for the link answers, because I
was--but I was afraid that you might take out the link which
would take out the impact, and I think, you know, even if we are
losing the case, we are winning these turns cold.

Case.   (Observation I)   All the inherency is granted.   First
advantage.   (Advantage I)   They say that you cannot solve, the
hard-line increases, etc.   First of all, it's not true.   We can
solve.   The 1AC evidence says most bilateral relations and things
can be solved, etc.   Second of all, the evidence from the 2AC

says, you can make it an orderly transition which means even if we don't decrease the number of refugees we still get orderly which all of their stuff about hard-line, I mean soft-line increases and staff does not matter, because with relations we make this better.

Now, the exile stuff is flipped by the 2AC evidence that says the hard-line increases that. There is at least some risk of nuclear war on this advantage. All the 1AC solvency evidence is granted here as well.

Second advantage (Advantage II): U.S.-Cuban War. He says, all of our evidence is outdated, etc. First of all, it's not true. The Fall '82 evidence, March '83 evidence, and the 1AC means it's not outdated. Second of all, none of their evidence talks about our scenarios. We talk about hard-line, Radio Marti, '62 missile crisis agreement, and Cuban subversion. All those are different things that could cause this in the future. She may be right, all of these things don't cause the present system to go to war which is sort of empirically proven, but none of these talks about what happens in the future. So these are irrelevant.

(B) subpoint: Escalation. He says, only rhetoric, assume, etc. First of all, we read good evidence in the first affirmative that says it will be the end of the world which means even if that win Mideast Shift, it does not weigh. This is still the same impact. Second of all, they are under the nuclear umbrella. We read '82 evidence. They read '79. And this Whalen stuff is all biased. He's Heritage Foundation.

(B10) Mideast Shift. Draft. They never proved that Reagan perceives that we don't have logistical-political support. Now, Mideast support. We read [unintelligible] definite evidence in '82 that says if we go into Cuba they can respond in Europe and the Middle East. That 2AC evidence also says that this is true which at least gives us the same risk of turnaround. Also, this is not the number one risk, because West Germany is the greatest threat to peace in Europe which they say is the most likely cause of nuclear war. Remember the evidence in the 2NC. Also, Cuba is the end of the world which means, if we win that, I don't see how this could outweigh anyway. And there's at least some risk that we flip it, because Cuban attack causes it too.

Now, I've really enjoyed my debate career. I think the same thing could be true for Mark. Thank you for a fine NDT. This is a good round. [Applause]

FIRST JUDGE CRITIQUE: DALE A HERBECK, UNIVERSITY OF IOWA

Much like a first negative, I feel compelled to begin my critique with a few preliminary "observations." First, I extend sincere congratulations to all of the participants in the final round. It is an honor just to attend the National Debate Tournament [NDT]. To qualify for elimination rounds signifies substantial

skill and talent. To have progressed through the elimination
rounds to participate in the final round reflects well on these
debaters, their coaches, and their respective institutions.

Second, I feel compelled to comment briefly on the procedure
that I used in evaluating this debate. Ordinarily I would not
engage in such an enterprise, confident in my belief that my
decision would reflect on my methods (or lack thereof). But, it
seems to me that such comments are especially justified this year
given the new "normative" rules adopted by the NDT Committee. In
particular, I feel a need to comment on the normative rule
suggesting that judges "should not read evidence." This is a
rule that I did not abide by during the preliminary rounds, nor
in any of the elimination rounds that I judged.

As I understand the rule it makes no logical sense. I
believe that it is based on suspect rationales and that it
furthers no constructive end. Obviously, academic debate is far
from a perfect activity. There is certainly room for improvement. Still, I cannot understand how this rule will benefit the
participants at this or any other NDT. Perhaps some judges do
read too much evidence, and perhaps some debaters are encouraged
to speak at even quicker rates of speed on the assumption that
when the judge reads the evidence after the round that he/she
will construct the round according to the evidence. These are,
no doubt, legitimate concerns. But I do not see how this particular rule will remedy these problems. Judges who interject
themselves into rounds will continue to do so, even if the NDT
rules say that they should not read evidence. And debaters will
continue to speak quickly as long as they perceive this practice
to be to their strategic advantage. Encouraging judges not to
read evidence will not solve this problem either. I know of few,
if any, judges who read evidence that they do not understand
because it was not delivered in an intelligible fashion.

Rather, by discouraging judges from reading evidence I
believe this rule will reduce the quality of some decisions.
Furthermore, such a rule will encourage debaters to stretch their
evidence to fit their arguments. If judges are unable to read
evidence the debaters have every incentive to overclaim their
evidence, confident that their opponents will not be able to
catch each and every overstatement.

I am not saying that all judges should read evidence, nor am
I saying that all judges who do not read evidence are making bad
decisions. Instead, I am trying to say that this should be a
matter for the given judge to decide. Personally, I believed
that I make better decisions by reading and comparing evidence
that was introduced into the round in a comprehensible fashion.
I think that such determinations are vital to deciding a round of
debate--particularly among teams as evenly matched as those
participating in this debate. Other judges may believe that
judges should not read evidence on principle, that reading
evidence does not help their decisions, or that reading evidence
actually distorts their decisions. My point is this--I do not
believe that the NDT Committee or anyone else should try to

discourage a particular judge from reading evidence. That is a decision that should be left to the individual judge.

Having dispensed with these preliminary observations I now turn to my critique of the final round. It seems to me that this debate hinges on the answer to three different questions. First, what is the harm to our current policy of antagonism toward Cuba? Second, does military intervention in Cuba prevent military intervention in the Middle East? And third, would this plan prevent the disintegration of the North Atlantic Treaty Organization [NATO]? I will consider the first two questions very briefly, and then progress to the pivotal question of whether the plan would save NATO.

CASE. First negative concedes inherency and argues that there is no substantive harm to our current policy of belligerency toward Cuba. The first harm claimed by the affirmative is based on immigration. First negative responses to this harm are generally very good. The best responses suggest that a softer line would actually increase Cuban immigrants, that a softer line toward Cuba would cause backlash by Cuban exiles already in this country, and that the affirmative solvency assumes an improvement in relations with Cuba which will not necessarily happen once the plan is adopted. Affirmative has adequate responses on the causal link and on backlash. But, the affirmative never addresses the negative evidence which suggests that improved relations are required to solve the migration problem. Thus, I see little chance for stemming the tide of Cuban immigrants.

The second harm claimed by the affirmative is based on direct U.S. military intervention in Cuba. First negative has a myriad of responses to this particular argument. She suggests that the affirmative evidence is rhetorical, that the United States will not undertake military actions, that political checks preclude intervention, that our threats are just threats to discourage Castro from undertaking actions counter to American interests, that Cuban military might deter U.S. attack, and that the United States would not attack Cuba because of Castro's role as leader of the Third World. While she offers many other responses, these are the responses substantively extended in first negative rebuttal. And to be honest, I find them compelling. Affirmative answers to most of these evidenced arguments amount to assertions that we will intervene in the future. Unfortunately, second affirmative does not address many of the specific barriers and checks on intervention outlined in first negative constructive and extended in first negative rebuttal.

Instead, the affirmative spends most of their time on this particular issue developing "scenarios" for intervention. They suggest that the construction of Radio Marti, the Symms Amendment, and our hard-line policy will eventually culminate in war. All of this is well and good, but I do not find any of the scenarios to be independent of the specific negative responses. Phrased in different language, I think that the different scenarios are adequately answered by the first negative arguments.   There is, in my mind, little chance of direct military intervention against Cuba.

The third harm claimed by the affirmative is based on the current military embargo against Cuba.   The affirmative case maintains that this embargo encourages and fosters repression within Cuba.   This advantage is not substantively extended by either the second negative rebuttalist or by the second affirmative rebuttalist.   Furthermore, the impacts claimed are miniscule when compared to the broader issues in the debate.

Thus, at the end of this debate there is very little advantage left of the original affirmative case.   The negative has diluted the solvency of the first advantage on immigrants, proved that the disastrous military intervention identified in the second advantage probably will not occur, and the third advantage is confused beyond recognition by the end of rebuttals.

MIDEAST SHIFT DISADVANTAGE.   This argument is premised on the idea that if the United States intervened in Cuba it would not be possible for the U.S. to intervene in the Middle East. Being tied down in Cuba is desirable, the negative argues because while the Soviets would not confront the U.S. in Cuba they would surely confront the U.S. in the Middle East.   Such a Mideast confrontation is undesirable because U.S.-U.S.S.R. confrontation in Latin America over Cuba.

This is, I think, an interesting argument.   Unfortunately, it is a very difficult argument for the negative to win.   Simply put, to win this argument the negative must lose the argument that military intervention in Cuba will occur.   Absent such intervention the U.S. will not be tied down and we will go into the Middle East.   Only by losing the argument that America will not intervene will not occur the Middle East argument is rendered impotent.   Absent affirmative proof of military intervention in Cuba there is no unique disadvantage to the affirmative case. Thus, when the first negative wins that there will be no military intervention in Cuba she necessarily loses to the disadvantage.

Furthermore, even if I award the affirmative some risk of intervention the resulting disadvantage does not seem sufficient to outweigh the NATO disadvantage.   The evidence regarding West German proliferation suggest that it is the greatest possible danger.   Hence, even if the negative wins something on this disadvantage it is still dwarfed by the NATO disadvantage.

NATO DISADVANTAGE.   Affirmative arguments with respect to this disadvantage are either a masterstroke of strategy or incredibly fortuitous.   As presented in first negative this disadvantage claims that by prohibiting military intervention the plan would pacify NATO.   This would prevent NATO from disintegrating.   Saving NATO would be disadvantageous because NATO's NATO's disintegration would necessarily engage the U.S. in a war with the Russians over Europe.   The DA literally claims it would be better to "Finlandize" Europe than to have a military confrontation with the Soviets over the fate of Europe.

Second affirmative has a multiplicity of arguments in response to this disadvantage.   Second negative spends almost the

entirety of his speech responding to this list of arguments.
First affirmative rebuttalist extends most of the list, and all
of his specific extensions are answered by the second negative
rebuttalist.   It is in the second affirmative rebuttal that the
affirmative claims the issue.   Rather than extending all of the
issues he grants the entirety of the disadvantage concedes the
link and the impact, and attempts to win the debate on a turnaround.

The turnaround, as presented in second affirmative argues
that were NATO to disintegrate, then West Germany would proliferate.   West German proliferation would in turn spark a
Russian attack that would certainly end the world.   The original
negative response to this position was based on anti-ballistic
missiles (ABMs).   Second negative constructive suggests that in
response to West German proliferation that Soviets would develop
ABM's (proved by the Dunn evidence).   Because of these systems,
he suggests that the Soviets would not be concerned about West
German proliferation (proved by the Coffey evidence).

It is at this point that the round becomes confusing.   The
negative response to the affirmative argument is based on Russian
ABM's.   It assumes that the Soviets would find the ABM an adequate guarantee against West German proliferation.   Unfortunately, most all of the analysis and evidence introduced into the
debate on this issue is referring to American acquisition of
ABMs.   While this evidence may have a certain probative value, it
does not directly relate to the question at hand.   The question
is, will ABM's pacify the Soviets and thereby eliminate the need
to respond to West German proliferation?

Ultimately I conclude that ABMs will not be sufficient to
prevent a Soviet attack.   I resolve the issue this way for two
reasons.   First, I believe the affirmative response on time-
frames.   Negative never explains how the Soviets can respond to
West German proliferation by instantaneously developing ABMs.
Both affirmative rebuttalists argue that West Germany would
proliferate before the Soviets could develop ABMs.   Thus, there
would be reason for the Soviets to attack West German nuclear
weapons in the interim.   Second negative rebuttalist simply does
not respond to this argument.   Additionally, the only reference
to time contained within any evidence is found in the affirmative
evidence suggesting the West German proliferation could occur
within a matter of days.   At the end of this debate I see no
reason to believe that the Soviets can develop ABMs as fast as
West Germany can proliferate.   Thus, it seems doubtful that the
Soviets will be fully pacified by the development of ABMs.

Second, affirmative evidence on ABMs is much better than the
negative.   Admittedly, neither side has evidence which pertains
to this specific scenario.   Still, the affirmative evidence on
ABMs is sufficient to prove that they are not a viable alternative.   Pugwash Symposium evidence suggests that the dangers
outweigh the benefits, and the Kruzel evidence suggests that they
might actually increase the risk of preemptive attacks.   Second
affirmative rebuttal evidence from <u>Denver Post</u>, Steinberg [sic],
and others supports this position.   Both the preponderance and

the quality of evidence support the affirmative. The negative extensions of ABMs are crushed. ABMs, when they happen, will actually increase the risk of war.

Having progressed this far there is only one question yet to be resolved. Is it worse to let NATO disintegrate or is it worse to have West German proliferation? Both the analysis and the evidence support the latter. NATO's disintegration reduces the risk of war with the Soviets and prevents deployment of TNFs. The evidence on these impacts is specific. Still, these impacts are dwarfed by the consequences of West German proliferation. Evidence from Fisher, Dunn, Passin, Calder, Kissinger (quoted by LeFever), Wolf, and others, all indicates that West German proliferation is the greatest possible evil. All of the evidence suggests that compared to any other harms West German prolifer- ation is of a greater magnitude. This argument is clear for the affirmative.

So, the negative disadvantage is turned. While the plan might increase the risk of war with Russia it prevents West German proliferation. According to the evidence this is a totally compelling risk. This advantage, coupled with the absence of any other disadvantage to the affirmative case is more than sufficient to carry the round for the affirmative.

SECOND JUDGE CRITIQUE: DWAINE R. HEMPHILL
KANSAS STATE UNIVERSITY

My warmest congratulations are extended to the four participants of the 1983 Final Round. I would also like to congratulate the non-advancing semifinalists from Samford and Dartmouth. We should remember that while only one team can win in the end, many teams consistently exhibit the excellence necessary for that victory.

REASONS FOR DECISION: Kansas wins West German prolifer- ation. The chain of arguments culminating in Rodger's 2AR strategy is interesting and in many ways confusing.

The development of the NATO Alliance disadvantage by Robin was rapid and a bit unclear. When I realized that Dartmouth was maintaining that the collapse of NATO would be beneficial, I knew it would be an interesting round. By 2AR, the links were granted by the affirmative, so the only question remaining was "Which impact is more probably?" And, in a nutshell, Tom never effect- ively denied the proliferation links or impact.

The negative held that US military intervention and a hard-line foreign policy would "tear the alliance at its seams." NATO is already teetering on the "brink of collapse"; and Tom claimed that the specific intervention Kansas would prohibit--that into--Cuba would be enough to destroy NATO. Rodger conceded all of these points in 2AR.

The impact claimed in the disadvantage is a bit counter- intuitive. The collapse of the alliance would be good, because its existence guarantees nuclear war. Robin and Tom's evidence indicates that Europe is the most likely theater for the next world war, and this war will probably occur before the year 2000. If the alliance collapsed, as Dartmouth held it should, the nations of Western Europe would slowly and peacefully "Finlandize" into the Sovietsphere of influence, thus defusing this volatile area of East-West confrontation.

The second impact in the disadvantage is more specific. A hawkish U.S. policy was proven to fuel the massive grass roots movement against nuclear weapons in Europe. Tom explained that this would make the scheduled deployment of intermediate range missiles less likely. Actual deployment of these US missiles would "increase the level of confrontation," encourage "launch-on-warning strategies," and "increase the probability of war."

In 2AC and 1AR, Mark pressed these impacts and questioned the unique application of the disadvantage to the affirmative policy. 2AR made these arguments moot by conceding them and focusing on one position that was relatively unscathed in 2NC and 2NR: West German proliferation.

Mark's fourth argument in 2AC developed the proliferation position: A strong NATO provided an alternative to the development of a nuclear force by West Germany. If the alliance collapsed, West Germany would clearly fear for its defense and develop an indigenous missile force. The disastrous implications of such a development were impacted in 2AC; the Soviets would attack if Germany built the bomb. A ballot to prohibit intervention would save the alliance and preclude the proliferation.

Many arguments come to mind when the issue of nuclear proliferation enters an academic debate round. Perhaps to intentionally avoid debating these details of proliferation, Tom chose a different strategy in 2NC. Tom granted the link to proliferation and argued that it would not necessarily mean war. Why? Because if Germany built the bomb, the Soviets would have more incentive to develop anti-ballistic missile systems. Once these systems were developed, Tom claimed global stability and enhanced deterrence would result. Mark pointed out the flow in this scenario with his first 1AR extension. The development of ABMs and realization of the subsequent stability would involve a "time lag." ABM development certainly could not occur in a matter of weeks. Mark attempted to put the competing impacts into focus through the timeframe analysis, something Tom failed to do in his constructive. And in 2NR, Tom does not answer this "timeframe" view of the arguments. A serious mistake, as the 2AR pointed out. The evidence in 2AC says West German proliferation guarantees war. This evidence is not indicted. Tom does claim that the German missiles would not be as accurate as the tactical U.S. weapons, but this is irrelevant. Acquisition of an indigenous capability would spark Soviet aggression, and Dartmouth did not argue this point in 2NR.

2NR extensions on the proliferation arguments appear sparse on my flow. Tom only argued the ABM scenario and none of his extensions beat the timeframe analysis. Mark claimed that the harms of ABM systems outweigh their benefits. Tom responded by calling the evidence a "blurb." Rodger pointed out that the source of this "blurb" was a Pugwash symposium of experts. While the affirmative evidence was conclusionary, it was not unclear. And the source qualifications add credibility to the conclusionary statements cited.

The relationship between ABMs and the arms race was discussed in 1AR and 2NR, but neither team indicated the level of risk involved in an arms race. And Rodger was correct when he pointed out in 2AR that none of the ABM scenarios for war and peace assumed development of the bomb by West Germany. The only evidence specific to this is affirmative, and it remained unindicted. I concluded that there would never be the opportunity for ABM development if Germany built the bomb; we'd be ashes, and the cockroaches would be ruling.

If ABMs would result from proliferation, the round still goes affirmative. Mark proved that the temptation to launch strategic first strikes would be greater during deployment of the systems. This claim is not answered in 2NR, and is extended by 2AR.

2AR did a fine job of clarifying what had become a very confused disadvantage. The structure of the attack was not effectively rebuilt in 2NC. And 2NR's superficial coverage on the proliferation add-on gave Rodger considerable room to maneuver in 2AR. Rodger claimed the unanswered link to proliferation and extended the impact with evidence that made the risk evaluation relatively simple. West German proliferation is "the number one threat to peace," "means the end of the world," and could occur "in a matter of days." Given the dropped timeframe argument, this impact so clearly outweighs the "nuclear war by 2000" that Dartmouth wins with the disadvantage. The TNF "launch-on-warning" impact is never given a time perspective. Finlandization is clearly a long term process. The TNF impact is also never clarified in relation to West German proliferation. There is simply not enough in the disadvantage to outweigh the advantage Kansas claims by saving the NATO alliance.

OTHER ISSUES: The remainder of the issues become secondary. Robin effectively reduces the impact of "racial tensions" to an unquantifiable level of advantage for Kansas. Rodgers extends this advantage, but claims no real impact from it. Hence, it does not weigh in my decision.

The risk of war with Cuba is uncertain. We may invade in the future, but Tom extends current political barriers that are not specifically answered in 2AR. Kansas provides no criteria to evaluate the risk of a future war with Castro. Additionally, our nation will probably be deterred from invading by the threat of Soviet nukes. 2AR is nonresponsive on this point. (Note-- loss of this advantage does not undermine the basis of the Alliance DA; it was clearly linked to a hard-line policy, not actually U.S. intervention. However, the Middle East shift DA does appear to be undercut by the negative position. If no invasion will occur, we will have troops to use in the Mideast, and the shift DA could occur regardless of my decision. The credibility of the DA is diminished.)

The Mideast Shift DA was extremely muddled in the last three rebuttals. The application of evidence in rebuttals was not well explained, and reading it after the round did not help to clear up the issues. I lean affirmative on the perception analysis, and Reagan's ability to call up the draft hurt the uniqueness of the disadvantage. 2NR and 2AR both needed a clearer explanation of their positions on this issue. Finally, the turnaround claimed in 2AC balances out the DA risk. A blockade of Cuba would probably result in a Soviet response in the Mideast or Europe. The Bailer and Stepan evidence is clear, and Dartmouth's only real indictment is that the evidence says "possible" and is "only rhetoric." The clear rhetoric is enough to balance out the risk of a Mideast conflict.

Advantage III is dropped by 2AR; and the "any" equals "every" topicality claim is conceded in 2AR. The plan thus prohibits intervention into all nations in our hemisphere. This feeds the affirmative position on the Alliance DA—such a move would certainly improve relations between our nation and the NATO alliance.

Despite some strategic mistakes, the round was fun to listen to. Indeed, the outcome was close until 2AR. Rodger effectively brought the debate down to the one issue Mark had clearly won. The move eliminated a lot of confusing issues and focused the panel's attention on affirmative ground. If 2NR had employed the same type of strategy to clarify the negative issues, the outcome of the round would certainly have been more difficult to determine.

Again I congratulate Robin, Tom, Rodger, and Mark for their fine season and tournament. Best of luck to you all in the future.

THIRD JUDGE CRITIQUE: DALLAS PERKINS, HARVARD UNIVERSITY

To properly appreciate the drama of this round one must begin at the end with the 2AR, the speech for which the debate will likely be remembered. The speech focused on two issues which one would not have expected to be crucial: the harms of ABM deployment and West German nuclear proliferation (WGP). While the speaker spent some time on case arguments, he was primarily concerned with achieving a draw on those issues. Intervention shift was almost conceded, with only the disadvantage implications questioned. A turnaround on genocide in Cuba was treated similarly, and the nuclear war impacts on immigration were dropped for fear of losing a turn there as well (the most recent empirical evidence that Carter's softness toward Cuba caused the Mariel exodus.)

The strong point of the 2AR was the way it "put things together," explaining how the vast number of arguments in the round were interrelated. Three examples come to mind: "Even if we can't decrease the number of immigrants, we can make the process orderly;" "A war with Cuba is at least as bad as a war in the Mideast;" and, "The negative reads no evidence saying ABMs mean Russia won't attack Germany to stop its nuclear weapon development." All three of these claims were wrong, though to varying degrees. However, the speaker was sufficiently persuasive to convince all but the most astute and diligently attentive listeners.

A glance at even the most casual of flowsheets would reveal that vast portions of the negative position were simply conceded: the affirmative uniquely saves NATO, causes TNF modernization, stops Finlandization, increasing the risk of war in Europe. That such a high-risk strategy was necessary is a tribute to a 2NR of truly awesome proportions. When Tom announced that he was going to cover every set of arguments in the debate (three affirmative advantages with a disadvantage against each, voluminous link arguments on the NATO disadvantage, ABMs, WGP, TNF, Finlandization, and Topicality), I laughed aloud. But he did it.

In what was surely the most poignant moment in the round, and in retrospect the most provocative, Tom concluded by wishing he were "as good as Lenny," and hoping he had been, "good enough." I beg to differ.

Debate is an uncomfortable combination of information processing and oral communication. In terms of amassing facts and logic to support a position, this 2NR was brilliant. I have never heard Lenny do anything like it. However, it was notably lacking in the qualities which made the 2AR so persuasive. There are those who would have thought it abominable, who proclaim that this activity is progressively failing to reward excellence in oral communication, emphasizing research and blocks instead. The outcome of this round stands in stark refutation of such claims. As was even more clearly the case last year, the team with evidential and argumentation superiority was defeated by the team displaying superior communication skills. Of course, both teams were in each case very well prepared, and information processing is an important part of any policy dialectic, but the argument that excellence in oral communication is not also rewarded is plainly wrong. It is surely advanced mostly by persons who did not witness the last two final rounds, and who have not heard Lenny very much either. Indeed, slow rhetoric, in small doses, wins a good portion of all debates, and many of the debaters are awesomely talented at it already. Many of them join other students in polishing these skills both here and in other forums. This diversity is to be encouraged. But we should strive to preserve and enhance the value of NDT debate as the uniquely broad and spirited academic competition that it is.

The usual comment to the rebuttalist in a debate like this is "cover fewer issues." Here, examination of the entire debate reveals such facile advice to be misguided. The 2NR could have conceded the links on the NATO disadvantage and dropped it. The first negative did have the case in serious trouble. However, the case arguments might well have been salvaged by a highly focused 2AR. In particular, if the case of Carter's soft-line leading to Mariel could have been distinguished more clearly, especially with evidence, the affirmative might have won the immigration advantage. The 1AR had spent a lot of time talking up the nuclear war risk from rioting Cubans. The 2NR could not profit from dropping any of the NATO disadvantage impacts, since they were all interrelated. Topicality was important on the links to the NATO disadvantage. And the case had to be at least minimized, since the disadvantage links were still contested and might also be minimized. In short, it was all or nothing. Tom gave it his all, and he probably should have won.

That he lost is attributable entirely to the clarity, persuasiveness, in short, the superior communication skills of the 2AR. The pivotal point was the previously mentioned assertion that there is no negative evidence showing the ABM's will stop Russia from going to war over WGP. It was argued that ABMs might make the Russians feel more secure, but this would take a long time and they would attack in the interim. Then came a parade of new evidence saying the Russians would attack. If one sees this merely as increasing the significance of an argument which the negative had been conceding all along, the new evidence in 2AR may be appropriate. And the quality of this evidence, at least rhetorically, was far superior to the negative's impact evidence on TNF. Proliferation sounds like the end of Finlandization as well, and the affirmative evidence might outweigh that too (though it would be close).

That was how I viewed the debate and the time and for several weeks thereafter: the case was close, ABM was a tie, proliferation substituted for Finlandization, and the harms of WGP outweighed the conceded TNF impacts and dwarfed any marginal advantages on other issues. And a super 2AR had come back from an apparently desperate situation.

The problem with all of this is that its fundamental premise is wrong: The 2NC did read evidence which said that ABMs might decrease or end Russian concerns about a Western German nuclear strike. Without benefit of the transcript now before you, it is my memory that the 2NC labeled this subpoint, "Instead of attacking, the Russians will build ABMs," implying a tradeoff. Furthermore, the scenario of an attack to interrupt the proliferation process is clearly inconsistent with a decision to renegotiate the ABM Treaty to promote long run security. However, the first two cards read said only that ABMs would be deployed, and I have on my flowsheet for the third card, the one alluded to above, only the single word "concern." I examined all of the evidence read under the "ABMs are good" subpoint, but since the fact of ABM construction was not contested, I neglected to look at the "link" cards, one of which was in fact a key "impact" card as well. The negative never reiterated this point or specifically applied it in refutation of the affirmative evidence on the point. My colleague Roger Solt, whose quickness of ear and hand exceed my own, and who routinely reads far more evidence after the round than I, informed me of it one month after the round.

This card makes all the difference. In the first place, the 1AR had substantially dropped all of this, arguing mostly that ABMs are bad. Allowing the 2AR to read lots of new evidence on the contested issue of what the Russians will do, as opposed to the uncontested issue of the likelihood of attack, is suspect. No explanation is offered as to why they would both attack and deploy ABMs, and no defense of the affirmative evidence is offered in response to the question of whether it assumes ABMs. Much of this evidence is old; Kissinger is 1969, before ABMs were viable.

Second, probabilities are critical. WGP might provoke Russian attack, but we ought not be blinded by conclusionary evidence calling this the greatest threat to world peace when the specific evidence and analysis in the round indicate otherwise. TNF will certainly be modernized under the affirmative and this is certainly very bad.

Finally, ABMs may save Finlandization, as the Europeans may see little security in nuclear weapons of which the Russians have little fear. Also, collapse of NATO may so sap European resolve that Russia will no longer fear its suddenly pliant and even solicitous neighbors, with or without the bomb. Neither side discusses the relationship of Finlandization to WGP and ABMs in detail. The argument that NATO collapse will assure peace through Finlandization is conceded by the 2AR however, and this cuts against the probability of Russian attack.

Neither side has a big edge on the value of ABM in the strategic context, debating the issue at a very superficial level and confusing silo and city defense. Thus, while WGP is unambiguously bad in that it risks war with Russia, the magnitude of the risk is all-important, as it must be weighed against TNF, Finlandization (which at least may survive), net risk on the shift disadvantage, and other miscellaneous case arguments. My impression is that the affirmative did no better than a tie on the case, and the balance of WGP against TNF and Finlandization favors the negative except for the quality of affirmative evidence saying WGP is the greatest risk (which evidence is, however, new in 2AR).

In a debate this close, the "persuasiveness" of the speakers and individual judgments about how the round should be put together are inevitably important. So are clarity of explanation and emphasis of superior evidence. Dartmouth chose an attack so large that brevity demanded sacrifice of some of these. A less ambitious strategy might have been better, but Kansas may well have defeated it on the merits. We should aspire to improve our listening and analytic skills to fully appreciate the subtleties of this attack, but we need offer no apologies for underestimating it at the time. The burden of successful communication must fall primarily on the speaker.

FOURTH JUDGE CRITIQUE: ROGER SOLT, UNIVERSITY OF KENTUCKY

This was a round which pitted against each other perhaps the two best researched debate teams in the country. Both teams have obviously accumulated a wide range of data, and they managed to pack a good deal of it into this round. The major problem with the round, as with many contemporary debates, is that too much attention is given to the accumulation of information and too little to its processing or assimilation.

This problem has several manifestations. The first is presentational: in the attempt to condense so much material into an hour of speaking a good deal of the information content, the subtleties and distinctions of the evidence is lost--to the debaters, I suspect, as well as the judges. The second problem relates to assessment of source credibility. Despite the fact that most of the major issues in the round eventually turn on the assessment of highly speculative and authoritative evidence, almost no attention is given to evaluating source qualifications. Professors of international relations, newspaper columnists, and extremist rag sheets are given an indiscriminately equal credibility. The third problem relates to synthesis of issues. Both sides clearly establish credible scenarios for catastrophe, but neither side does nearly enough to indicate the comparative probabilities of these occurrences. Ultimately, I think the affirmative does a better job of selling the impact of its scenarios. Rhetorically, the risks of Soviet ABM deployment and or Russian attack on West Germany sound very compelling at the end of the second affirmative rebuttal. I believe, of course, that a proper assessment of issues would assign greater risk to the scenarios outlined by the negative. As impactful as these risks may be, however, they are given relatively little rhetorical weight in the final rebuttals. The conclusion that one could draw from this is that, in competitive terms at least, it may be better to be persuasive than right. A conclusion that I would prefer to draw is that current debate neglects, to its severe detriment, sufficient emphasis on presentational clarity or analytical thoroughness in issue assessment. The result is debates filled with half understood and half processed information, a defect from which this in many ways excellent debate also clearly suffers.

The first key set of issues in this round involves comparing the risks of European war with or without the plan. It is critical here to realize that if the affirmative plan is adopted the risk of war will be very high. Negative evidence, substantially undisputed after constructives, indicates that Europe is ripe for nuclear war, implying in my mind a greater than fifty percent war risk. Further, it is undenied that TNF deployment will create a major increase in war risk. My assessment at the end of the round is that if the affirmative position is upheld the probability of war should be regarded as being in the neighborhood of eighty percent.

Absent the plan this risk figure to be largely mitigated. NATO breakup clearly removes the incremental risk due to TNF deployment. It also appear to remove most of the current war risk by breaking up the alliance and leading to Finlandization. The question might be raised as to whether West German proliferation would preclude Finlandization, thereby undercutting the impact of the disadvantage. I reject the conclusion for a number of reasons. First, the affirmative, as best I can tell, never claims that proliferation precludes Finlandization. Second negative rebuttal specifically claims the Finlandization impact. Second, even with West German proliferation, the rest of Europe could be Finlandization. Negative evidence obviously envisions the Finlandization of France and Great Britain, both already nuclear powers. Fourth, as I understand the negative's evidence, must of the war risk is attached to the existence of the Alliance itself; thus, even without full Finlandization most of the current war risk should be mitigated.

The breakup of NATO thus figures to remove a large and increasing probability of war. The question is whether West German proliferation can be assigned a war probability greater than the already high war risk. My conclusion is that it cannot. One key to my assessment of this issue is a perception that Russian attack on West Germany and Russian ABM deployment represent alternative rather than additive risks. It seems logical that Russian invasion of West Germany would remove its incentive to deploy an AMB system, and likewise that ABM deployment would remove the incentive for attacking West Germany. The Coffey evidence read in second negative constructive makes this latter point (despite the assertion of the second affirmative rebuttalist to the contrary).

Given this understanding, a comparison must be made between the current war risk and the risk under both the Soviet ABM deployment and non-deployment scenarios. (Parenthetically, I assess both scenarios as comparably credible. The only on point evidence in the round is the negative evidence saying that Russia would deploy the ABM--affirmative evidence does not explicitly consider the ABM option. The affirmative does mitigate this probability by means of the time lag argument, but this position is not very well explained in first affirmative rebuttal, and the assertion of a lag time, while intuitively credible, must be weighed against the negative evidence on the issue.) It seems to me clear that if Russia deploys ABMs the war risk is less than under the present system. It is implicitly conceded by the affirmative that ABMs would stabilize the European theatre; what affirmative evidence suggests is that ABMs might have a destabilizing effect on the strategic balance at large. Both sides read a good deal of contradictory evidence on this point, and even if one regards the affirmative as having an edge here (primarily on volume of evidence), it seems unreasonable to assess the war risk from ABMs as anywhere close to the current European war risk. If the European war risk is regarded as eighty percent, the war risk from ABMs can hardly be assigned more than a fifty percent probability and probably should be assessed as closer to twenty percent or thirty percent.

The next question is: what if Russia does not deploy ABMs? Based on the evidence read this risk would appear to be very high; affirmative evidence makes some very strong statements about this being the greatest nuclear risk. A couple of factors, however, mitigate this probability. First, this evidence appears to assume a non-Finlandized Europe. Given the Finlandization described above, West German proliferation might be a good deal less provocative. (Though this argument is not specifically applied here by the second negative rebuttalist, he does argue elsewhere that Finlandization means peace). Second, in the second negative constructive it is argued that for several reasons a West German nuclear force would be less provocative than U.S.-sponsored TNF (West German nuclear weapons would lack counterforce capacity, would not be backed by the U.S. arsenal, and would not lead to Russian launch-on-warning policies). These reasons are dealt with only briefly by the first affirmative rebuttalist and are dropped altogether by the second, suggesting that despite strong conclusionary evidence West German nuclear weapons would be no more provocative than currently planned NATO tactical nuclear weapons and might even be less so. I, therefore, doubt that relative war risk would be greater than that existing at present even under the non-ABM deployment scenario. Even if war was certain under this scenario, however, the war probability under the deployment scenario is enough lower than the current war risk that the net probability of war given West German proliferation (a weighted average of the two scenarios) would still be less than that which currently exists. That is, the current war risk of eighty percent is greater than the average of fifty percent and one hundred percent under scenarios one and two. Obviously, the specific numbers I have assigned to these scenarios are somewhat arbitrary; however, the war risks assigned to both ABM deployment and non-deployment in the above equation appear to be biased toward the affirmative. Only a systematic biasing of assumptions against the negative can lead to an on balance affirmative advantage. Finally, in terms of timeframe, TNF deployment appears to be the most immediate danger, giving the negative still another edge.

The second major set of issues involves assessment of the relative risks of Cuban versus Middle Eastern intervention, and this leads in my mind to a comparable advantage for the negative. The affirmative does not deny that the U.S. will intervene in the Mideast unless intervention in Cuba prevents it. Nor do they deny Mideastern intervention would result in confrontation with Russia and probable war. In contrast, there is at least opposing evidence concerning the Russian response to intervention in Cuba. The affirmative clearly wins some risk of Russian response under that scenario; however, this evidentally contested scenario seems less risky than the undenied risks of intervention in the Mideast. The weight which can be assigned to the negative based on Middle Eastern intervention is of course significantly minimized by the arguments the negative makes minimizing the probability of intervention in Cuba. The affirmative, however, clearly wins some risk of intervention into Cuba, thus leading to the ultimate conclusion that allowing the Cuban intervention option lowers the probability of nuclear war in the Mideast at least marginally. Thus, even if the war risk in Europe is regarded as equal both with and without the affirmative plan (or even if the affirmative is seen as having a slight edge

here), the Mideast intervention turnaround on case should outweigh. The affirmative can win only if they have a substantial
edge in terms of European war, and in my mind they clearly do
not.

The other two affirmative advantages seem relatively trivi-
al. The first advantage on immigration does claim a nuclear
impact, but it is obvious at the end of the round that this risk
should be regarded as minimal. Clearly it doesn't weigh significantly against the other risks being argued.

Although in places the tone of these remarks has been
critical, I definitely feel that two of the finest debate teams
in the country participated in this year's final round. Obviously there are other teams also eminently deserving of such a
distinction. The Samford team of Walker and Gardner, as recipients of the number one first round bid certainly merit mentioning in this regard, and so does the second Dartmouth team of Gail
and Koulogeorge--their 10-0 record at the NDT will probably never
be equalled. Nonetheless, this year's final round was made up of
four state-of-the-art debaters, whose excellence has been demonstrated over long and distinguished college careers. Most of
their argumentative weaknesses are characteristic of the current
state of debate; one would wish that more of their strengths were
equally so.

FIFTH JUDGE CRITIQUE: GEORGE ZIEGELMUELLER
WAYNE STATE UNIVERSITY

The debaters and coaches at Dartmouth College and the University
of Kansas should be congratulated not only for advancing to the
final round of the National Debate Tournament but also for the
fine debate which ensued. Although the rate of delivery was
rapid, both teams were clear in their organization and their
articulation so that the debate was easy to follow for anyone
schooled in the topic and in the activity. Despite the intensity
of the exchange between these two teams, I especially appreciated
the genuinely friendly manner in which they responded to each
other's questions and in which they conducted themselves generally throughout the contest.

This particular debate demonstrated both some of the major
strengths and major weaknesses of current intercollegiate debate
practice. The major strengths demonstrated in this round were
the debaters' breadth of understanding of the topic and their
ability to draw complex relationships among the issues. While
such breadth of analysis is commendable, it also contributed to
the major weakness of the debate: the tendency to develop
arguments linearly rather than in-depth. The NATO disadvantage
is perhaps the best example of this. The affirmative gave a
number of responses to this disadvantage, but none of them
explored very deeply the initial causal link or the predicted
impact. The primary effect of the second affirmative's response

was to shift the focus of the analysis to a consideration of the possible effects of West German proliferation. The negative in turn gave literally dozens of responses to the affirmative responses, but once again, the analysis was extended linearly by adding the anti-ballistic missile turnaround to the West German proliferation turnaround. Thus the linear development of the argument gained precedence over the in-depth analysis of the original issue.

My decision was based upon an evaluation of the NATO disadvantage, the shift to Mideast disadvantage and the second advantage. By rebuttals the inherency was pretty much granted to the affirmative, and the first and third advantages did not receive very much emphasis by either team.

Because of the great impact of the two disadvantages and the second advantage, they became the critical issues in the debate. The NATO disadvantage was an interesting one but because of the various turnarounds, the original focus of the argument became less important. The ultimate question with regard to this disadvantage revolved round whether or not Soviet ABMS would or would not be desirable. In the end, the affirmative persuaded me that the harms of Soviet ABMs would outweigh any possible benefits for the following reasons: (1) the only evidence which considered both the advantages and disadvantages of ABMs was the evidence from the Pugwash conference which indicated that the consensus of experts is that the disadvantages of ABMs outweigh any advantages; (2) the negative evidence which indicated reduced chances of war did not assume that West Germany would have nuclear weapons prior to the deployment of the ABM system and a time lag would be necessary for the deployment of such a system; (3) the affirmative's 1983 evidence indicated West German proliferation would be the greatest threat to peace. By winning the issue the affirmative was able to demonstrate that they would avoid a major threat of nuclear war in the future from West German proliferation.

The affirmative established a more immediate threat of nuclear war with their second advantage. The three specific scenarios for nuclear war outlined in the first affirmative speech were not directly refuted by the negative and at least one piece of the affirmative evidence did indicate a continuing threat of U.S. intervention in the fall of 1983. In addition to winning the scenarios the affirmative also carried the risk of 40 to 50,000 U.S. lives lost, the risk of an expanded regional war and ultimately the risk of nuclear war with Russia. While the negative had several responses to Soviet escalation, none of these denied that Cuba was under the Soviet nuclear umbrella nor did any of them deny that the presence of Soviet personnel in Cuba serves as a tripwire for Soviet involvement.

The final question of the debate, thus, became would the likelihood of a Soviet shift to the Middle East pose a greater and more immediate threat than U.S. intervention in Cuba. It seemed to me that the affirmative successfully minimized the probability of this risk with the arguments which said: (1) empirically our non-intervention to date has not led to the Rapid

Deployment Force being used in the Middle East; (2) there is no reason to use the RDF in the Middle East since Israel is winning; and (3) there is no evidence that Reagan perceives any linkage between Cuban intervention and the deployment or non-deployment of forces in the Middle East.

Overall the affirmative succeeded in keeping the debate focused more on its ground than did the negative. Substantively the risk of nuclear war from U.S. intervention in Cuba seemed more immediate and probable than the risk of a war because of U.S. shifting forces to the Middle East and the avoidance of West German proliferation and Soviet anti-ballistic missiles was clearly an advantage to the affirmative proposal.

ENDNOTES

[1] The tournament director was Professor Michael Hazen of Wake Forest University, and the tournament host was Professor Al Johnson of The Colorado College.

[2] The debate was held in the Armstrong Theatre on The Colorado College campus on April 2, 1983. Coaches of the two teams were Professor Donn W. Parson of the University of Kansas and Professors Herb James, Steve Mancuso, and Ken Strange of Dartmouth College. The sixteen teams qualifying for the elimination rounds were from the University of Arizona, Augustana College (South Dakota), Baylor University, Darmouth College (two teams), Emory University (two teams), Georgetown University, Harvard University, University of Kansas, University of Louisville, Loyola Marymount University, Northwestern University (two teams), Samford University, and West Georgia College.

[3] Judges for the debate were Professors Dwaine Hemphill (Kansas State University), Dale Herbeck (University of Iowa), Dallas Perkins (Harvard University), Roger Solt (University of Kentucky), and George Ziegelmueller (Wayne State University). The decision was 4 1 for the affirmative team.

[4] The debate was edited from a tape recording. Except for the correcton of obviously unintended errors and, where necessary, the insertion of case outline references (I, A, 1, etc.), this is as close to a verbatim transcript as was possible to obtain from the recording. An outline of arguments developed in the debate is provided in the Editorial analysis section at the end of the transcript, which the reader may wish to consult occasionally for clarity. Evidence cards and other materials used in the debate were supplied to the editor immediately following the debate by the participants. Sources of the evidence have been verified as indicated in the footnotes, which also supply the exact quotatation and other information when necessary. When the source was not located after a reasonable

search or was not available to the editor, the term "source indicated" is used in the footnote, together with any additional information provided by the debaters. The editor gratefully acknowledges the assistance of the library staff of Illinois State University in locating sources in this debate.

[5] Dr. Robert Rowland, Baylor University, Paul Reader, David Rhaesa, Kansas' other team at the NDT. Jerry Gaines, another Kansas debater at the NDT. Hicks was Gidley's high school debate coach, and Holmes was Payne's high school debate coach.

[6] Sergio Roca, "Cuba Confronts the 1980's," Current History, February 1983, p. 78.

[7] William M. LeoGrande, "Cuba Policy Recycled" Foreign Policy, Spring 1982, p. 108.

[8] LeoGrande, 1982, p. 105.

[9] Michael J. Kryzanck, "President Reagan's Caribbean Basin Formula," AEI Foreign Policy and Defense Review, Vo. 4, No. 2, 1983, p. 135.

[10] LeoGrande, 1982, p. 117.

[11] Jorge I. Dominguez, "On U.S.-Cuban Ties," New York Times, 26 February 1981, p. A19.

[12] LeoGrande, 1982, p. 111.

[13] T.B. Miller, The East-West Strategic Balance (London: George Allen & Unwin, 1981, 1981), p. 156.

[14] R. Bruce McColm and Francis X. Maier, "Fighting Castro from Exile," The New York Times Magazine, 4 January 1981, p. 40.

[15] "The World's Poor Flood the U.S.: The Economic Consequences of a New Wave," Business Week, 23 June 1980, p. 86.

[16] "A Racial Outburst in Miami," Newsweek, 10 January 1983, p. 23.

[17] Steven Mumford, "Population Growth and Global Security," The Humanist, January/February 1981, p. 10.

[18] Louis H. Masotti, et al., A Time to Burn? (Chicago: Rand McNally & Company, 1969) p. x.

[19] LeoGrande, 1982, p. 119.

[20] Jo Thomas, "Castro Says Reagan Foreign Policy Will Pose a Threat to World Peace," New York Times, 18 December 1980, p. A5.

21 Press Release by the Council on Hemispheric Affairs, 4 November 1981, p. 1.

22 Flora Lewis, "Who's Scaring Whom?" Congressional Record, 3 May 1982, p. S4397.

23 Editorial, The Philadelphia Inquirer, 25 February 1981, reproduced in Editorial on File, 16-28 February 1981, p. 237.

24 "Cuba," Quarterly Economic Review of Cuba, Dominican Republic, Haiti, Puerto Rico, 4th Quarter 1981, p. 6.

25 William Safire, "Sand in My Shoes," New York Times, 12 February 1982, p. A35.

26 Edward Gonzalez, "To the Editor," Foreign Policy, Fall 1982, p. 180.

27 Carl T. Rowan, "Salvador at Topo of Another 'Slippery Slope,'" The Kansas City Star, 10 March 1983, p. 6A.

28 Lynn-Darrell Bender, Cuba vs. United States: The Politics of Hostility (San Juan, Puerto Rico: Inter American University Press, 1981), pp. 87-8.

29 Press Release by the Council on Hemispheric Affairs, 4 November 1981, p. 2.

30 Jorge I. Dominguez, "Cuban Military and National Security Policies," in Martin Weinstein, ed., Revolutionary Cuba in the World Arena (Philadelphia: Institute for the Study of Human Issues, 1979), p. 90.

31 LeoGrande, 1982, p. 109.

32 Bender, p. 88

33 Edgar O'Ballance, "The Cuban Factor," RUSI: Journal of the Royal United Services Institute for Defense Studies, September 1978, p. 46.

34 Charles Krauthammer, "There Is One Quick, Simple Plan for Arms Control: Salt II," The Kansas City Star, 25 April 1982, p. 4B.

35 Statement of Dr. Roman Kolkowicz, "Future of Arms Control," Hearings before the Subcommittee on Arms Control, Oceans, International Operations and Environment of the Committee on Foreign Relations, United States Senate, Ninety-seventh Congress, Second Session on Control of Nuclear Arms, January 20, 21, and 25, 1982 (Washington, DC: U.S. Government Printing Office, 1982), p. 123.

[36] Sen. Lowell Weicker, Congressional Report, 14 April 1982, p. S3464.

[37] Abraham F. Lowenthal quoted in "The IPS Connection: Shultz' Latin American Briefers," Human Events, 11 December 1982, p. 3.

[38] James M. Wall, "A Hopeful Sign in U.S.-Cuban Relations," The Christian Century, 5 May 1982, p. 523.

[39] Hon. Baltasar Corrada, "Human Rights in Cuba," Congressional Record, 20 July 1977, p. 24188.

[40] "Cuba," Country Reports on Human Rights Practices, Report submitted to the Committee on Foreign Relations, U.S. Senate and Committee on Foreign Affairs, U.S. House of Representatives by the Department of State in accordance with Sections 116(d) and 502B(b) of the Foreign Assistance Act of 1961, as amended, February 2, 1982 (Washington, DC: U.S. Government Printing Office, 1981), p. 397.

[41] Irving Louis Horowitz, "The Cuban Lobby: Supplying Rope to a Mortgaged Revolution," in Horowitz, ed., Cuban Communism, Fourth Ed. (New Brunswick and London: Transaction Books, 1981), p. 517.

[42] Abraham F. Lowenthal, "Reagan's Best Weapon Against Cuba May Be the Threat of Peace," Los Angeles Times, 5 April 1981, quoted in Congressional Record, 3 May 1982, p. 54398.

[43] Carmelo Mesa-Lago, Cuba in the 1970s, Rev. Ed., (Albuquerque, New Mexico: University of New Mexico Press, 1978), p. 145.

[44] Herb James and Ken Strange, Co-Directors of Debate, and Steve Mancuso, Assistant Coach, at Dartmouth. Tom Isaacson and Cy Smith, former Dartmouth debaters. Karen McGarrey, a current Dartmouth debater. Dusty is Jacobsohn's golden retriever. Lenny Gail and Mark Koulogeorge were undefeated in preliminary rounds of the tournament and proceeded to the semi-finals where they were scheduled to meet Jacobsohn and Lyon. The Dartmouth group decided which team would debate the final round.

[45] William E. Griffith, "Europe: Cold War and Threatened Alliance," Freedom at Issue, January-February 1983, p. 18.

[46] Robert Leiken, "Reconstructing Central American Policy," Washington Quarterly, Winter 1982, p. 56.

[47] Jonathan Sanders quoted in Daniel Southerland, "Who gets credit for keeping the Soviet bear at home?" Christian Science Monitor, 30 September 1982, p. 3.

[48] Sen. Sam Nunn, "NATO: Can the Alliance Be Saved? Report of Senator Sam Nunn to the Committee on Armed Services United States Senate, May 13, 1982," The Atlantic Community Quarterly, Summer 1982, p. 126.

[49] Joseph F. Pilat, "West Europe's New Antinuclear Wave," Contemporary Review, May 1982, p. 228.

[50] Stanley R. Sloan, "Crisis in NATO: A Problem of Leadership?" NATO Review, August 1982, p. 18.

[51] Michael Novak, "Making Deterrence Work," Catholicism in Crisis, November 1982, quoted in Congressional Record, 2 February 1983, p. E247.

[52] Jeffrey Record, "NATO's Theatre Nuclear Force Modernization Program: The Real Issue," A Special Report, November 1981, Institute for Foreign Policy Analysis, Inc., Cambridge, Massachusetts, and Washington, DC., p. vii.

[53] Source indicated.

[54] "The Role of Alliances and Other Interstate Alignments in a Disarming and Disarmed World," a report by a Study Panel of Research Associates of the Washington Center of Foreign Policy Research, School of Advanced International Studies, The Johns Hopkins University, Washington, DC, July 1965, p. 19.

[55] Edwanrd Gonzalez, "U.S. Policy: Objectives and Options," in Jorge I. Dominguez, ed., Cuba: Internal and International Affairs (Beverly Hills, California: Sage Publications, 1982), p. 197.

[56] John McMullan, "United States Sleeps While Castro Acts," Miami Herald, 23 January 1983, quoted in Congressional Record, 14 February 1983, p. E454.

[57] Lourdes Casal, "Cubans in the United States: Their Impact on U.S.-Cuban Relations," in Martin Weinstein, ed., Revolutionary Cuba in the World Arena (Philadelphia: Institute for the Study of Human Issues, 1979), p. 131.

[58] Casal, p. 128.

[59] Ambler Moss, "A U.S. Policy Option: Treat Castro as Irrelevant," The Miami Herald, 3 October 1982, p. 5E.

[60] William M. LeoGrande, "Foreign Policy: The Limits of Success," in Dominguez, ed., Cuba: Internal and International Affairs, p. 188. "While these preparations may seem overdrawn, given the implausibility of an actual U.S. military assault on Cuba, they underline the Cubans determination to stand firm in the face of threats, serious or not."

[61] Bernard Gwertzman, "Shultz Says U.S. Told Salvadorans to 'Clean Up' Their Rights Record," New York Times, 23 March 1983, p. A3.

[62] William M. LeoGrande, "Foreign Policy: The Limits of Success," p. 188.

[63] Jorge I. Dominguez, Cuba: Order and Revolution (Cambridge, Massachusetts: The Belknap Press of Harvard University, 1978), p. 345.

[64] Dominguez, 1979, p. 90.

[65] Jorge I. Dominguez, "The Armed Forces and Foreign Relations," in Cole Blasier and Carmeto Mesa-Lago, eds., Cuba in the World (Pittsburgh, PA: University of Pittsburgh Press, 1979), p. 77.

[66] William M. LeoGrande, "Foreign Policy: The Limits of Success," p. 168.

[67] Dan Oberdorfer, "Raising the Ante in Salvador and Reagan's more direct role," The Boston Globe, 11 March 1983, p. 8.

[68] Patrick E. Tyler, "Nicaragua: Hill Concern on U.S. Objectives Persists," The Washington Post, 1 January 1983, p. A10.

[69] Source indicated.

[70] Carl J. Migdail, "Inside Cuba: Castro Thumbs His Nose at Reagan," U.S. News & World Report, 3 August 1981, p. 28.

[71] Cole Blasier, "The Soviet Union in the Cuban-American Conflict," in Blasier and Mesa-Lago, eds., Cuba in the World, p. 48.

[72] Source indicated.

[73] Dean Rusk, Robert McNamara, George Ball, Roswell Gilpatrick, Theodore Sorensen, and M. George Bundy, "The Lessons of the Cuban Missile Crisis," Time, 27 September 1982, p. 85.

[74] Dev Murarka, "Five Fetters on Soviet Policy in Central America," South Magazine, May 1982, p. 12.

[75] Murarka, p. 12.

[76] Testimony of Robert S. Leiken, "U.S. Policy Options in El Salvador," Hearing and Markup before the Committee on Foreign Affairs and Its Subcommittee on Inter-American Affairs, House of Representatives, Ninety-Seventh Congress, First session on H.

Con. Res. 197, II. Con. Res. 212, November 19, 1981 (Washington, DC: U.S. Government Printing Office, 1981), p. 134.

[77] Robin Montgomery, "Middle Eastern Maelstrom," National Defense, June 1980, p. 32.

[78] Michael T. Klare, Beyond the "Vietnam Syndrome": U.S. Interventionism in the 1980s (Washington, DC: Institute for Policy Studies, 1981), p. 80.

[79] Christopher Paine, "On the Beach: The Rapid Deployment Force and the Nuclear Arms Race," MERIP Reports, January 1983, p. 4.

[80] Paine, 1983, pp. 7-8.

[81] Klare, 1981, p. 27.

[82] Deborah Shapley, "Helpers in the Persian Gulf," The New Republic, 26 April 1980, p. 19.

[83] Benson Grayson, "Soviet Intentions and American Options in the Middle East," National Security Affairs Monographs Series 82-3 (Washington, DC: National Defense University Press, 1982), p. 58.

[84] Michael T. Klare, "Have R.D.F., Will Travel," The Nation, 8 March 1980, p. 266.

[85] John F. Davis, "We Are Latin Africans," New York Amsterdam News, 29 January 1983, p. 2.

[86] Dominguez, 1978, p. 6.

[87] Davis, 1983, p. 2.

[88] Testimony of Bahakn Dadrian in "Investigation with Certain Past Hearings before the Subcommittee on Future Foreign Policy Research and Development," Committee on International Relations, House of Representatives, Ninety-Fourth Congress, Second Session, May 11, 1976 (Washington, DC: U.S. Government Printing Office, 1976), p. 21.

[89] Dadrian, 1976, p. 8.

[90] "Any," Words and Phrases, Permanent Ed., Volume 3A (St. Paul, Minnesota: West Publishing Co., 1953), p. 60.

[91] "Any," The Century Dictionary and Cyclopedia, Vol. 1 (New York: The Century Company, 1911), p. 253.

[92] "Pennsylvania Casualty Co. v. Elkins et al, No. 461, District Court, E. D. Kentucky, 30 April 1947," Federal Supple-

ment, Volume 70 (St. Paul, Minn., West Publishing Co., 1947), p. 158.

[93] Leiken, 1982, p. 56: "In this context, U.S. military actions in Central America would give credibility to Soviet propaganda that the United States, and not the U.S.S.R., is the imperialist power and the main threat to peace, thus serving to heighten pacifist and neutralist tendencies in Japan and Europe and further dividing the alliance."

[94] Testimony of Hon. Adrian S. Fisher, "Nuclear Proliferation: Future U.S. Foreign Policy Implications," Hearings before the Subcommittee on International Security and Scientific Affairs of the Committee on International Relations, House of Representatives, Ninety-Fourth Congress, First Session, October 23, 1975 (Washington, DC: U.S. Government Printing Office, 1975), p. 57.

[95] Lewis A. Dunn, Controlling the Bomb: Nuclear Proliferation in the 1980s (New Haven and London: Yale University Press, 1982), p. 123.

[96] Ernest W. Lefever, Nuclear Arms in the Third World (Washington, DC: The Brookings Institute, 1979), p. 7.

[97] Fisher, 1975, p. 57.

[98] Bernard Weintraub, "Reagan Policy in Central America: After 2 Years, Tough Tone Softens," New York Times, 25 January 1983, p. A1.

[99] David Rogers, "The Dilemma in Congress," The Boston Globe, 5 March 1983, p. 2. Thomas O. Enders is Assistant Secretary of State for Inter-American Affairs.

[100] Wall, p. 523.

[101] James A. Donovan, ed., U.S. Military Force--1980: An Evaluation (Washington, DC: Center for Defense Information, 1980), p. 10.

[102] Philip W. Dyer, "Tactical Nuclear Weapons and Deterrence in Europe," Political Science Quarterly, Summer 1977, p. 248.

[103] Leslie H. Gelb, "Moscow's Problems, Dilemmas," New York Times editorial quoted in Congressional Record, 30 July 1980, p. 510363.

[104] Fred M. Kaplan, "Enhanced-Radiation Weapons," in Bruce G. Blair, ed. Progress in Arms Control (San Francisco: W. H. Freeman and Company, 1979), p. 161.

[105] The Boston Study Group, The Price of Defense: A New Strategy for Military Spending (New York: New York Times Books, 1979), p. 156.

[106] "Prohibit," The Oxford English Dictionary, Vol. VIII (Oxford: Oxford University Press, 1961), p. 1441.

[107] Jewell Cass Phillips, et. al., Essentials of National Government (New York: American Book Company, 1966), p. 456.

[108] "Embargo," Webster's New World Dictionary of the American Language, Second College Ed. (New York and Cleveland: The World Publishing Company, 1970), p. 455.

[109] Saul Landan, "Warm Up to Cuba," New York Times, 4 March 1982, quoted in Congressional Record, 3 May 1982, p. S4398.

[110] Jorge I. Dominguez, "Cuban Foreign Policy," Foreign Affairs, Fall 1978, p. 106.

[111] G. D. Loescher and John Scanlon, "'Mass asylum' and U.S. Policy in the Caribbean," The World Today, October 1981, pp. 393-4.

[112] Loescher and Scanlon, p. 394.

[113] Testimony of William M. LeoGrande, "Impact of Cuban-Soviet Ties in the Western Hemisphere, Spring 1980," Hearings before the Subcommittee on Inter-American Affairs of the Committee on Foreign Affairs, House of Representatives, Ninety-sixth Congress, Second Session, May 14, 1980 (Washington, DC: U.S. Government Printing Office, 1980), p. 96.

[114] Ronnie Lovler, "Training for the Counterrevolution," The Nation, 26 September 1981, p. 265.

[115] Masotti, 1969, pp. x-xi.

[116] Rep. Tom Harkin Quoted in Tim Gallimore, "80-Plus Amendments Pending: House Struggles with a Bill Creating Broadcasts to Cuba," Congressional Quarterly Weekly Report, 7 August 1982, p. 1900.

[117] Sen. Dodd, Congressional Record, 14 April 1982, p. S3467.

[118] Sen. Lowell Weicker, Congressional Record, 14 April 1982, p. S3465.

[119] Press Release by the Council on Hemisphere Affairs, 4 November 1981, p. 2.

[120] Tom Wicker, "A New Political Reality," New York Times, 15 December 1981, p. A31.

[121] Carla Anne Robbins, "Cuba," in Edward A. Kolodziej and Robert E. Harkavy, eds., Security Policies of Developing Countries (Lexington, Massachusetts: Lexington Books, 1982), p. 73.

[122] George Anderson, "The Cuban Blockade: An Admiral's Memoir," The Washington Quarterly, Autumn 1982, p. 87.

[123] LeoGrande, 1982, p. 109.

[124] "Removing Soviet Influence from Cuba," National Security Record: A Report on the Congress and National Security Affairs (Washington, DC: The Heritage Foundation, July 1981), p. 3.

[125] LeoGrande, 1982, p. 118.

[126] Roger W. Fontaine, On Negotiating with Cuba (Washington, DC: American Enterprise Institute for Public Policy Research, December 1975), p. 56.

[127] Fred C. Ikle, "Allies Criticized for Salvador Reaction," The Boston Globe, 15 March 1983, p. 12.

[128] Lewis, p. S4398.

[129] Tad Szule, "Confronting the Cuban Nemesis," New York Times Magazine, 5 April 1981, p. 117.

[130] George J. Church, "Facing a World of Worries," Time, 3 May 1982, p. 10.

[131] Lawrence Freedman, "Limited War, Unlimited Protest," Orbis, Spring 1982, pp. 101-2.

[132] James Reston, "The Two Dangers," New York Times, 13 February 1983, p. E17.

[133] Joseph Joffe, "Europe and America: The Politics of Resentment," Foreign Affairs, Vol. 61, no. 3, 1983, p. 590.

[134] Source indicated.

[135] Phil Williams, "Europe, America and the Soviet Threat," The World Order, October 1982, p. 380.

[136] Lawrence Freedman, "Is NATO Obsolete?" World Press Review, November 1982, p. 21.

[137] Melvyn B. Krauss, "It's Time to Change the Atlantic Alliance," The Wall Street Journal, 3 March 1983, p. 24.

[138] Joseph C. Harsch, "How to Contain the Bomb," Christian Science Monitor, 4 November 1982, p. 23.

[139] Dave Myers, "The Last Europe," Bulletin of the Atomic Scientists, March 1982, pp. 22-23.

[140] Myers, 1982, p. 22.

[141] "Reagan's Euromissiles: Trigger for WW III," Workers Vanguard, 11 February 1983, p. 1.

[142] Frank Barnaby, "War-fighting weapons for Europe," Bulletin of the Atomic Scientists, March 1980, p. 9: "The mutually suicidal threat of the use of these weapons is simply not credible. 'Modernizing' them will not make the threat any more credible. But it may increase the probability of a nuclear war in Europe."

[143] Christopher Paine, "Pershing II: the Army's strategic weapons," The Bulletin of the Atomic Scientists, October 1980, p. 31.

[144] Steven Erlanger, "Easing Difficulties for NATO Alliance," The Boston Globe, 7 March 1983, p. 8.

[145] Guido Goldman, "Kohl, the Anchor," The New York Times, 8 March 1983, p. A31.

[146] Griffith, 1983, p. 19.

[147] Eric R. Alterman, "An Alternative to Zero Option," The Nation, 5 March 1983, p. 265.

[148] Lawrence Freedman, "Limited War, Unlimited Protest," Orbis, Spring 1982, p. 95.

[149] Myers, 1982, p. 22.

[150] Lewis A. Dunn, "U.S. Strategic Force Requirements in a Nuclear-Proliferated World," Air University Review, July–August 1980, p. 32.

[151] Lewis A. Dunn, "U.S. Defense Planning for a More Proliferated World," A final report prepared for the Office of the Assistant Secretary of Defense, Program Analysis and Evaluation by the Hudson Institute, April 1979, p. 43.

[152] J. I. Coffey, "Soviet ABM Policy: The Implications for the West," International Affairs, April 1969, p. 208.

[153] Source indicated.

[154] Daniel O. Graham, "Toward a New U.S. Strategy: Bold Strokes Rather Than Increments," Strategic Review, Spring 1981, p. 15.

[155] Source indicated.

[156] Herbert Scoville, Jr., "Confrontation is only a prescription for nuclear disaster," The Center Magazine, November/December 1982, p. 28.

157 Dusko Doder, "Euromissile May Spur New Soviet Retaliatory Plan," The Washington Post, 30 November 1982, p. A19.

158 "Senate Blocks Attempt to Curtail Covert Acts," Miami Herald, 17 December 1982, p. 1A.

159 Ibid.

160 Walter Isaacson, "'Not Our Finest Hour,'" Time, 3 January 1983, p. 43.

161 Quoting Joseph Eldrigde of the Washington Office on Latin America in Arthur Jones, "The Thin Man," The Progressive, February 1983, p. 15.

162 John Barrett of Georgetown University was top speaker in the 1983 NDT.

163 Jira Valenta, "Soviet Options in Poland," Survival, March/April 1981, p. 53.

164 Source indicated.

165 Seweryn Bailer and Alfred Stepah, "Cuba, the U.S., and the Central American Mess," The New York Review of Books, 27 May 1982, p. 17.

166 Roy A. Werner, "How Sharp the Teeth If Tail Won't Thrash?" Army, February 1982, p. 33.

167 C. F. Barnaby, "Arguments For and Against the Deployment of Anti-Ballistic Missile Systems," in C. F. Barnaby & A. Boserup, eds., Pugwash: Implications of Anti-Ballistic Missile Systems, Pubwash Monograph II (New York: The Humanities Press, 1969), p. 33.

168 John Spanier and Eric M. Uslander, How America Foreign Policy Is Made (New York: Praeger Publishers, 1974), pp. 118-9.

169 Joseph J. Kruzel, "Arms Control and American Defense Policy: New Alternatives and Old Realities," Daedalus, Winter 1981, p. 146.

170 "Brown Declared ABMs too Risky," The Dallas Morning News, 18 January 1981, p. 23A.

171 Bailer and Stepah, p. 17.

172 Source indicated.

173 Herman Kahn, "The Case for a Thin System," in Johan J. Holst & William Schneider, Jr., eds., Why ABM? Policy Issues in the Missile Defense Controversy (New York Pergamon Press, 1969), p. 67.

174 Richard Burt, "Official Interest in Antimissiles Is Being Reviewed," New York Times, 14 August 1980, p. A4.

175 Lenny Gail, member of Dartmouth's other team, undefeated in the 1983 NDT, and placed second in speaker points at the end of eight preliminary rounds.

176 "Colo. Senators Split on Outer-Space Arms," The Denver Post, 31 March 1983, p. 8A.

177 John Steinbruner, et. al., "Strategic Stability," Current, November 1981, p. 21.

178 John Quirt, "Washington's New Push for Anti-Missiles," Fortune, 19 October 1981, p. 144.

179 Alan Wolf, "The ABM--The End of Deterrence," The Nation, 12 April 1982, p. 417.

180 Herbert Passin, "Nuclear Arms and Japan," in William H. Overhold, ed., Asia's Nuclear Future (Boulder, Colorado: Westview Press, 1977), p. 120.

181 Nigel Calder, Nuclear Nightmares: An Investigation into Possible Wars (New York: The Viking Press, 1979), p. 74.

182 Field Marshal Lord Michael Carver, "Nuclear Nonsense," Bulletin of the Atomic Scientists, April 1982, p. 7.

183 Calder, 1979, p. 157.

Notes

Notes

Notes

Notes

Notes

Notes

Notes

Notes

Notes

Notes

Notes

NTC Debate Books

1987/88 Topic
Establishing a U.S. Foreign Policy Toward
  Latin America, *Goodnight, Gander, Deatherage*
Paths of Peace, *Hynes*
Politics of Power in Latin America, *Flaningam*

Debate Theory and Practice
Advanced Debate, Third Edition, *Thomas, Hart*
Basic Debate, Second Edition, *Fryar, Thomas, Goodnight*
Cross-Examination in Debate, *Copeland*
Forensic Tournaments: Planning and
  Administration, *Goodnight, Zarefsky*
Judging Academic Debate, *Ulrich*
Modern Debate Case Techniques, *Terry, et al.*
Strategic Debate, *Wood, Goodnight*
Student Congress & Lincoln-Douglas Debate,
  Fryar, Thomas

Debate Aids
Debate Award Certificates
Debate Lectern
Debate Pins
Debate Timer
Case Arguments Flow Charts
Plan Arguments Flow Charts
Lincoln-Douglas Debate Casette Tape

For further information or a current catalog, write:
National Textbook Company
4255 West Touhy Avenue
NTC Lincolnwood, Illinois 60646-1975 U.S.A.